To Ann

With the and
compliments
wishes

Vaughan Young

November 1979.

From the Vikings to the Reformation

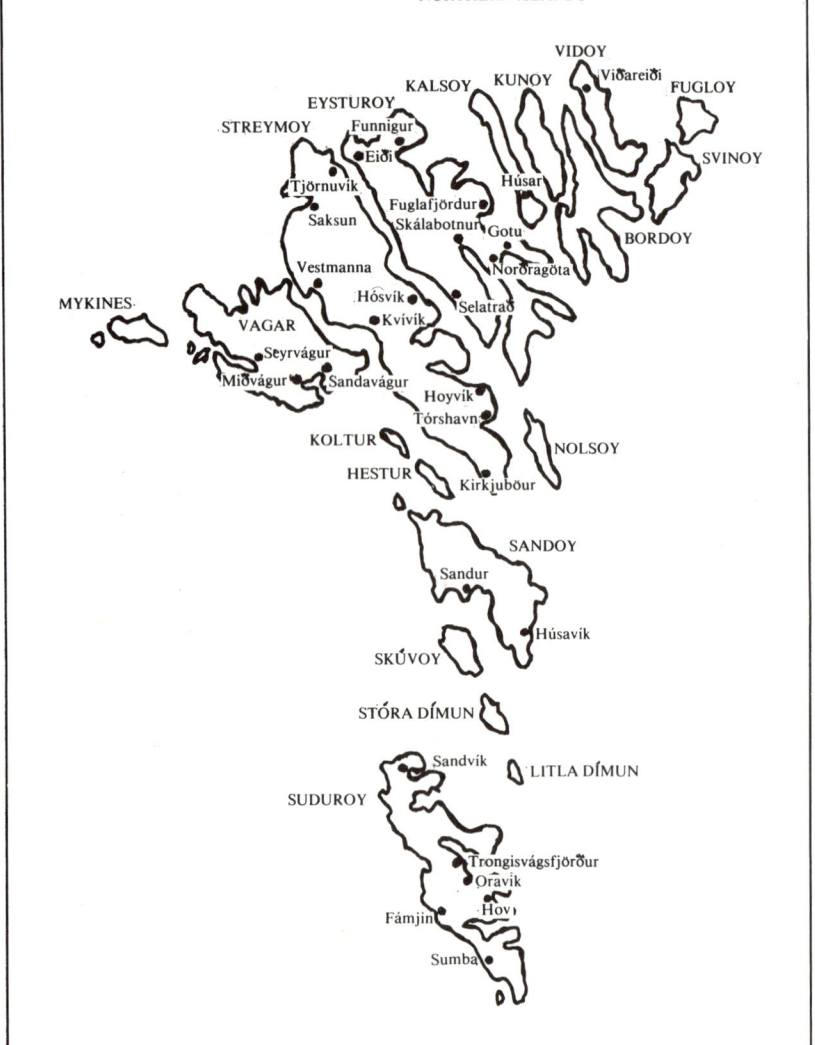

The Faroe Islands

From the Vikings to the Reformation

A Chronicle of the Faroe Islands up to 1538

G. V. C. YOUNG

SHEARWATER PRESS
DOUGLAS   ISLE OF MAN

Author's Note

This book was written in 1974 so that the money-values relate to those in that year and not those in 1978. I have also given living people referred to in the book the positions and marital status which they held in 1974.

© G. V. C. Young 1979

First Published 1979

All rights are reserved. Except for the purpose of review, criticism or private study no part of this publication may be reproduced, stored in a retrieval system, or transmitted, in any form or by any means, electronic, electrical, chemical, mechanical, optical, photocopying, recording or otherwise without the prior permission of Shearwater Press Limited.

ISBN 0 904980 20 0

Distributed in the Faroe Islands by

FØROYA SKÚLABÓKAGRUNNUR

Printed in the Isle of Man
by Bridson & Horrox Limited,
for Shearwater Press Limited,
Welch House, Church Road,
Onchan, Isle of Man.

CONTENTS

Table of Abbreviations.
1 Introduction. 1
2 825 to 968. 5
3 969 to 971. 9
4 971 to 994. 13
5 994 to 1005. 19
6 1005 to 1035. 25
7 Sixty-five years in the Faroes (970-1035). 35
8 1035 to 1100. 39
9 Religion pre-1100. 41
10 1100 to 1538. 49
11 Religion 1100 to 1538. 59
12 The legislature, courts and the law. 79
13 Relations with the outside world. 93
14 Farming, fishing and fowling. 99
15 Culture. 107
16 Coinage. 109
17 Historic remains. 115
Appendix 1 Scandinavian monarchs having jurisdiction over the Faroes prior to the Reformation. 123
Appendix 2 Ecclesiastical hierachy of the Church in the Faroes prior to the Reformation. 126
Appendix 3 The decree of Magnus the Law Reformer, son of Hakon, made for the Faroes in the spring of 1271. 139
Appendix 4 The Sheep Letter. 140
Part I Translation of the Stockholm copy by Michael Barnes, M.A. 140
Part II Translation of the Lund copy by Michael Barnes, M.A. 145
Part III Notes on the Sheep Letter. 150
Part IV Table of comparison between the Stockholm and Lund copies. 152
Appendix 5 Translation of documents about goods and property of Gudrun, daughter of Sigurd. 155
Document 1 dated 22nd August, 1403. 155
Document 2 dated 7th September, 1403. 156
Document 3 dated 7th October, 1403. 157
Document 4 dated 22nd March, 1404. 158
Document 5 dated 13th October, 1405. 158
Document 6 dated 9th November, 1405. 159
Document 7 dated 3rd July, 1407. 160

Appendix	6	Bull of Pope Anastasius IV erecting the see of Nidaros.	160
Appendix	7	Open Letter from Bishop Mark of Sodor dated 1299.	164
Appendix	8	Translation of a letter from Bishop Signar of the Faroes to Bishop Audfinn of Bergen dated 1320.	165
Appendix	9	Translation of documents about John, Bishop in Kirkjubøur, and Haraldur Kálvsson Lawman.	166
Document	1	dated 1412.	166
Document	2	dated 15th August, 1443.	167
Document	3	dated May, 1479.	167
Appendix	10	Mortgage, etc., by Greip Ivarsson in favour of Gaute Eiriksson.	168
Document	1	Mortgage dated 12th May, 1399.	168
Document	2	Parchment note supplementary to Document 1.	169
Appendix	11	The law about travelling allowances for members attending the Løgting.	170
Appendix	12	Important events in, or affecting, the Faroes.	171
Acknowledgements			175
Index of names of persons and places.			176

ABBREVIATIONS IN RELATION TO SOURCE NOTES.

AB	The History of the Archbishops of Hamburg-Bremen by Adam of Bremen: Translated, etc., by Professor Francis J. Tschan (1952).
AD	Færøske Kongbonder 1584-1884 by A. Degn.
ADJ	De hamborgske arkebispers forsøg pa at generhvenve primatet over den nordiske kirke by A. D. Jørgensen.
AJ	The Megalithic Yard Reconsidered: Rods, Poles or Barleycorns? by Anthony Jackson (published in Northern Studies 1974:4).
CFM	Case for the Millennium by G. V. C. Young. Published in The Manxman for Winter 1977/78.
CM	The Chronicle of Man and the Sudreys by Professor P. A. Munch, edited by Right Rev. Dr. Goss (1874) published in MSJ Vols. XXII and XXIII.
D	Denmark (published 1961 by the Danish Ministry of Foreign Affairs).
DB	Fra de færøske bygder by Daniel Bruun (1919).
DD	Diplomatarium Danicum.
DEO	The Dansk/Engelsk Ordbok by Vinterberg and Bodelsen (revised by Bodelsen and others, 1966).
DF	Diplomatarium Færoense by Jakob Jakobsen (1907).
DM	The Vikings in the Irish Sea Area c.850-c.980 by Danial McCall (Unpublished).
DN	Diplomatarium Norvegicum.
DW	The Viking Age in the Isle of Man by David M. Wilson (Odense University Press 1974).
F	Tingstaðurin á Tinganesi by Sámal Petersen (published in Froðskaparrit Annales Societatis Scientiarium Færoensis 20 Bok.)
FB	Tillæg til Forslag og Betænkninger by the Faroese Landbokommission (1911).
FJ	Føreyingasaga edited by Finnur Jônnson (1927).
FR	Frðóskaparrit (Annal Societ. Færoensis).
FS	The Faroese Saga by G. V. C. Young and Miss C. R. Clewer (1973).
GJ	A History of the Vikings by Professor Gwyn Jones (1968).
GL	Gyldendals Leksikon.
H	Sandö Fundet by C. J. Herbst.
HK	Den danske kirkes historie by Professor Hal Koch, (Vol I) (Copenhagen 1950).
JHWP	Seyðabrævið by Jóhan Hendrick W. Poulson (published in Føroyar 1974).
JJ	Færøske Folkesagn og eventyr by Jakob Jakobsen.
JM	Føroysk-Dansk Orðabók (second edition) by M. A. Jacobsen and Chr. Matris (1961).
KJK	Guardians of Church History by Knud J. Krogh (published in Føroyar 1974).
KL	Kulturhistorisk Leksikon for Nordisk middelalder.
L	Løgtingssøga frá landnámstið til Sverra kong by Dr. Scheel (private circulation 1953).
LW	Skånes kyrka från äldsta tid till Jacob Erlandsens död 1274 by L. Weibull in Lunds domkyrkas hist. 1145-1945, I, Lund 1946.

LZ	Føroyar sum raettarsamfelag 1535-1655 by Louis Zachariasen (1961).
M	A History of the Isle of Man by A. W. Moore (1900).
MA	Medieval Archæology, Vol. XIV (1970) — The Norse Settlements of the Faroe Islands by Sverri Dahl.
MD	Viking Coins of the Danelaw and of Dublin by Michael Dolley (1965).
MO	Mondul, Nr., 1, árg 1, 1945.
MS	The Ancient Ordinances and Statute Laws of the Isle of Man (1841).
MSJ	The Manx Society Publications.
MSR	The Statutes of the Isle of Man (Revised Edition).
NL	Necrologium Lundense.
OE	Rekneskapsböker 1532-1538 by Olav Engelbriksson, edited by J. A. Seip (1931).
OS	The Orkneyinga Saga translated by Jon A. Hjaltolin and Gilbert Goudie and edited by Joseph Anderson (1973).
P	Panteprotokol 1706-22.
RDHD	Regesta Diplomatica Historiæ Danicæ (822 to 1536) Vol. I.
RL	Fornnorrøn Lesibók by Richard Long.
RS	Føroya Søga by Petur M. Rasmussen and Hanus A. Samuelson.
S	Seyðabrævið (limited circulation).
SD	Fortidslevn by Sverri Dahl contained in Færøyerne.
SH	Sønderjyllands Historie, Vol. I.
St.	The Isle of Man by Canon E. H. Stenning (1950).
T	Danmark by T. J. Trap (Fifth edition, Gads Forlag, Copenhagen, 1968).
TBL	The article on "Bjarnasteinur" by J. Simun Hansen contained in Part II of Tey Byggja Land.
Ú	Útiseti, Vol. VI.
V	Varðin.
W	Søga og Søgn by A. Weihe.

CHAPTER 1
INTRODUCTION

The Faroe Islands lie in the North Atlantic between about 61° 24' and 62° 24' N. and 6° 15' and 7° 41' W. and are approximately halfway between the north of Scotland and Iceland, and about 335 miles west of Norway.

The main islands amount to eighteen in number, of which seventeen are inhabited, and their total area extends to about 540 square miles or 1,399 square kilometres.[1]

The written sources covering the pre-Reformation history of the Faroes are very few in number and the main work on the subject is the *Faroese Saga* which is compiled from Icelandic Sagas, but only covers the period from about 970 to 1035 and cannot be treated as a true historical work. The lack of records is due, in part, to the fact that there was a very bad fire in Nidaros (now known as Trondheim) in 1531 and that two important libraries in Copenhagen were destroyed by fire in the eighteenth century. To make matters worse, when the Reformation reached Denmark, King Christian III ordered that all the records in Lund, then in Denmark, should be packed up and sent to Copenhagen. This was done, but nothing further has ever been heard of the twelve packing cases which contained the records. Further old Faroese records were destroyed by fires on Tinganes, now part of Tórshavn on the island of Streymoy which took place in the seventeenth century.

The first reference to the Faroes having been inhabited is contained in a book written in Latin in 825 A.D. by Dicuil, an Irish monk, under the title *Liber de Mensura Orbis Terrae*. The following is a free translation of the relevant extract from this book:

"There are many other islands north of the British seas. One arrives there after sailing direct from the north of Britain for two days and two nights with full sail and a favourable wind all the time. A pious priest has told me that he, in two summer days and the night between, went there in a small boat with two thwarts and landed in one of the islands. The majority of the islands are small and have, in most cases, narrow sounds between them, and, for nearly a hundred years, hermits who have come from our Scotia (Ireland) have lived on the islands. But,

1

even as from the beginning of time they (the Faroes) have been uninhabited, so have the Norse Vikings made the monks desert them, but they are full of innumerable sheep and many different types of sea birds. At no time have we seen the islands referred to in the books of the authors"[2].

Although the Faroes are not mentioned by name by Dicuil, it is generally accepted that he was referring to them. It would seem from this that the first Irish monks came to the Faroes in about 725 A.D.[3] This, however, would appear to conflict with recent pollen tests which indicate that the Faroes were probably inhabited about 650, so Dicuil's "hundred years" may be on the short side as he gives no indication of the Faroes having been inhabited when the monks first went there.

Dicuil also mentions Iceland and, from what he says it would seem that the first priests went there about 795 (30 years prior to the date of his book), probably driven westwards as a result of the visitations of the Vikings to the Faroes[4].

There is some conflict as to when exactly the Faroes were first settled by the Vikings, but the generally accepted view nowadays is that the first settlement was made about 825 by Grim Kamban[5].

The *Faroese Saga*[6] states that Grim Kamban first settled the Faroes and made his home in Eysturoy, but the *Saga* goes on to state that this was in the time of Harald Fairhair's tyranny, which would have placed it between 885 and 890 or thereabouts. This is not now generally accepted, and it is possible that the writer of the *Saga* was confusing Grim Kamban's settlement with a later settlement in Harald Fairhair's time. It seems fairly clear that, somewhere about 867, Thoralf Smør moved west from the Faroes to Iceland with Floki Vilgerdason, a Norwegian, who called in at the Faroes on his way west, and that one of his daughters married in the Faroes[7].

It has generally been considered that Grim Kamban (whose name is considered to be Celtic and not Norse in origin) did not come to the Faroes direct from Norway, but that he came via either the Hebrides or Ireland[8]. Dr. Scheel expressed the view that Grim Kamban came to the Faroes from Ireland[9]. It would have been in accordance with the Viking pattern if he had brought Celtic slaves and women with him to help in the settlement, and it is of interest to note that the only other place, apart from the Faroes, in Western Europe where their women carried creels or panniers on their backs supported by a headband appears to have been in County Donegal in the north of Ireland. However, another possibility is that Grim Kamban came from the Isle of Man (another Celto-Norse country) rather than from the Hebrides or from Ireland. There does not appear to have been any Norse settlement in Ireland early enough for Grim Kamban to have been born there[10], but there is archaeological evidence which seems to indicate that there was a wealthy and settled Norse community on the Isle of Man by the first half or middle of the ninth century[11]. This would appear to prove that the Norse must have settled there some time earlier than that period. Professor David Wilson has expressed the view that the first Norse raids on the Isle of Man took place in about 800[12], and it is suggested that the first landnamsmen settled there shortly after that, which would make it possible for Grim Kamban to have been born in Man. The fact that he was born in the Isle of Man would not, however, rule out the possibility that he collected his slaves and women from Ireland, which was the subject of frequent Norse raids about the time when Grim Kamban settled in the Faroes.

Further evidence of the Celtic connection with the Faroes is found in the fact that Aud the Extremely Rich (or Deep-minded), daughter of a chief in the Sudreys [13] and wife of Olaf the White of Dublin, landed in the Faroes on her way to Iceland and gave away in marriage Thorstein the Red's daughter, Olive (Olúva)[14], from whom stemmed the famous Faroese family, the Gøtuskeggs, who lived at Gøta on Eysturoy. Another indication of the Celtic connection is to be seen in the name Gille which is of Celtic origin,[15], and in certain place names such as Dimun[16] and names beginning in the northern islands with Argi—and in Suðuroy with Ergi, such as Argisa, Argisfossur, Ergibyrgi and Ergidalur[17].

A list of the Scandinavian monarchs who had jurisdiction over the Faroes is set out in Appendix I. An attempt has been made to anglicize, as far as possible, the names of individuals referred to in the book, but, so far as place names are concerned, the author has endeavoured to give the names by which they are known at the present time in the relevant countries.

1 d p. 62.
2 RS pp. 142; GJ pp. 269 and 70.
3 S, facing page; GJ p. 270.
4 GJ p. 270.
5 FS p. 1.
6 RS p. 1, S facing page, RS p. 4.
7 GJ pp. 273-5, and RS p. 4.
8 *Ibid.* p. 270.
9 L p. 7.
10 See p. 6 *post.*
11 DM p. 8.
12 DW p. 8.
13 *Ibid.* pp. 28-9.
14 FS p. 1, L p. 15. Thorstein the Red was Aud's son, see CM p.14.
15 See chapter 6, note 9.
16 MA p. 62.
17 *Ibid.* p. 73. See also "Um aergistaðir or aergitoftir" by Sverri Dahl Fr. b. 18, pp. 361-8.

Stone with Celtic cross from Skúvoy. (By courtesy of Sverri Dahl, Tórshavn.)

CHAPTER 2

825 to 968

    The period in Faroese history from 825 to about 950 is one in respect of which conjecture and legend must have supremacy over proven fact, but it is felt that an attempt to give a background to the events which lead up to those covered by the *Faroese Saga,* is justified.

    From what has been stated in the previous chapter, it would seem likely that the Faroes were first settled by the Norsemen in about 825 and that there was a second period of settlement, probably around 885 to 890. The majority of the Faroese settlers came from the area around Bergen in Western Norway, which is apparent from the surnames "landsynningur", "útsynningur", "útnyroingur" and "landnyrðirgur".[1] The language connection between that area of Norway and the Faroes still exists today and it has been known for a Faroese to be able to speak in Faroese with a person from a country district outside Bergen who spoke in the local Norwegian dialect and for the two of them to understand each other perfectly. Contact was maintained by the Faroese with the rest of the Viking world and Vikings had called in at the Faroes on their way to Iceland and people from the Faroes, like Thoralf Smør (Thoralf Butter), had migrated from the Faroes to Iceland.[2] Another example of this intercourse can be seen from the fact that Aud the Extremely Rich (or Deep-minded) visited the Faroes while *en route* to Iceland[3] No date is given for this, but it seems likely that it took place somewhere between about 890 and the end of the ninth century which would coincide with the movement west from Norway and would be consistent with the fact that the Gøtuskeggs were well established by the middle of the tenth century. At any rate by about the middle of the tenth century, Thorbjørn (by then an old man) was rich and the head of the Gøtuskeggs[4]. Thorbjørn had, by his wife Gudrun (a sister of Svinoy-Bjarni), two sons, Thorlak and Thrand[5]. The latter is the central character in the *Faroese Saga.* Thrand is a fascinating individual, but it is doubtful if his character was as bad as the *Saga* paints it. In this connection, it must be remembered that the sagas from which the *Faroese Saga* is compiled were written by monks, and Thrand was a reluctant Christian, if he was really one at all.

It would seem that Thrand was born between 950 and 960 or thereabouts and that his father died between about 965 and 975[5]. In the later 960's the rule of the Faroes was shared between Hafgrim of Suðuroy, who held half the Faroes in fief from Harald Greycloak, King of Norway, and Brester and Beiner (sons of Sigmund the Elder, the grandfather of the famous Sigmund Bresterson) who held the other half in fief from Earl Hakon who had control of Trondheim[6]. The brothers lived in Skúvoy and they were related to Einar the Sudreyan who lived on Suðuroy[6]. Thrand was a cousin of Brester and Beiner, Thorbjørn Gøtuskegg and Sigmund having been brothers[7], but the cousins did not get on too well together.

It would appear that, by this period, the Faroes had a fairly settled form of Government, with a Thing or Council Meeting *(Alting)*, representing all the freemen in the islands, held at Tinganes, on Streymoy[8].

After Thorbjørn's death, Thrand drew lots with his older brother, Thorlak, in order to decide the division of their father's property, as a result of which the estate at Gøta went to Thrand[9]. Thrand was, however, short of money, so he leased his land at rack rents and went on a journey to Denmark where, by certain clever manoeuvres, he made a lot of money and then returned to the Faroes a wealthy man[10].

The following is the description of Thrand given in the *Faroese Saga:*—[11]

"Thrand was a big man with red hair and a red beard, freckled and stern in appearance, sombrely disposed, cunning and obsequious in all his schemes, unsociable and bad to ordinary people, yet sweet-spoken to all his superiors, but always deceitful in his heart."

It must, however, be remembered that it is more than likely that the monks who wrote the sagas were biased against Thrand.

As has been mentioned earlier in this chapter[12], the rule of the Faroes was, at this time, divided between Hafgrim of Suðuroy and Brester and Beiner of Skúvoy. Hafgrim was powerful and rich and a son-in-law of Snæulf the Sudreyan, who had left the Sudreys, because he had murdered someone, and lived in Sandoy[13]. He was, however, of an impetuous disposition and was not very intelligent. Brester and Beiner, on the other hand, are given glowing characters[13]. Both Brester and Beiner had sons, Sigmund and Thorer, by their respective mistresses, Cecilia (who later became Brester's wife) and Thora[14].

It is interesting to note that there were at this time in the Southern Faroes at least two families, namely Einar's and Snæulf's, who came from the Sudreys. It is relevant in this connection to mention that the words in the original text of the *Faroese Saga* which are translated into English as the Hebrides or Hebrideyan mean the southern islands or the Sudreys, that is the Hebrides (which consist of the Outer Hebrides or Lewis group, the Skye group, the Mull group and the Islay group of

Scottish islands) and the Isle of Man[15]. This view is supported by the fact that the diocese of Sodor (derived from the same word as that from which the Sudreys came) comprised the same Scottish Islands and the Isle of Man. It is therefore conceivable that Einar's and Snæulf's families could have come from the Isle of Man and not from the Hebrides. The expressions Sudreys and Sudreyan will be used in this book instead of Hebrides or Hebrideyan, which are used in the translation of the *Saga*.

Thrand's maternal uncle, Bjarni, lived in Svínoy and was known as Svínoy-Bjarni. He was a good farmer and owned a considerable amount of property[16].

These are the principal actors in the scene which opens in the next chapter.

1   RS pp. 6 & 7.
2   FS Table A; GJ p. 274.
3   See p. 3. *ante*.
4   FS p. 2.
5   See the family tree at FS, Table B.
6   FS p. 4. c. 4. See also p. 6.
7   *Ibid*.
8   RS p. 6. Tinganes is now part of Tórshavn. See also ch. 12.
9   FS p. 2.
10 FS p. 4. c. 3.
11 FS p. 4. c. 3.
12 See p. 5. *ante*.
13 FS p. 4. c. 4. The reference to Suðuroy in FS is incorrect, see FJ p. 5.
14 FS p. 4. c. 4. and p. 7. c. 7.
15 St. p. 62.
16 FS p. 6. c. 5.

A facsimile from Svabo's *Indberetninger fra en Reise i Færoe, 1781-1782.*

CHAPTER 3

969 to 971

Hafgrim of Suðuroy was a great idolator, being, like all the other Faroese of that period, a pagan[1]. One harvest time, probably in around 969, Hafgrim was singeing sheep's heads at his home in Hov with two friends, Einar the Sudreyan and Eldjarn Kamhat, alias Kambhøtt, who was a stupid, malicious, lazy but impetuous person[1]. A discussion arose concerning certain people, during which Einar praised his kinsmen, Brester and Beiner, and Edljarn Kamhat supported Hafgrim[1]. A quarrel arose and Eldjarn hit Einar with a piece of wood, at which Einar picked up an axe and wounded Eldjarn on the head[1].

After the fight Einar went to Brester who was learned in the law and asked his advice[2]. That winter Hafgrim went to Brester and Beiner and demanded compensation for the injury to Eldjarn. Brester tried to persuade Hafgrim to go before "the best men" for judgement in order to obtain an amicable settlement, but Hafgrim would not agree[2].

Hafgrim then summoned Einar before the Thing on Streymoy (i.e. at Tinganes)[3]. Immediately after the incident had occurred, Brester had let it be known that Eldjarn had attacked Einar before the latter had hit him[3]. At the Thing, Brester and Beiner and their followers supported Einar when he was prosecuted by Hafgrim on behalf of Eldjarn[3]. Brester submitted that Eldjarn was in breach of the ancient law because he had first struck an innocent man[3]. The case went against Hafgrim, who went away saying that he would be avenged[3].

It would appear from the above that the Thing at Tinganes exercised judicial functions in addition to executive ones and that there was a distinction between proceedings before "the best men in the Faroes" and proceedings before the Thing at Tinganes[4].

Shortly after the case was heard, Hafgrim went to Sandoy to see his father-in-law, Snæulf the Sudreyan, to ask him for his help[5]. Snæulf, however, said that he was surprised that Hafgrim was supporting a bad case and the two of them quarrelled, as a result of which Hafgrim went home[5].

Hafgrim then sailed from his home on Suðuroy to Eysturoy to visit Thrand, who gave him a warm reception. Hafgrim asked Thrand for advice[6]. Thrand agreed to help Hafgrim to attack Brester and Beiner if Hafgrim would agree to pay him the value of 2 cows every spring and of 200 ells (that is 480 feet) of homespun every autumn during his lifetime, and that the same should be a charge on his estate after his death, but said he would not take part in the enterprise unless Hafgrim would get Thrand's maternal uncle, Bjarni of Svínoy, to join in the expedition[6]. Hafgrim agreed to these terms[6]. Hafgrim then went to Bjarni who agreed to take part in the expedition subject to a similar payment but, in his case, of the value of 3 cows every spring and of 300 ells (that is 720 feet) of homespun every autumn[6].

Brester and Beiner had two farms, one on Skúvoy and the other Stóra Dímun[7]. They also jointly kept sheep on Lítla Dímun (which was then, and still is, uninhabited)[7]. One day, about the spring of 970, Brester and Beiner sailed to Litla Dímun with their sons, Sigmund and Thorer, who were then 9 and 11 years old respectively[7]. On their way back from Lítla Dímun to Stóra Dímun, the party sighted three ships heading for them with twelve armed men on each ship and recognised Hafgrim, Thrand and Bjarni among the people on board the ships[7]. The three ships steered between the brothers' boat and Stóra Dímun to prevent them going ashore at the landing place, but the brothers landed on a beach and took up a defensive position on a steep rock[7]. Hafgrim and his companions then came ashore and Hafgrim and Bjarni immediately launched an attack on the brothers, but Thrand and his men stayed on the beach[7]. The battle went on for some time without any definite result[7]. Hafgrim then asked Thrand for assistance, but Thrand said that surely twenty-four men could defeat two[7]. Hafgrim then attacked again.

The result of the fight was that Brester and Beiner were eventually killed and, of the attackers, Hafgrim and five others were slain[7].

Sigmund and Thorer, the sons of Brester and Beiner, had watched the whole fight and had seen their fathers killed[8]. After the fight, Thrand suggested that they should kill the two boys to prevent them avenging their fathers' death later on. Bjarni, however, refused to agree to this. Thrand then said that he would bring up the boys himself and, accordingly, took them back to Gøta[8].

Hafgrim's corpse was taken back to Suðuroy and buried there according to ancient custom[9]. There is at Hov a place known as "Hafgrim's Grave"[10]. The bodies of Brester and Beiner were taken back to Skúvoy where they too were buried according to ancient custom[11].

That summer, a ship came to Tórshavn under a captain, Rafn the Sailor from Novgorod[12]. When the ship was about to sail, Thrand came and offered to sell Rafn two slave boys, but Rafn refused to buy when he realised that the boys were the sons of Brester and Beiner[12]. Thrand then paid Rafn a sum of money to take the boys to Norway and to see that they would never return to the Faroes[12]. Rafn agreed to this and they sailed to Tønsberg, near Vik in southern Norway, where they spent the winter and were well treated by Rafn[12].

Thrand adopted Hafgrim's ten year old son, Ossur, and brought him up at Gøta[13].

The result of all this was that of the four people who had controlled the Faroes only Thrand remained, Hafgrim, Brester and Beiner having been killed. In addition, Hafgrim's son, Ossur, was under Thrand's control, while Brester's and Beiner's sons had been sent away to Norway. Thrand then seized the property which had belonged to Brester and Beiner and took over supreme control of the Faroes, and there was no one in the islands strong enough to stand up to him[14].

1 FS p. 6. c. 5.
2 *Ibid.*
3 *Ibid.*
4 See c. 4. *post.*
5 FS pp. 6 & 7. c. 6.
6 FJ pp. 7 & 8. (x) The references in the original text to 200 and 300 are to 200 and 300 ells of homespun, one ell being 2 feet and the hundred being the long or great hundred or 120. The references to the value of 2 cows and 3 cows are references to the kúgildi which was worth about 1 mark of nunted silver in later years, but probably worth 1 mark of pure silver at this time. For values see c. 16, esp. pp. 111-113.
7 FS pp. 7 & 7. c. 7.
8 FS pp. 8 & 9. c. 7.
9 FS p. 9. c. 7. Holmgaard was the Swedish name for Novgorod.
10 RS p. 23.
11 FS p. 9. c. 7.
12 FS p. 9. c. 8.
13 FS p. 9. c. 9.
14 *Ibid.*

Making fishing line in the Faroes in the eighteenth century.

CHAPTER 4

971 to 994

As has been mentioned in the previous chapter, Sigmund, son of Brester, and Thorer, son of Beiner, went with Rafn to Norway in about 970 and spent the winter in Tønsberg. The following spring Rafn gave the boys their freedom and a sum of money before he sailed to the East (i.e. to the Eastern Baltic)[1].

Sigmund and Thorer stayed in Vik for two years, by which time the money which Rafn had given them had run out. They had, by that time, reached the respective ages of twelve and fourteen[2]. This would be in about 973.

The boys heard that Earl Hakon, from whom their fathers had held half the Faroes in fief[3], had become very powerful, having succeeded Harald Greycloak three years before, so they decided to visit him[4]. They set out through the uplands, and then went east through Hedemark and subsequently north to Dovrefjell which they reached at the beginning of winter[4]. Despite the time of year, the boys went up into the mountains, but lost their way and only just succeeded in getting down from the mountain and finding a little valley, where they were taken in by a farmer called Ulf, his wife Ragnhild and their daughter, Thuride[4].

Sigmund and Thorer stayed with Ulf and his family for over five years, by which time they had reached the ages of eighteen and twenty years respectively[5]. This would be in about 979. Sigmund then told Ulf that it was time that he (Sigmund) and Thorer moved on, as a result of which Ulf went with the two young men north of Dovrefjell until they could see Orkedal[5].

Before parting, Ulf asked the young men for their story, which Sigmund related to him. Then, at Sigmund's request, Ulf told his own story: his real name was Thorkel Barfrost, son of Steingrim, and he had fallen in love with Ragnhild, the daughter of Thoralf, but Thoralf had not agreed to the marriage and Thorkel had run off with Ragnhild[6]. As a result of this, Thorkel had been banished and they had come to Ulfdal to live[6].

Sigmund then admitted to Thorkel that he had had an affair with Thuride, the daughter of Thorkel and Ragnhild, and that she was expecting his child[7]. Thorkel said that he was aware of what was going on and had not wanted to stop it[7]. Sigmund told Thorkel that he wished eventually to marry Thuride, and Thorkel gave his consent[7]. In return for this, Sigmund promised Thorkel to try and obtain permission for Thorkel to return from exile[7].

Sigmund and Thorer then left Thorkel and went to Lade near Trondheim, where Earl Hakon had his seat, and told him their story[8]. Earl Hakon allowed Sigmund and Thorer to remain at his court for the winter, but made no decision about the cousins' future until the spring[8].

In the spring, Earl Hakon agreed to provide Sigmund and Thorer with a ship and crew so that they could go on a Viking expedition, and each of the Earl's sons, Erik and Sven, also gave them a ship and crew[9]. Sigmund and Thorer went with their ships to the Baltic and, at the end of the summer, they had a successful engagement with Randver of Holmgaard (or Novgorod)[10]. Earl Hakon gave Sigmund and Thorer a very good reception on their return to Norway and made them his courtiers: they spent the winter with him[11].

The following summer, the cousins went on a very successful expedition with their ships to Sweden and Russia, during which they fought with the Swedes, Bjørn and Vandil, and killed them before returning to Norway to spend the winter with Earl Hakon[12].

In the following year (about 982) Sigmund and Thorer went, at Earl Hakon's request, to British waters to destroy an enemy of the Earl, Harald Ironhead[13]. Eventually, towards the end of the summer, they came to Anglesey, in the Irish Sea, where they met Harald Ironhead and a fierce battle ensued[13]. At the end of the day, the two factions (according to custom) broke off the engagement until the following morning[13]. Next day, however, the two leaders got together and decided that they should not continue the fight and instead they joined forces and went raiding together[13]. At the end of the summer, Sigmund persuaded Harald to return to Norway and promised to plead on his behalf with Earl Hakon[13]. This he did, and eventually Sigmund managed to persuade Earl Hakon to become reconciled with Harald Ironhead[13]. Sigmund and Thorer spent the winter with Earl Hakon, but Harald went north to Helgeland on the border of Finnmark[13].

By this time, Hafgrim's son, Ossur, had grown up and Thrand had obtained the daughter of the best farmer in the Faroes as a wife for him[14]. He had also divided the Faroes into two parts and had given Ossur the part which his father Hafgrim had formerly controlled and also, as compensation for Hafgrim's death, the property which Brester and Beiner had owned and which should have gone to Sigmund and Thorer[14]. Word had, by this time, reached the Faroes of Sigmund's successes and, as a result, Ossur fortified his home in Skúvoy[14]. Next to Thrand, Ossur was the most powerful man in the Faroes, but Thrand was the richest man there and, being a wilier man than Ossur, it was he who had, in fact, control over all the islands[14].

After the expedition in which he had encountered Harald Ironhead, Sigmund told Earl Hakon that he wished to return to the Faroes to avenge his father's death, a request to which Earl Hakon agreed and allowed him to take two *knørrir* (ships more suitable for the Faroes than the normal longships)[15]. Before Sigmund left for the Faroes, Earl Hakon took him to a pagan priestess and gave her an offering of silver and persuaded her to give Sigmund a ring which would ensure his safe return[15]. The Earl told Sigmund never to part with the ring[15].

Sigmund then set out with Thorer and Harald Ironhead in two ships, each manned by sixty men[16]. This was in about 983. They had a fair passage to the Faroes and made a landfall at Eysturoy, but there they encountered bad weather so they went to Svínoy, arriving there at daybreak; and, when they had landed on that island, they seized Svínoy-Bjarni, who was in bed[16]. Bjarni admitted having been present when Sigmund's father was killed but reminded Sigmund that he had advised Thrand against killing him and Thorer[16].

Sigmund wanted Bjarni to go to Eysturoy with him and his companions, but Bjarni said that that would be impossible with the weather as it was and advised Sigmund to go to Skúvoy, where he thought they would find Ossur[17]. Sigmund and his companions, plus Harald Ironhead and fifty men provided by Bjarni, went to Skúvoy and attacked Ossur[17]. Ossur suggested that the case between them should be determined by the "best men in the Faroes" but Sigmund would not agree to this and, as a result, a battle ensued which ended in Ossur being killed by Sigmund and Ossur's men surrendering[17].

After the fight on Skúvoy, Sigmund was joined by Thorer who had, in the meantime, gone to Suðuroy[18]. Negotiations were then carried out between Sigmund and Thrand and a truce was declared and arrangements made for a meeting to be held at Tinganes on Streymoy[18]. Thrand was delighted with this and requested Sigmund to judge the case, but Sigmund insisted that Thrand should come back with him to Norway so that Earl Hakon could adjudicate on the matter[18].

Sigmund and Thorer spent the winter in the Faroes and, in the spring, prepared their ship for the journey to Norway: Thrand also prepared a cargo ship[19]. Sigmund and Thorer returned to Earl Hakon in Norway but Thrand did not turn up[19]. Later, reports arrived that his ship had been driven back by the weather to the Faroes and that damage to it had prevented it putting out to sea again[19].

Sigmund then asked Earl Hakon to determine the case, and this he did[20]. Earl Hakon ordered Thrand to pay four penalties by way of blood-money—one for the killing of Brester, one for the killing of Beiner, one for advising that Sigmund and Thorer should be killed when their fathers were slain and one for having delivered Sigmund and Thorer into slavery[20]. He also ordered that sufficient land should be taken from Thrand's share of the Faroes, and from what Ossur had inherited, to make Sigmund's share up to one half of the Faroes: the other half, however, was to be forfeited to him (the Earl)[20]. He further said that Sigmund should give Thorer such part of the blood-money as he

(Sigmund) thought fair[20]. Earl Hakon also said that Thrand could remain in the Faroes if he complied with his (the Earl's) ruling[20]. Finally, the Earl told Sigmund that he should have all the Faroe Islands in fief and pay tribute to him on his (the Earl's) share[20].

Sigmund thanked the Earl for his decision and spent the winter with him[21]. In the spring, Sigmund and Thorer returned to the Faroes and, on their arrival, Sigmund summoned a meeting of the Thing at Tinganes at which he informed Thrand of Earl Hakon's decision and said that Thrand could make up his mind whether or not he would keep to the terms of the settlement[21]. Thrand still wanted Sigmund to determine the case himself, but Sigmund refused[21]. Thrand finally agreed to accept the terms, but he asked for more time in which to pay the blood-money, as the Earl had ordered that the money should be paid within six months[21]. As a result of the petition of the people present at the Thing, Sigmund agreed to extend the period of payment to three years[21].

Thrand said it was perfectly reasonable for Sigmund to have control over the Faroes as he (Thrand) had had it for too long, to which Sigmund replied by telling Thrand not to be a hypocrite and at that they parted[22]. Thrand invited Leif, Ossur's son, to come home with him to Gøta and he brought Leif up there[23].

Sigmund sailed for Norway in the summer and, before his departure, Thrand reluctantly paid him one third of the blood-money[24]. Sigmund and Thorer had a good journey to Norway and, on their arrival, Sigmund paid over the tribute to Earl Hakon with whom they spent the winter[24]. This would be in about 985/6.

According to the *Faroese Saga*[25], in the year after the Christmas when Earl Hakon made Sigmund a courtier they went to the summer Thing at Frosta. This would suggest that it was in the summer of about 981 when Sigmund was away on his expedition to Sweden and Russia, but this does not seem to fit in. The summer after Sigmund returned from the Faroes after receiving the first third of the blood-money[26] could, however, fit in with the facts and this would place it at about the summer of 986, but exact dates after a lapse of nearly one thousand years are hard to fix and can be only approximate.

At any rate, when Sigmund went to Frosta with Earl Hakon, Sigmund applied to the Earl on behalf of Thorkel Barfrost for permission for Thorkel to return from exile[27]. This the Earl readily granted and he invited Thorkel and his family to spend the winter with him, which they did[26]. In the following spring, Earl Hakon gave Thorkel control of a district in Orkedal which Thorkel accepted[27]. After Sigmund had obtained permission for Thorkel to return, he asked Thorkel's leave to woo Thuride, who had given birth to his daughter, Thora, in the same summer that Sigmund and Thorer had left Ulfdal (viz: in about 979)[27]. Thorkel agreed to this, and Sigmund and Thuride were married at Earl Hakon's residence, the wedding celebrations lasting for seven days[27]. In the autumn, Sigmund returned to the Faroes with Thuride and Thora[27]. This would appear to have been in about the autumn of 986, but again the exact year is in doubt.

The winter following the journey of Sigmund and his family to the Faroes was quiet, and in the spring a meeting of the Thing was held at Tinganes[28]. Sigmund and Thrand both attended and the latter demanded the second third of his blood-money: Thrand, for his part, asked Sigmund to pay blood-money to Leif Ossurson for having killed Ossur on Skúvoy[28]. Sigmund refused to pay the blood-money and Thrand, cowed by threats from Sigmund, handed over the second third of the blood-money to Sigmund[28]. Sigmund made a short trip that summer to pay Earl Hakon the tribute due to him and returned to the Faroes for the winter[28]. Sigmund was popular in the Faroes except with Thrand, with whom he was continually having disputes, as a result of which Svínoy-Bjarni was constantly having to make peace between them[28]. In the spring, another meeting of the Thing was held at Tinganes at which Sigmund demanded the third third of the blood-money, while Thrand counter-claimed for blood-money for Leif Ossurson. In the end, neither Thrand nor Sigmund paid over any money[28].

Sigmund and Thorer sailed again to Norway that summer but Thuride and Thora remained behind in the Faroes[29]. They arrived at Trondheim late in the autumn, and, when Sigmund had handed over the tribute to Earl Hakon, he and Thorer stayed with the Earl[29]. By this time, Sigmund was twenty-seven years of age[29], and the year would be about 988. Sigmund would appear to have spent the winter there before returning to the Faroes.

The *Faroese Saga* refers to Sigmund killing Bue the Stout in a battle between the Jomsvikings and Earl Hakon and his sons who were supported by Sigmund and Thorer[30]. This engagement would appear, from the *Saga,* to have occurred in the winter referred to in the preceding paragraphs, but the accuracy of the whole incident is queried by some authorities: it is more than probable that, if the incident did occur at all, it was at an earlier period.

The *Saga* does not relate what took place in the six years following 988, but Sigmund probably spent them in the Faroes.

1   FS p. 7. c. 9.
2   FS p. 10. c. 10.
3   See p. 6. *ante.*
4   FS p. 10. c. 10.
5   FS p. 12. c. 13.
6   FS pp. 13-15.
7   FS p. 15.
8   FS p. 15.
9   FS p. 16. c. 17.
10 FS pp. 16 & 17. c. 18.
11 FS p. 17.
12 FS pp. 18-20, cc. 19 & 20.
13 FS pp. 20 & 21.
14 FS p. 22. c. 22.
15 FS pp. 22 & 23, c. 23.
16 FS pp. 22 (c. 24) & 25.

17 FS p. 25. c. 24. See also p. 82 *post* regarding the "best man in the Faroes".
18 FS pp. 25 & 26. c. 24.
19 FS p. 26. c. 24.
20 FS p. 26. c. 25.
21 FS pp. 26 & 27. c. 25.
22 FS p. 27. c. 25.
23 *Ibid.*
24 *Ibid.*
25 FS p. 27. c. 26.
26 See previous paragraph.
27 FS p. 27. c. 26.
28 FS pp. 27 & 28. c. 26.
29 FS p. 28. c. 27.
30 *Ibid.*

CHAPTER 5

994 to 1005

Olaf Tryggvason ousted Earl Hakon as ruler of Norway somewhere about 995. The precise date is not certain but the better view seems to be that, having been converted to Christianity in England in 994, he returned to Norway, reputedly via the Orkneys, with a following of war-hardened Vikings and, so it is said, with a complement of English or English-trained priests [1].

According to the *Orkneyinga Saga*[2], King Olaf, while in the Orkneys, met Sigurd, Earl of the Orkneys, and gave him the choice of becoming a Christian or being beheaded, as a result of which the Earl was baptized[2]. King Olaf then ordered the Earl to convert all his people to Christianity and, in order to ensure that the Earl obeyed his command, he took the Earl's son, Hundi or Hvelp (Whelp), to Norway with him as hostage[2]. This incident probably also assisted the cause of Christianity in the Sudreys[3] as about this time the Sudreys came under the Earl of Orkney, who administered them through his brother-in-law, Earl Gille[4]. This name Gille, which is Celtic, is taken to indicate that the original holder of it was a Norseman who had been converted to Christianity[5].

According to the *Faroese Saga*[6], after King Olaf had been two years on the throne, he sent a messenger to the Faroes inviting Sigmund Bresterson to come to see him in Norway and saying that he would make Sigmund the most powerful man in the Faroes if he became the King's man. This must have been somewhere about 997.

Sigmund came to Norway and met King Olaf at Sunnmøre[7]. The King gave Sigmund a warm welcome, and had a long talk with Sigmund in which he related his life story and explained that it was very similar to that of Sigmund[7]. King Olaf exhorted Sigmund to become a Christian, to which Sigmund agreed and, as a result, Sigmund and all his followers were baptized and spent the winter with the King[7].

In the spring, King Olaf came to Sigmund and asked him to go to the Faroes and convert the inhabitants to Christianity[8]. At first, Sigmund declined to do this but he finally agreed to do what the King wished[8]. The King then put Sigmund in charge of all the Faroes and sent priests with him to teach the Faroese Christianity[8].

Sigmund sailed to the Faroes and summoned the farmers to a meeting of the Thing at Tinganes on Streymoy[9]. When Sigmund informed the meeting that King Olaf had appointed him to be in charge of the Faroes the information was well received by most of those present[9]. However, when he announced to the Faroese people that the King wished him to convert them to Christianity, he met with very strong opposition from the farmers led by Thrand and, to save his own life, he had to back down and swear to the people that he would abandon the idea of converting them[9]. Sigmund spent the winter, which would appear to be about that of 998-9, at his home in Skúvoy and he harboured resentment against the way in which the farmers had acted[9].

One day, in the following spring, when the currents were so strong that people did not think that anyone would put out to sea, Sigmund set out with thirty men from Skúvoy determined to carry out the King's command or to die in the attempt[10]. The party having landed on Eysturoy and encircled the farm at Gøta, made their way into the house and seized Thrand[10]. Sigmund gave Thrand the choice of agreeing to being baptized or being put to death[10]. Thrand said he did not wish to be converted but, when threatened with an axe, he finally agreed to become a Christian[10]. Thorer wanted Sigmund to kill Thrand, as otherwise he considered that Thrand would eventually be the cause of their death, but Sigmund did not agree with him[10]. Then Thrand and all his household were baptized and the conversions continued throughout the islands until all the Faroese had become Christians[10].

In the summer, Sigmund set out with Thrand for Norway with the tribute for King Olaf, but the ship was wrecked and the tribute lost, although most of the people on board were saved, Thrand being rescued by Sigmund[11]. Sigmund then prepared another ship, but Thrand said that the journey would be unlucky if he was forced to go[11]. Sigmund, however, made Thrand come with him, but once again the ship was wrecked[11].

Sigmund then let Thrand, who said that they would never succeed in their voyage if he was forced to go against his will, remain behind in the Faroes on condition that he swore a sacred oath that he would uphold the Christian faith in the Faroes, and that he would be faithful to King Olaf[12]. Sigmund himself spent the winter in the Faroes and went to Norway in the spring, with tributes for that year and the previous one, and stayed with King Olaf[12]. During his visit, which lasted far into the spring, King Olaf and Sigmund took part in swimming and shooting contests and in other sports. King Olaf came first in each contest, but Sigmund was not far behind[13].

According to legend, one evening King Olaf noticed Sigmund's gold ring (the one which Earl Hakon had obtained for him from the priestess) and tried to persuade Sigmund to give it to him in exchange for another one equally good[14]. Sigmund, however, said he could not do this because he had promised Earl Hakon not to part with the ring[14]. The King then said that the ring would be the cause of Sigmund's death[14]. The incident closed, but relations between the two were never as good as they had been previously[14].

Sigmund left for the Faroes in the summer and he and King Olaf never met again[15]. This event would appear to have taken place in about the year 1000[16].

After King Olaf's death, Norway was ruled by Earl Erik and Earl Sven[17]. Somewhere about 1001, the Earls invited Sigmund to come to Norway, and, as a result, he travelled to Lade, near Trondheim, to meet them; and on his arrival they gave him a warm welcome, made him a courtier and assigned the Faroes to him in fief[17]. Sigmund returned to the Faroes in the autumn[17].

At this time, there lived at Gøta with Thrand, in addition to Leif Ossurson, three other young men who were all about the same age as Leif[18]. These were Sigurd, the son of Thrand's elder brother Thorlak, Sigurd's brother, Thord the Short, and Gaut the Red, the son of Thrand's sister[18].

Sigmund and Thuride had, by now, in addition to their eldest daughter Thora, four sons, namely, Thoralf, Steingrim, Brand and Heri[19].

During the rule of the Earls, Christianity had waned throughout the Kingdom of the Earls, although the Earls themselves and Sigmund and his people remained good Christians[20]. Moreover, Sigmund allowed a church to be built on his farm at Skúvoy[20]. Thrand, on the other hand, almost reverted to paganism[20].

One day a meeting of the Thing was summoned (presumably at Tinganes on Streymoy) and Thrand demanded blood-money from Sigmund on behalf of Leif Ossurson. Sigmund demurred and said that the whole case had been settled by Earl Hakon and that he owed no blood-money. Thrand replied by saying that he had not forgotten how Sigmund had humiliated him and made him change his faith and warned Sigmund that the people would not put up for long with the violation of their rights[21]. Sigmund was not, however, alarmed by these threats[21].

Shortly after this, Thrand and his companions made two attacks on Sigmund[22]. The first of these took place when Sigmund, Thorer and Einar the Sudreyan (the same person who some thirty-five years previously had been involved in the quarrel with Eldjarn Kamhat which led to the killing of Brester and Beiner) were on a visit to Lítla Dímun to kill some of the sheep which grazed on that island[22]. Sigmund and his friends managed, however, to outmanoeuvre Thrand's party and escaped, taking Thrand's ship with them[23]. The second attack was made later in the summer when a fight took place at sea as Sigmund was going around collecting land dues: once again Sigmund defeated Thrand and his companions[23]. These events would appear to have taken place in about the year 1005.

In the late autumn of the same year, Thrand made his final attack on Sigmund[24]. He collected a party, sixty strong, which, apart from himself, included his nephews Sigurd, Thord the Short and Gaut the Red, Leif Ossurson, Steingrim, a neighbour of Thrand's, and Eldjarn Kamhat, the enemy of Einar the Sudreyan[24]. Svínoy-Bjarni did not take part in the raid as he and Sigmund had made their peace[24].

Thrand and his party landed on Skúvoy and attacked the farm when Sigmund, his wife Thuride and their children were there, and also Thorer and Einar the Sudreyan[25]. Thrand set fire to the house as well as attacking it, but Sigmund, Thorer and Einar escaped through a secret passage[25]. After a time, Thuride opened the door and told the attackers that the leaders had left, as a result of which the attackers searched for them and a short engagement took place at the gorge which crosses the island[25]. During the engagement, Sigmund killed Steingrim but lost his sword. Eventually, Sigmund and his companions, considering discretion to be the better part of valour, dived into the sea and swam for Suðuroy[25]. Such a swim seems incredible unless the swimmers had the benefit of a very strong tide for the whole of the time. The distance to be swum would seem to be about fifteen kilometres.

Einar was the first of the three swimmers to give up, but Sigmund carried him on his back until Thorer pointed out that Einar was dead[26]. Thorer carried on for some time but then he too became exhausted and Sigmund carried him on his shoulders until they approached Suðuroy, when Thorer was torn from his shoulders by a large wave and drowned. However, Sigmund managed to get ashore at Sandvík on the north-east coast of Suðuroy at dawn and lay down on a pile of seaweed and remained there until broad daylight[26]. This account must, however, be considered as mere surmise, not historical.

A farmer known as Thorgrim the Evil lived with his two sons, Ormstein and Thorstein, on a farm not far from where Sigmund came ashore[27]. Thorgrim, who was a copyhold tenant of Thrand, went to the beach with a wood axe on the morning Sigmund came ashore and discovered Sigmund under a pile of seaweed. When asked by Thorgrim who he was, Sigmund told him his story[27]. Thorgrim's sons then arrived and Sigmund asked for help[27]. However, Thorgrim had seen Sigmund's gold ring (the one which Earl Hakon had obtained for him from the priestess) and proposed that he and his sons should dispose of Sigmund in order to get possession of it[27]. His sons at first opposed this proposal, but finally agreed, at which Thorgrim cut off Sigmund's head and he and his sons removed Sigmund's clothes and valuables and buried him under an earth bank[27]. Thus King Olaf's prophecy that the ring would cause the death of Sigmund came true[28].

Later, Thorer's body was washed ashore and Thorgrim and his sons buried it beside Sigmund's[29].

1   GJ pp. 132 & 133.
2   OS pp. xxvii and 3.
3   Christianity seems to have survived in the Isle of Man throughout the ninth and tenth centuries, albeit in low profile.
4   M p. 94.
5   See M p. 163 *n*.

6   FS p. 29. c. 29.
7   FS pp. 29 & 30. c. 29.
8   FS p. 31. c. 30.
9   *Ibid.*
10 FS pp. 31 & 32. c. 31.
11 FS p. 32 & 33. c. 31.
12 FS p. 33. c. 31.
13 FS p. 33. c. 32.
14 FS pp. 33 & 34. c. 33.
15 FS p. 34. c. 33.
16 GJ p. 393, note 1.
17 FS p. 34. c. 34.
18 FS p. 34. c. 35.
19 *Ibid.*
20 *Ibid.*
21 FS pp. 34 & 35. c. 35.
22 FS pp. 35 & 36. c. 36.
23 *Ibid.*
24 FS p. 36. c. 37.
25 FS pp. 36-38. c. 37.
26 FS pp. 38 & 39. c. 38.
27 FS p. 39. c. 38.
28 See p. 21 *ante.*
29 FS p. 39. c. 38.

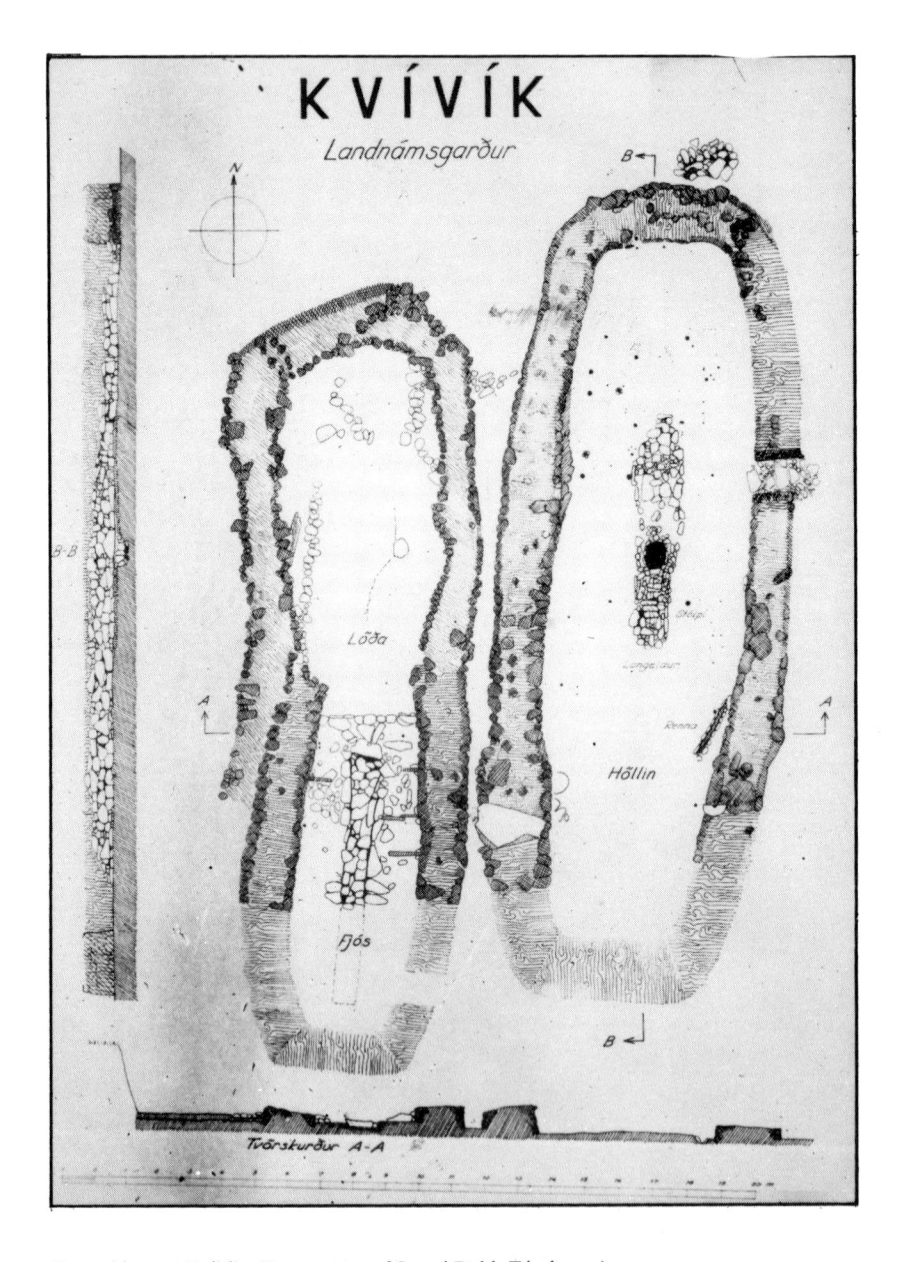

Excavations at Kvíkík. (By courtesy of Sverri Dahl, Tórshavn.)

CHAPTER 6

1005 to 1035

Thrand and his companions returned to Gøta after the fight on Skúvoy[1]. The farm at Skúvoy had not been badly damaged by the fire and Thuride, who now received the additional name of "the Principal Widow", ran it[1]. Thrand and Leif Ossurson had by this time complete control of the Faroes[1]. They tried to obtain a reconciliation with Thuride and her sons and offered to agree to such terms as "the best men in the Faroes" would decide, but Thuride and her sons did not, however, wish to accept that solution[1]. On the other hand, while they were young, the sons did not try to get help from Norway and the Faroes were peaceful for some time[1].

After a while, Thrand suggested to Leif Ossurson that he should woo Thora, the daughter of Sigmund and Thuride[2]. Leif was pessimistic about the outcome, but they went to Skúvoy, where they met with a chilly reception[2]. Thrand again offered Thuride and her sons such reconciliation as "the best men in the islands" might determine[2]. Thrand then wooed Thora on Leif's behalf, believing that that would be the best way in which to effect a reconciliation between the two parties, and offered to give Leif a large fortune if Thora accepted him as a husband[2]. Thora was not a very beautiful woman but she was a wise one, and she said that she was not lusting after marriage and would lay down certain conditions for the acceptance of the proposal of marriage, namely, that Leif should swear that he had taken no part in killing Sigmund and that he should find out who the killers were[2]. Thora went on to say that, if this was done, a reconciliation would be concluded on such terms as her brothers, mother and kinsmen would recommend[2]. Everyone agreed that this was a wise decision and the meeting broke up[2].

Shortly after this, Thrand left Gøta and sailed to Sandvík on Suðuroy with Leif and went to the farm of Thorgrim the Evil[3]. Thrand questioned Thorgrim about Sigmund's death and, after hearing his answers, accused Thorgrim of having killed Sigmund, which Thorgrim denied[3].

Thrand then had Thorgrim and his sons bound and chained, and according to the *Faroese Saga*[4] (although this is undoubtedly legend and not fact), he then held a séance in which he conjured back to life Einar the Sudreyan, Thorer and Sigmund[4]. When Sigmund appeared he was covered in blood and carried his head under his arm[4]. From these manifestations, Thrand deduced that Einar and Thorer had died of cold or were drowned, but the prisoners had killed Sigmund[4]. This deduction was accepted as the truth by all Thrand's companions[4]. Thrand then ordered his men to search the whole house and eventually they found Sigmund's gold ring (the one which Earl Hakon had obtained for him from the priestess)[4]. When Thorgrim saw the gold ring, he confessed everything and took Thrand and his companions to the place where Sigmund and Thorer were buried[4]. The two corpses were removed and were later re-buried in the church on Skúvoy[4].

Thrand took Thorgrim and his sons to Tórshavn where a full meeting of the Thing was summoned at Tinganes[5]. At this meeting, Thorgrim the Evil and his sons publicly confessed to Sigmund's murder and to secreting his corpse, and, as a result, all three of them were hanged on the spot[5].

After this Leif and Thrand pressed Leif's courtship with Thora and offered reconciliation on such terms as would suit Thora and her mother[6]. The end result was that Leif married Thora and there was a complete reconciliation[6]. Leif settled down in his ancestral farm at Hov in Suðuroy[6]. This would all appear to have occurred in about 1010.

For a time there was peace in the Faroes, during which Thora's brother, Thoralf Sigmundson, married and made his home in Stóra Dimun[7].

About this time, King Olaf the Holy of Norway[8] enacted legislation taxing the whole of his kingdom except Iceland[9]. The Orkneys were the first to be taxed, followed by the Shetlands, then the Faroes and finally Greenland[9].

In about the year 1024, in answer to a summons from King Olaf, Gille the Lawman[10], Leif Ossurson and Thoralf from Stóra Dimun (the eldest son of Sigmund and Thuride) travelled to Norway[11]. Thrand should have accompanied them but, just before they left the Faroes, he suddenly became ill and was unable to travel[11].

When the Faroese met King Olaf, he told them that he wanted an assurance from them, confirmed on oath, that they would uphold his laws, submit to his justice and pay the taxes which he imposed[12]. He further said that, if they did so, the most distinguished of them would become his men and receive his friendship and honours[12]. The Faroese felt that they would suffer if they did not agree to the King's demands and, accordingly, they did so and became the King's courtiers and took the oath which the King demanded[12]. The three Faroese then left for home taking with them gifts which the King had given them[12].

King Olaf sent a ship to the Faroes to collect the taxes which were due, but the crew never returned and no taxes arrived the following summer[13]. People said that the ship never arrived in the Faroes and no one collected any taxes there[13].

In the following spring, about that of 1026, a ship came to the Faroes with a message from King Olaf requiring Leif Ossurson, Gille the Lawman or Thoralf from Stóra Dímun to come to him [14]. The three of them met and tried to guess what the King wanted, but they all felt that it had something to do with the missing emissaries who had been sent to collect the taxes in the Faroes [14]. They then decided that Thoralf should be the one to go to Norway [14]. Thoralf prepared a cargo ship for the journey and got a crew together, the total complement amounting to ten or twelve men [14]. When all was ready, they waited for a fair wind [14]. One day at about this time, when the weather was fine, Thrand went into the main room of his house and, seeing his three nephews, Sigurd, Thord the Short and Gaut the Red, lounging around, he said that things had changed since his young days and that their forefathers would never have believed that Thoralf could have been braver than the three nephews [14]. He further said that, if he had been some years younger, he would have set out to sea himself and taken to Norway the wool which was lying in the houses [14]. Sigurd then jumped up and went out and called Thord, saying that he would not be insulted in this way [14]. They prepared a ship, also manned by ten or twelve men, and set out for Norway [14].

Both ships set sail at the same time and were within sight of each other throughout the journey to Norway [15]. Both made a landfall in the dark at Herna, Sigurd's ship being anchored further out to sea than Thoralf's [15]. During this evening, Thoralf and one of his men went ashore and were attacked [15]. Thoralf was killed and the other man was thrown into the sea, but got ashore again [15]. When his crew heard of the incident, they brought Thoralf's body on board and sent a message to King Olaf who was then staying at Lygra [15]. A meeting of the Thing was immediately summoned by an arrow (to indicate the martial nature of the meeting [15]).

When the meeting was assembled, the King said that a brave young man had been killed and asked if anyone could tell him who was responsible, but no one replied [16]. The King then said that he believed that Sigurd had killed Thoralf and that Thord the Short had thrown the other man into the sea [16]. He believed that they had committed these acts because they did not want Thoralf to tell him about the murder of the King's emissaries in the Faroes, for which Thoralf must have known that Sigurd and Thord were responsible [16].

Sigurd then got up and said that if he had wanted to kill Thoralf he could have done so in the Faroes instead of in Norway right under the King's eyes [17]. He denied the charge and offered to confirm his denial on oath according to Norweigan law or "to carry the hot iron" as proof of his innocence [17]. After some discussion and in accordance with the wish of the people present, the King accepted Sigurd's offer to "carry the iron" [17] and it was arranged that Sigurd should go to Lygra in the morning where the ordeal would be supervised by the bishop [18]. The King then went back to Lygra and Sigurd and his companions returned to their ship [18]. On his return to the ship, Sigurd told his crew that the King had been responsible for Thoralf's death and that he now wanted to make the rest of them outlaws[18]. He suggested that they should leave immediately, to which the rest of the crew agreed, and they set sail and kept well out to sea[18]. When they returned to the Faroes, Thrand expressed his disapproval at what they had done[18].

King Olaf soon learned what Sigurd and his companions had done and they were severely criticised[19]. There was considerable support for the view that Sigurd's conduct raised a reasonable presumption that he was guilty of the offences with which the King had charged him[19].

King Olaf went south the following spring and at one of his regular House Things raised the question of his emissaries who had been killed in the Faroes and of the taxes which had not been collected from those islands[20]. He then said he wanted to send men to the Faroes to collect the taxes and asked several people to undertake the mission, but they all excused themselves from doing so[20]. Then a man stood up and offered to go to the Faroes to collect the taxes: this was Carl of Møre, who had been a great Viking in his day, but, in the past, the King and Carl had been enemies[20]. King Olaf accepted Carl's offer and invited him to come and stay with him as his guest[20].

The King sent messages by Carl to his aides in the Faroes, Leif Ossurson and Gille the Lawman[10], and asked them to co-operate with Carl[21]. As soon as Carl was ready, he sailed for the Faroes with nineteen companions[21]. When he arrived in the Faroes, Carl berthed in Tórshavn, and immediately a meeting of the Thing was held at Tinganes and a large crowd of people attended, including Thrand and his supporters and Leif and Gille and their supporters[21].

After Leif and Gille had pitched their tents and the Thing had got under way, they went and called on Carl, who gave them the messages from King Olaf[22]. These they much appreciated and they invited Carl to come and stay with them and promised to help him with his mission[22]. Shortly afterwards, Thrand arrived, welcomed Carl to the Faroes and invited him to spend the winter with him[22]. However, Carl pointed out that he had already promised to spend the winter with Leif[22]. When Thrand asked if he could assist him in any other way, Carl said it would be a very great help if Thrand could collect the taxes from the Northern Islands, namely Kalsoy, Kunoy, Borðoy, Viðoy, Svínoy, and Fugloy. Carl of Møre spent the winter with Leif·Ossurson, who collected taxes from Streymoy and from all the islands south of it[23].

In the following spring, Thrand became very ill with eye trouble, asthma and other complaints, but, all the same, he came to the meeting of the Thing in the spring as usual[23]. When he arrived at the Thing, he had a curtain placed inside his tent with a black curtain under the first one with the object of preventing the sun shining brightly into the tent[23].

After the Thing had been in session for some days, Leif and Carl went to Thrand's tent with a large crowd of supporters[24]. They entered the tent and Leif went behind the black curtain and asked where Thrand was[27]. Thrand answered him and, after they had exchanged greetings, Leif asked Thrand if he had collected the money from the Northern Islands, to which Thrand replied that he had not forgotten his promise to

Carl and handed Leif a purse which he said contained silver[24]. Leif looked round and saw that there were only a few people present[24]. He then took the purse to Carl and asked him to look at the money[24]. They examined the silver and discovered that it was of the lowest grade that could be found in the Northern Islands[24]. Thrand then took the silver back and gave them another bag[24]. Carl and Leif examined it and, although the silver was better than the first lot, they considered it was not good enough to take back to King Olaf[24]. Gaut the Red objected to this view, but Thrand rebuked him and gave Leif yet another bag of silver which the people from his own island (i.e. Eysturoy) had given him[24]. Thord the Short then got up and threatened Carl for having criticized the earlier silver[24]. Carl and Leif were perfectly satisfied with the grade of the third bag of silver and they began to pour it into Carl's helmet in order to weigh it[25]. At that moment, someone came in and said that Sigurd Thorlakson had killed one of Gille the Lawmen's men[25]. Leif immediately left the tent but Carl remained surrounded by the Norwegians[25]. Gaut the Red then hit Carl with an axe and seized a weapon which had been sticking in the ground and struck the axe with it so that it went right down into Carl's brain[25].

Thrand condemned the murder but offered blood-money on behalf of his kinsmen. However, Leif and Gille, who were parties to the case, would not accept the blood-money[26]. Then, probably as a result of a decision of the Thing at Tinganes, Sigurd was banished for killing Gille's man and Gaut the Red and Thord the Short were banished on account of the murder of Carl of Møre[26]. Thrand gave them a ship in which to leave the country, but after it sailed there was a heavy storm and there were rumours that it had been wrecked[26].

The Norwegians returned to Norway but no one came from Norway to avenge Carl's death for there was trouble in that country, and so ended the episode which had occured as a result of King Olaf demanding taxes from the Faroes[27].

After the death of Carl of Møre (probably in about 1028), there were many quarrels between Thrand on the one hand and Leif Ossurson and Gille the Lawman[10] on the other[28]. In the following spring, Thrand arranged a meeting with Leif and suggested that they should pass a law prohibiting the carrying of arms to the Thing[29]. He also said that the Thing should be a place where cases were debated and reconciliations made[29]. Leif discussed the proposal with Gille the Lawman[10] but, not trusting Thrand, they decided that only the officals and their followers should bring arms to the Thing, and that the common people should go unarmed[29]. This solution was agreed to by all parties[29].

A meeting of the Thing was held at Tinganes that summer[30]. One day in the course of the meeting, Gille and Leif came out of their tent which was on a hill and saw a party of about thirty armed men coming from the East, led by Sigurd Thorlakson, Gaut the Red and Thord the Short, approaching[30]. On seeing this, Leif and Gille went back to their tent[30]. Sigurd and his party came to the tent and were joined by Thrand and his followers, who were all fully armed[30]. Leif and Gille had only a few men to oppose these people and only a small number of those were armed [30]. Thrand said that he and his kinsmen would no longer be subject to Leif and Gille and that if they did not submit to his ruling he would let Sigurd and his companions dispose of them [30]. Seeing that they had no alternative, Leif and Gille agreed to abide by Thrand's judgement in the case [30].

Thrand ruled that Sigurd, Gaut and Thord should be allowed to live where they wished in the Faroes, despite the fact that they had been banished and that no blood money should be payable for what they had done [31]. In addition, he declared that the Faroes should be divided into three equal parts, one part going to him, one to Leif and the third to the sons of Sigmund Bresterson [31]. Finally, he offered to bring up Leif's son, Sigmund (i.e. the grandson of Sigmund Bresterson) [31]. Leif replied that he would leave to his wife, Thora, the question of the upbringing of their son [31].

When Thora was told of Thrand's offer, she said that she would not deprive Sigmund of a good upbringing and that Thrand was far superior to most people in the Faroes [32]. And so Sigmund, who was three years old, went to Gøta to be brought up by Thrand [32]. This was in about the year 1029.

The *Faroese Saga* states [33] that, during the time when Sven was King of Norway and ruled with his mother Aelgifu (the English mistress of King Canute the Great), Thrand lived at Gøta and his nephews, Sigurd, Gaut and Thord resided with him. This would be around the early 1030's.

After some time, Thrand's patience with his lazy nephews became exhausted and he made them leave his house [34]. The three nephews then went to live on Streymoy [34]. Sigurd went into partnership with a wealthy Streymoy farmer called Thorhal the Rich who had a young wife called Birna, who had married him for his wealth [34]. As a result of their agreement, Sigurd went over all the Faroes collecting money due to Thorhal and made a lot of money out of this enterprise, of which he was allowed to retain half [34]. In the following spring, Sigurd and Birna took over the running of Thorhal's house, and Thorhal had no longer any say in it [34].

In the summer of that year, a cargo ship was wrecked on Suðuroy, but there were seven survivors including the masters of the ship, three brothers called Hafgrim, Bjarngrim and Hergrim [35]. Sigurd invited the brothers to stay with him in Thorhal's house [35]. The three guests were well looked after there, better in fact than Thorhal was [35]. Thorhal was a very stingy man and he and Bjarngrim often quarrelled: on one occasion the quarrel ended in blows [35]. In spite of this, the brothers spent the winter in Thorhal's house and in the spring Sigurd gave them a cargo ship of which he was part owner with Thorhal [33]. The brothers slept on the ship at night but returned to the farm during the daytime [35].

One evening, Sigurd returned to Thorhal's house and asked for Thorhal and was told he was asleep, but he discovered later that Thorhal had been killed [36]. Sigurd, Gaut the Red and Thord the Short then went down to the ship and killed the three brothers, Hafgrim, Bjarngrim and Hergrim[36]. They then went home, taking the three brothers' property with them and claiming that they had avenged Thorhal's death[36]. However, rumours went around blaming Sigurd and his kinsmen for Thorhal's death[36]. At all events, Sigurd married Birna and they had a large family[36].

Later on, Gaut the Red entered into an arrangement with a farmer called Thorvald, who lived in Sandoy, similar to the arrangement which Sigurd had had with Thorhal: he also made a great deal of money from it[37]. Gaut spent as much time with Thorvald as he did with Sigurd, and it was rumoured that he had seduced Thorvald's wife, Thorbera[37]. Sigurd's arrangement with Thorvald ended with the murder of Thorvald one evening in the dark in his house when Gaut and some of his men, and a fisherman who owed Thorvald some money, were present[37]. Gaut killed the fisherman as soon as he saw that Thorvald was dead, accusing the fisherman of having murdered Thorvald[37]. After Thorvald's death, Gaut the Red married Thorbera and together they ran Thorvald's farm[37].

Beiner's son, Thorer, had a son, Leif, who traded between Norway and the Faroes and, when he was in the Faroes, he took turns in staying with Leif Ossurson and with Thuride, Sigmund Bresterson's widow[38]. On one occasion, however, Sigurd Thorlakson invited Leif Thorerson to stay with him and Leif accepted the invitation, much to the displeasure of his namesake, Leif Ossurson[38].

Leif Thorerson spent that winter with Sigurd and was well treated[39]. One day in the spring, Sigurd asked Leif to go with him to a neighbour called Bjørn who owed him some money[39]. According to Sigurd, Bjørn became offensive when he asked him for the money and took an axe and tried to hack Sigurd with it[39]. However, Leif had run in between them and caught the blow from the axe, which killed him[39]. Sigurd said that he then killed Bjørn but there was no one who could corroborate Sigurd's story and nasty rumours began to circulate regarding Sigurd's role in the affair[39].

Thuride, Sigmund's Bresterson's widow, and Thora, Leif Ossurson's wife, reproached Leif for not having avenged the disgrace from which they suffered and accused him of cowardice and indolence[40]. However, according to the *Faroese Saga* [40], Sigmund Bresterson appeared to Thuride in a dream and told her not to be angry with Leif and said that he would, in due course, avenge her shame. After that, Thuride and Thora were more tolerant to Leif[40].

One day an eighteen man ship with a master called Arnljot came to Streymoy from Norway and berthed near Sigurd's farm[41]. Arnljot came from the Sudreys and he went to a man called Skofte who worked for the traders and lived near to where the ship was berthed[41]. Arnljot told Skofte that he was the father of the three brothers, Hafgrim, Bjarngrim and Hergrim, who had been killed by Sigurd and his kinsmen[41]. Skofte said that he "had no time for" Sigurd and would let Arnljot know when a suitable opportunity for revenge should occur[41].

As a result, one day that summer Arnljot and his men went to an island where Sigurd, Gaut the Red and Thord the Short had gone to slaughter sheep and a fight took place, which ended with Sigurd and his companions coming out the winners[42]. Sigurd made Arnljot pay treble bloodmoney to each of the kinsmen before he left the Faroes[42]. He also caused Skofte to be banished from the Faroes when he heard about the part Skofte had played in the affair[42], presumably by bringing him before the Thing at Tinganes.

After this, Sigurd Thorlakson tried to get his brother, Thord the Short, to marry Thuride, Sigmund Bresterson's widow, but the latter was not enthusiastic[43]. However, on the following day, Sigurd went to Skúvoy and put the proposition to Thuride[43]. When Sigurd told Thord of her answer, he was surprised and could not believe that Thuride had been serious[43].

After the meeting with Sigurd, Thuride had gone to her daughter, Thora, and her son-in-law Leif Ossurson, and told them of the proposal and said that she had rejected the proposal with less vehemence than she might have done in view of the fact that it could serve as a bait which would enable them to get their revenge on Sigurd and his kinsmen[44]. They all considered that this was a good plan, but Leif was worried about their son, Sigmund, who was being brought up by Thrand[44]. They then decided that they must visit Thrand on Eysturoy[44]. At that time, Sigmund was nine years old[44] and the year would, therefore, be about 1035, so that the events which occurred after the death of Carl of Møre must have taken place somewhere between about 1030 and 1035.

When the party arrived at Gøta, Thora asked to see her son and she questioned him about what Thrand had taught him[45]. She discovered that Thrand had taught Sigmund everything about instituting suits and legal proceedings but that he had taught Sigmund his own personal brand of Christianity, which was a very strange one[45].

The visitors were very well entertained that night and they drank heavily[46]. With some difficulty Thora persuaded Thrand to let Sigmund sleep with her and Leif[46]. When Leif came to bed, Thora told him to go and immobilize all the boats in Eysturoy and, according to the *Faroese Saga,* he did so in the course of the night[46]. This must, of course, be an exaggeration, as it would have been physically impossible to do so in view of the size of Eysturoy. It is more probable that Leif put out of action the boats in the immediate vicinity of Gøta.

Early next morning, Thora and Sigmund left for the ship while Leif said goodbye to Thrand[47]. He told Thrand that Thora wanted to take Sigmund home with her but Thrand would not agree to this. Leif then went down to his ship[47]. When Thrand discovered that Leif and Thora had taken Sigmund with them, he went down to his own ship, but when his crew boarded the ship, the water came in and they could not put out to sea and, as a result, Leif was able to sail home unmolested[47]. Leif and his companions arrived in Skúvoy on the day when Sigurd and Thord were expected to come and continue the courtship of Thuride[47].

Sigurd Thorlakson and Thord the Short made arrangements to go to Skúvoy to keep their appointment, but Thord was very dubious about the outcome and said that he would be surprised if they should return to Gøta unharmed[48]. However, Sigurd, Thord and ten companions sailed to Skúvoy[48]. Sigurd went up alone to the farm, but Thord and the others remained behind at the boat[48].

When Sigurd arrived at the farm, he met Thuride and they sat down on a bench and, at her suggestion, faced the church with their back to the house[49]. They talked and Sigurd courted Thuride on his own account (not on Thord's) saying that he could soon arrange things so that he would be free to marry her[49]. However, when Sigurd tried to embrace her, Thuride pulled his cloak towards her[49]. At this moment, the door of the house opened and Thuride's son, Heri, rushed out with a sword in his hand[49]. Sigurd managed to duck under the cloak and escape, chased by Heri and other men[49]. Heri seized a spear and threw it at Sigurd, but Sigurd avoided it, and picking it up, threw it back, killing Heri[49]. Sigurd then ran for his ship chased by Leif, who managed to wound Sigurd in the waist before he got on board[49]. Leif followed later with a party of eighty men and pursued Sigurd to Streymoy[49]. On his arrival at Streymoy, Sigurd went ashore but he died shortly afterwards from the wound which Leif had inflicted on him[49].

When Leif and his party arrived at Streymoy, they attacked the farm where Gaut the Red and Thord the Short were[50]. During the fight, Gaut the Red wounded Heri's brother, Steingrim, severely on the knee, as a result of which he, Steingrim, was given the nick-name "the Halt"[50]. Thord the Short killed Heri's other brother, Brand, but Leif killed both Gaut and Thord[50]. After this Leif returned home[51].

When Thrand heard the news of the death of his nephews, he was overcome with grief and died[51]. According to legend, when Thrand was on his death-bed, the Devil sent a halibut, black on both sides, for him, and, by the means of this transport, Thrand was conveyed to Hell: Leif Ossurson then became sole ruler over the whole of the Faroes[51]. This happened in the reign of Magnus I the Good, King of Norway[51], who came to the throne in 1035[52], and that is the year which is taken to be the one in which Leif Ossurson became sole ruler of the Faroes[53] and is also the date which the Faroese antiquarian, Sverri Dahl, considers to be the end of the Viking era in the Faroes and the beginning of the Middle Ages[54].

1 FS p. 39. c. 39 as to "the best men in the Faroes" see c. 12 *post*.
2 FS pp. 39 & 40. c. 39.
3 FS pp. 40 & 41. c. 39.
4 FS p. 41. c. 40.
5 FS p. 41. c. 41.
6 *Ibid*.
7 *Ibid*.
8 See Appendix I.
9 FS p. 42. c. 42.
10 Gille the Lawman is an interesting name, first because Gille is a Celtic word indicating the person concerned was a Norseman who had converted to Christianity (see M p. 163). In addition it indicates that he was the Lawman and it is of note that

he is the only person mentioned by that office in Icelandic literature outside Iceland and Greenland (L p. 12).
The son of Godred II, Crovan, of the Sudreys, was called Lagman, or Lawman in English (M. p. 104).

11 FS p. 42. c. 42.
12 *Ibid.*
13 *Ibid.*
14 FS pp. 42 & 43. c. 43.
15 FS p. 43.
16 FS pp. 43 & 44. c. 43.
17 FS p. 44. c. 43.
18 This would probably be Bishop Sigefrid the Younger as Bishop Grimkil,who preceded him, was King Olaf's legate to Archbishop Unwan of Hamburg-Bremen, see AB p. 214.
19 FS p. 44. c. 44.
20 FS pp. 44 & 45. c. 44.
21 FS pp. 45 & 46. c. 45.
22 FS p. 46. c. 45.
23 *Ibid.*
24 FS pp. 46-48. cc. 46 & 47.
25 FS pp. 47-8. c. 47.
26 FS p. 48. c. 47.
27 *Ibid.*
28 *Ibid.*
29 FS p. 48. c. 48.
30 FS pp. 48 & 49. c. 48. It has been suggested that Sigurd and his companions were probably coming from Hoyvík which used to be the harbour for boats coming to Tórshavn from Eysturoy.
31 FS p. 49. c. 48. Divisions into quarters, thirds and halves were common in the north (L. p. 7).
32 FS p. 50. c. 48.
33 FS p. 50. c. 49. Sven ruled Norway under King Canute the Great of Denmark and England, see Appendix I.
34 *Ibid.* According to legend, the three nephews settled at Kirkjubøur.
35 FS pp. 50 & 51. c. 50.
36 FS p. 51. c. 50.
37 FS pp. 51 & 52. c. 51.
38 FS p. 52. c. 52.
39 FS pp.52 & 53. cc. 52 & 53.
40 FS p. 53. c. 53.
41 FS p. 53. c. 54.
42 FS pp. 53 & 54. c. 54.
43 FS p. 54. c. 55.
44 *Ibid.*
45 FS pp. 54 & 55. c. 56.
46 FS p. 55.
47 FS pp. 55 & 56. c. 56.
48 FS pp. 56 & 57. c. 57.
49 FS p. 57.
50 FS pp. 57 & 58. c. 57.
51 FS p. 58.
52 See Appendix 1.
53 S facing page.
54 T vol. XIII *Fortidsminder* by Sverri Dahl p. 198.

CHAPTER 7

SIXTY-FIVE YEARS IN THE FAROES

970 to 1035

This is the period of pre-Reformation Faroese history about which we have the most written evidence, although it must be admitted that the authority for most of the events is the *Faroese Saga,* compiled from sagas written by monks living in Iceland, which is some 240 miles to the northwest of the Faroes and out of immediate contact with those islands, about 200 years after the events are alleged to have taken place.

It is conceded that one must approach the sagas with caution and it is appreciated that they are probably nearer to historical novels than to pure history, yet it is felt that, if cross-checking is done with other known facts, those given in the *Faroese Saga* can be seen to have a certain ring of truth.

The two outstanding Faroese personalties in the sixty-five years prior to 1035 are undoubtedly Thrand and Sigmund Bresterson, and it is equally obvious that the monks who wrote the sagas from which the *Faroese Saga* is compiled have been biased in favour of Sigmund and against Thrand. This is not an unreasonable bias in view of the fact that Sigmund supported Christianity while Thrand was, if one can call him a Christian, a very reluctant one![1].

Thrand was first and foremost a very astute, wily and not too honest politician but, if one gets down to basic facts, was he so very different from some of our so-called eminent politicians of the present era? Fundamentally, he was a supporter of his country and a Faroese nationalist opposed to outside interference from Norway.

Sigmund, on the other hand, was not without his faults. He tended to want his "pound of flesh" and he was not as merciful as he might have been. His refusal to go before "the best men of the Faroes" to settle his dispute with Hafgrim's son, Ossur, is an example of this[2].

Moreover, it could be said that Sigmund was no Faroese patriot, and that he was an adventurer and a "yes-man" of the Norwegian rulers whom he was quite prepared to support if it was to his personal advantage. It would appear that he was not really interested in Faroese self-government, and considered that he would benefit from being a lackey of the "Norwegian bosses." This view receives support from the fact that he did not object to becoming the liege man of Earl Hakon[3], Olaf Tryggvason[4] and Earls Sven and Erik[5].

In addition, it is doubtful whether Sigmund would have become a Christian and converted the Faroese unless he had been convinced that it would serve his own purposes, and it is quite obvious that King Olaf made it very clear that it would be to his advantage to become a Christian[6].

Despite the way in which the Saga is slanted in Sigmund's favour, it is doubtful whether in fact Sigmund was any more than a "rice-Christian"[7], and his reluctance to give King Olaf his gold ring might have been less strong if, in fact, he was a true follower of Christ! One is tempted to believe that both he and King Olaf still had a lot of faith in the powers of the ring just in the same way as the author of this book found, when in West Africa, that many a so-called Christian considered an oath on his "juju"[8] was more binding on him than an oath on the Bible.

Gwyn Jones has described King Olaf as Christ's best hatchetman of his day and place[9] but, as the *Faroese Saga* reveals in relation to the conversion of Thrand, Sigmund must have been Christ's axeman in the Faroes[10]!

It is also worth noting that, when Thrand was in control of the Faroes, the islands tended to be peaceful[11]. He was not an absolute dictator because, when Hafgrim's son, Ossur, became old enough, he divided the Faroes with him, although this apparently did not affect the practical situation to any great extent[12]. Also, he divided up the Faroes after the return of his three nephews from exile in such a way as to preserve peace[13]. A further example of his endeavours to make the Faroes peaceful was his effort, eventually successful, to effect a reconciliation with Thuride, the Principal Widow, and her sons[14].

Quite apart from the story of the persons involved during this period of Faroese history, the *Faroese Saga* gives one an insight into the operation of the political, judicial and legislative institutions affecting the Faroese. It indicates quite clearly that, apart from the rule of force in the islands, there was also a rule of law, and that, at any rate in certain respects, there was a form of democracy in the Faroes at that time[15].

With the death of Thrand, the real era of the Chiefs came to an end and, as will be seen, the Faroes came more under Norway and subsequently more under the Church[16].

The *Saga* shows the importance Thrand placed on having sons (albeit foster sons), he himself having been unmarried, although he is credited with having a daughter, Gudrun[17].

It also shows that women played an important part in Faroese life in those days as can be seen from the roles played by Thuride, the Principal Widow, and Thora[18].

1. FS pp. 31, 32 & 34.
2. FS p. 25.
3. FS p. 26. c. 25.
4. FS p. 31. c. 30.
5. FS p. 34. c. 34.
6. FS p. 30.
7. The name given in former days in China to Chinese who formally became Christians in order to collect the rations of rice given to their "flock" by the missionaries.
8. A powerful charm.
9. GJ p. 135.
10. FS p. 32.
11. See pp. 10, 25 and 26 *ante*.
12. See pp. 14 and 15 *ante*.
13. See p. 30 *ante*.
14. See pp. 25 and 26 *ante*.
15. See chapter 12.
16. He fostered Ossur and Leif Ossurson and brought up Sigurd Thorlakson, Gaut the Red, Thord the Short and Sigmund son of Leif and Thora.
17. FS p. 50. c. 49.
18. See pp. 25, 26 and 31-33 *ante*.

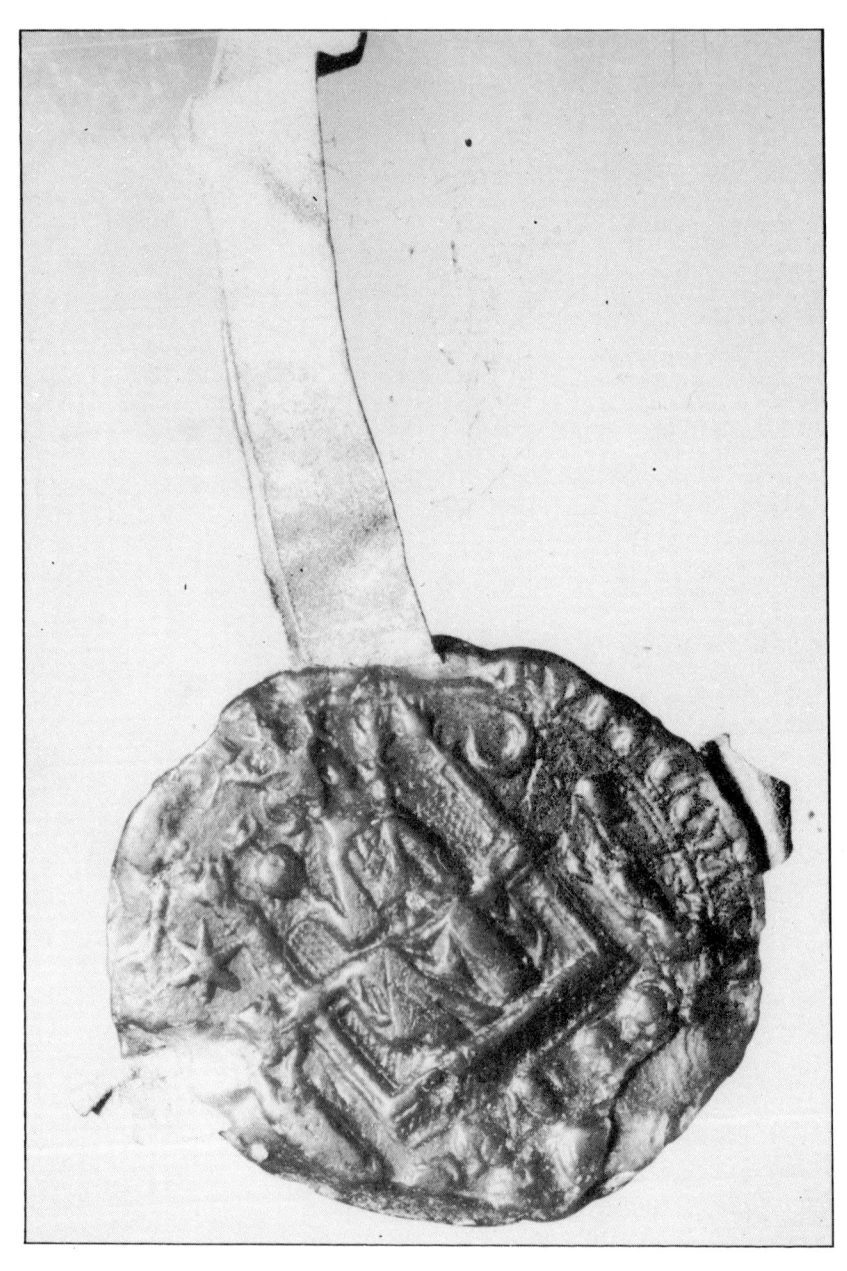

The seal of the Gulating. (By courtesy of the Norsk Historisk Kjeldeskreft Institut, Oslo.)

CHAPTER 8

1035 to 1100

As has been mentioned[1], Leif Ossurson became sole ruler of the Faroes in about 1035 when Magnus I the Good was King of Norway. Leif went to Norway and officially obtained the Faroes in fief from the King and then returned to the Faroes where he lived to an old age[2]. He and his mother-in-law, Thuride, died during the reign of Magnus I the Good[2] (i.e. prior to 1047). The only surviving son of Sigmund Bresterson and Thuride, Steingrim the Halt, lived in Skúvoy[2]. Leif's son, Sigmund succeeded Leif and he and his mother, Thora, lived together in Suðuroy[2]. Sigmund in his turn, was succeeded by his son, Hafgrim, who was followed by Einar and Skegge who were either his sons (or, as suggested by some authorities, his son and grandson, respectively), and were both district chiefs[2].

These descendants of Leif Ossurson would probably span the period of Leif's death to about the end of the eleventh century. Very little is known about this period except that the control of the Faroes came more and more under the King of Norway and, as the power of the Norwegian Kings increased, that of the chiefs in the Faroes decreased[3]. Thus Sigmund and his descendants can be said to have been largely responsible for the wane of Faroese "home-rule" in the Middle Ages.

The position of the Church during this period is dealt with in the next chapter.

1   See p. 33.
2   FS p. 58. c. 58.
3   RS pp. 13 & 14.

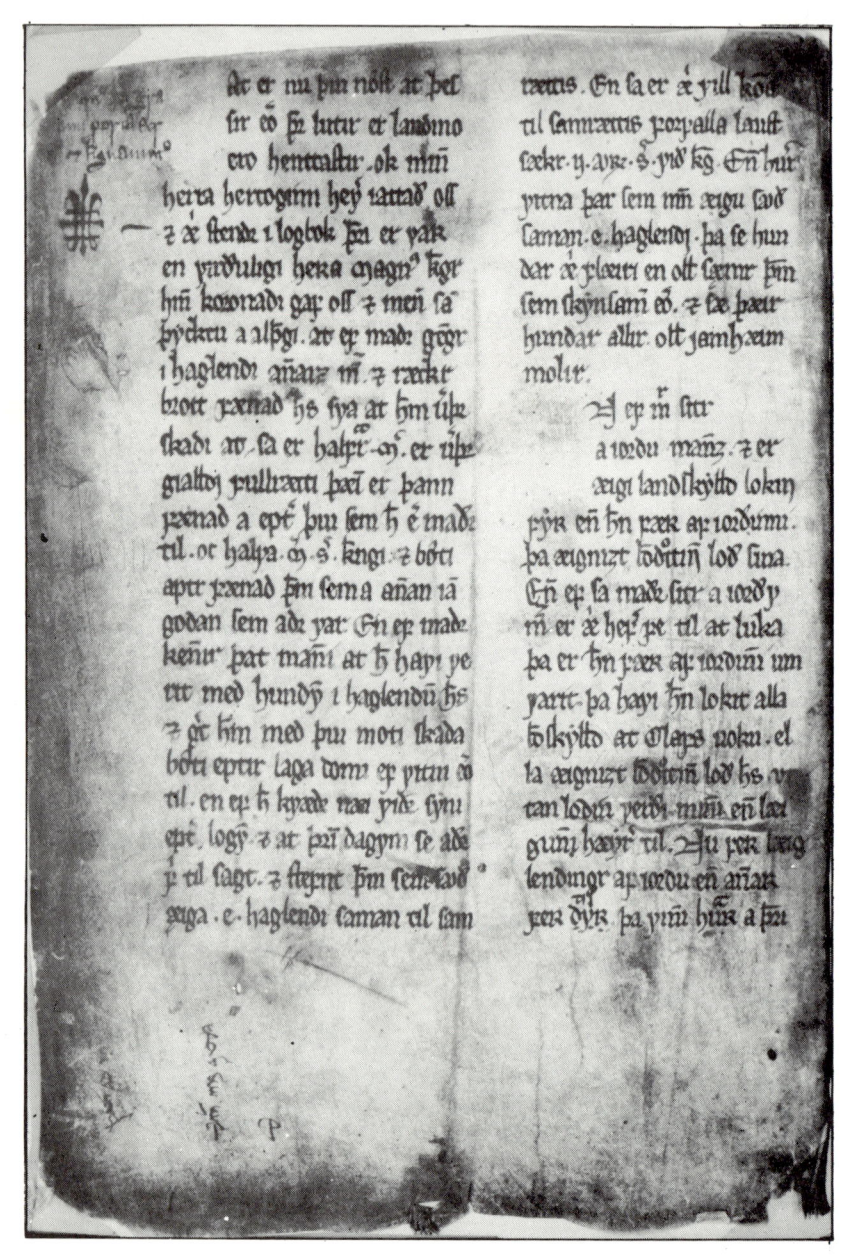

Facsimile of the Sheep Letter.

CHAPTER 9

RELIGION—pre 1100

The first people to live in the Faroes were, as has been mentioned,[1] Irish monks who were hermits and first came to the Faroes in about 725 or possibly, if the pollen tests are to be accepted, somewhat earlier, but were driven away prior to 825. These monks, however, had no real influence on the religious history of the Faroes as there were no inhabitants to convert or preach to and, when the Vikings did come, the monks left the Faroes and did not attempt to remain and convert the Norsemen to Christianity[2].

From the time of the first Viking settlement in about 825[3] until about 998, when Sigmund Bresterson went, on Olaf Tryggvason's instructions, to the Faroes to convert the inhabitants, the Faroese were pagans, and adhered to their belief in the old gods, whom most Faroese accepted[3].

The most respected of the old gods was Thor, the god of battle, who fought with the giants who were the enemies of humans[4]. He was also the god of the clouds who allowed the rain to fall so that vegetation could grow and cattle thrive[4]. People had a great deal of respect for Thor. His sign was the hammer and everything was consecrated with that sign, and that sign was also necessary for a marriage[4].

The old gods are still memorized in the Faroes[5]. On Suðuroy, Wednesday is called *"ónsdagur"* after Odin[5]. Words which begin *"hós"* or *"tórs"* are connected with Thor[5]. Here again a day of the week, Thursday, is called *"hósdagur"* in most of the islands and *"torsdagur"* on Suðuroy[5].

Place names like *"Tórshavn"* and *"Hósvík"* are also called after Thor[6]. It seems conceivable that these were places where sacrifices were made to Thor, but there has been no definite evidence to support this suggestion[6]. However, this may not be so strange as the Nordic people worshipped their gods in the open air and did not use buildings corresponding to churches until they came into contact with the Christians, from whom they learnt the custom of making use of

41

buildings for the purposes of worship[6]. The worship of the gods was carried out by the community (with their chief at the head) and not by the individual[6]. The normal offerings to the gods were food and drink; but, in special cases, live animals and humans were sacrificed[6]. The idea of worshipping the gods was to make promises to them so as to give the gods pleasure and to win their favour in order that the people concerned should prosper[6].

The *Faroese Saga* gives little assistance as far as the actual practice of pagan rites in the Faroes is concerned, although Hafgrim of Hov is described as being rich in property and a great idolator[7]. Gwyn Jones' view is that the pagan rights were carried out in the home of influential people rather than in temples as was indicated in some of the sagas[8]. The *Saga* also states that Hafgrim and Brester and Beiner were buried according to ancient custom[9]. As has been mentioned[9], there is a place at Hov on Suðuroy which is still called "Hafgrim's Grave." Unofficial excavations have been carried out there but the results are inconclusive[10].

It is very doubtful whether Sigmund Bresterson's so-called conversion of the Faroes was more than a theoretical conversion. In any event, in the time of the rule of Earls Sven and Erik, Christianity, as has been mentioned[11], waned throughout the Norwegian empire, although the *Saga* states that the Earls and Sigmund Bresterson remained good Christians and that Sigmund allowed a church to be built on his farm at Skúvoy. Thrand, however, practically reverted to paganism[11]. If Thrand did this, no doubt his companions and henchmen "followed suit" because (as is well known) when the chief is baptized, the missionaries have an easy task[12], so if he renounces the Christian faith his followers are likely to adopt the same course.

If one can place reliance on the *Saga*, it would seem that the church on Skúvoy was built about 1003[13]. It is of interest to note that, apart from the inference that the church in Skúvoy was built by clergymen, the only reference to priests in the *Saga*, is of those who accompanied Sigmund Bresterson to the Faroes on his mission of conversion[14]. However, it seems logical that the priests who came to the Faroes would have built churches and the most suitable place to build the first one would be where their patron, Sigmund, lived, that is on Skúvoy.

The church on Skúvoy is referred to again in the *Faroese Saga* in relation to the wooing of the Principal Widow by Sigurd in about the year 1035[15]. There is a stone on Skúvoy which is known as *Sigmundarsteinur* (Sigmund's stone). Sverri Dahl considers that this stone and others found in the vicinity could well date back to the era of Sigmund Bresterson or to very shortly after that period[16]. This evidence would to some extent support the story in the *Faroese Saga* of Sigmund having been buried in consecrated ground[17].

Another connection between the characters in the *Faroese Saga* and Christianity is *Bjarnasteinur* (Bjarni's stone) which was discovered in 1828 under the floor of the church which existed at that time[18]. According to legend the stone was the tombstone of Svínoy-Bjarni,

Thrand's uncle[19]. The stone resembles one of those found on Skúvoy[20] and could well come from the same period.

The first really reliable information of any church in the Faroes is that of the first church at Sandur on Sandoy which is stated to date back to the eleventh century[21]. It seems reasonable to assume that this church was built by Norwegian missionaries as it follows the style of a Norwegian stave church[21]. It is interesting to note that Sandur is the nearest village to Skúvoy and it is not beyond the bounds of probability to assume that, if the original church in Skúvoy was the first to be built in the Faroes, the church at Sandur, by reason of its proximity to Skúvoy, would have been the second. If one accepts this premise, then it can be reasonably assumed that the original church on Skúvoy resembled the first church at Sandur.

The first church at Sandur was only 27 feet long with a nave which narrowed into a choir towards the West and must have resembled the stave church at Holtalen in Norway[22]. The Nordic word for a nave has nautical undertones meaning, literally, the middle of a ship, which shows the approach the Nordic people adopted when building their churches[22].

In 1673, when one finds the first written descriptions of Faroese churches, they were built of boards and boulders[23]. The first churches, however, would seem to have been built entirely of wood[23]. The only two stone churches which date back to the Middle Ages are the unfinished cathedral at Kirkjubøur and the so-called parish church (but at one time an episcopal church) which is also situated at Kirkjubøur[23]. The cathedral dates back to about 1300 and the church to not much earlier (if at all) than the thirteenth century[23]. According to Krogh, there is every indication that only the bishops' churches were built of stone in the Middle Ages and that parish churches were built of wood, which is extremely perishable in damp climates such as in the Faroes[24]. There are minimal ruins of a third church at Kirkjubøur[25] which, according to legend, was built by Gaesa, daughter of Sigurd Thorlakson and Birna[26]. The stone church has been identified as an episcopal one not only by reason of its stone construction but also from the fact that a bishop's grave has been found under it[27].

The hundred years from 998 (when Sigurd came to convert the Faroes)[28], to shortly after 1100 (when the Faroes became an independent diocese[29]) was the period of the missionaries[30]. The eleventh century might also, however, be described, so far as the Faroes were concerned, as "the twilight of the gods"[30]. It was the period of transition from paganism to Christianity. The fundamental transition was gradual and many pagan customs have survived with the substitution of Christian words, names, prayers, etc., from their pagan predecessors[30].

A list of the various popes, archbishops and bishops having jurisdiction over the Faroes prior to the Reformation is set out in Appendix 2. This Table also gives the name of the various rival popes who appeared from time to time on the ecclesiastical scene together with the two Archbishops of Hamburg-Bremen who claimed jurisdiction over the Nordic churches after those churches had been transferred to other sees. The letter "K" is inserted after the names of the Bishops of the Faroes in Appendix 2 who are mentioned in Archbishop Henrik Kaltisen's copybook[31].

The first bishop mentioned in the Roll of Faroese bishops is Bernhardus, but it seems possible that there were earlier bishops who had theoretical connections with those islands even though they may not have, in fact, visited them. Adam of Bremen refers to three other bishops as well as Bishop Bernhard who came to Norway and also went to Sweden, Gothia and all the islands beyond Norway (which would, presumably, include the Faroes), preaching the Word of God and the Kingdom of Jesus Christ to the barbarians[32]. These three bishops are named by him as Siegfried, Grimkil and Rudolf[32]. Bishop Siegfried would seem to be the same person as the Bishop John who accompanied Olaf Tryggvason when he returned to Norway after having become a Christian and became the first Bishop of Trondheim[33]. Bishop Grimkil was Bishop John's successor at Trondheim and King Olaf the Holy's legate to Archbishop Unwan of Hamburg-Bremen[34]. Bishop Grimkil would seem to have returned to England eventually as he is reported as having been there between 1042 and 1046[35]. Bishop Rudolf also returned to England where he became Abbot of Abingdon and died in 1052[36].

There are four references by Adam of Bremen to a Bishop Bernhard[37] and Professor Tschan has suggested that they may refer to the same person[38]. However, this view is not supported by other facts. It would appear that, during the missionary period, there were two bishops called Bernhard. The first of these, called Bernhard the Learned, accompanied King Olaf II, the Holy, from England to Norway in 1014/15 and was sent by King Olaf to Iceland in 1016, where he remained for five years before returning to England[39]. In 1021, King Canute the Great appointed him to Skåne or Skania (then in Denmark but now part of Sweden)[40]. It is most unlikely that this is the Bishop Bernhard referred to in the Roll of Faroese bishops as, if he had visited the Faroes on his way to Iceland and carried out missionary work there, one would have expected to find a reference to him in the *Faroese Saga,* but there is no reference in that book to any Bishop who visited the Faroes during the reign of King Olaf, the Holy, or, for that matter, during any other period covered by the *Saga.*

The second Bishop Bernhard was Bishop Bernhard the Saxon or, according to some authorities, Bernhard the Englishman, who was a missionary bishop in Norway from about 1043 to about 1047[41]. He was consecrated by the then pope (probably Pope Benedict IX) but pledged allegiance to Archbishop Adalbert who was then Archbishop of Hamburg-Bremen[41]. Bishop Bernhard the Saxon left Norway in about 1047 on account of a disagreement with King Harald IV, the Ruthless, and went to Iceland where he arrived in 1048[41]. Bishop Bernhard remained in Iceland for nineteen years before returning to Norway in 1067[41]. It seems more than likely that this is the Bishop Bernhard referred to in the Roll of Faroese bishops. It is very probable that he called at the Faroes on his way to and from Iceland and possibly may also have visited the Faroes when he was living in Iceland. It seems likely (and this is a point worth noting) that Bishop Bernhard left Norway in 1047 but did not arrive in Iceland until the following year. It would have been consistent with this for Bishop Bernhard to have spent the intervening period in the Faroes. Apart from the two bishops referred to above, there is no mention of any other missionary bishop called Bernhard.

The second bishop referred to in the Roll of Faroese bishops is a Bishop Ryngerus who is also said to have been a missionary bishop [42]. The only missionary bishop in Norway in the relevant period with a name resembling a Norse form of the Latin Ryngerus is a Bishop Ragnar who was the fifth bishop to live in Trondheim, which was before a seat was established at Nidaros [43]. It is suggested that Bishop Ryngerus and Bishop Ragnar were probably the same person. Trondheim would, in view of its geographical situation, have been a suitable place from which a missionary bishop who wished to visit the Faroes could set out.

The Archbishops of Hamburg-Bremen always considered that they had ecclesiastical jurisdiction over all the Nordic churches and this was formally recognised in 1044 by Pope Benedict IX when he laid down in a papal bull that Archbishop Adalbert, who was at that time Archbishop of Hamburg-Bremen, had jurisdiction over the Nordic countries [44].

According to Munch [45], there were no defined dioceses in Norway and its dependencies prior to 1111 and the bishops were missionary bishops [46]. Modern historians tend, however, to the view that fixed bishoprics were established considerably earlier than that date, although Knud J. Krogh considers that the Faroes became a fixed diocese in about 1120. Archbishop Adalbert of Hamburg-Bremen is said by Adam of Bremen to have consecrated twenty such bishops for Denmark, Sweden, Norway and the islands of the sea as well as accepting allegiance from other bishops who had been consecrated elsewhere [48]. He consecrated Bishop Tholf for Trondheim and appointed Bishop Seward to the same area [49]. This does not, of course, take account of bishops like Bishop Bernhard who worked in Norway and its dependencies but were consecrated by the Pope and not by the Archbishop of Hamburg-Bremen [50].

Archbishop Adalbert also sent preachers to Iceland and Greenland, at the request of the inhabitants, and consecrated Bishop Turolf (or Thorolf) as Bishop of Orkney [51]. This would have been about the middle of the eleventh century [52]. This Bishop Thorolf or Turolf was probably the same person as the Bishop Rolf of the Isle of Man who is mentioned as the first bishop of that island after the Norse occupation [53], and appears to have lived about the same period as Bishop Turolf of Orkney [53]. It is of importance to note that between 1050 and 1060, or probably later, the Isle of Man and the Scottish isles were ruled by Thorfinn, Earl of the Orkneys [55], and it would be in accordance with the normal pattern of the day for the missionary bishop to have gone throughout the territories of his Earl administering to the inhabitants. If Bishop Turolf of Orkney was the same person as Bishop Rolf of Man, he is buried in Maughold, near Ramsey, in the Isle of Man [56].

The work of the missionary bishops would have been to travel around baptizing, preaching, teaching and saying Mass and solemnizing certain marriages [57]. Although these missionary bishops had no formal seat, they would in all probability have made their headquarters in a town or place of some importance in the same way as in the Middle Ages a cathedral was always built in the vicinity of a town, even it if was only a small one [58]. Kirkjubøur was chosen eventually as the episcopal seat of the Faroese diocese [59] and it is probable that it was previously used as the headquarters of the missionary bishops in the Faroes. Even though Kirkjubøur is not referred to by name in the *Faroese Saga,* legend has it that it was the place where Sigurd Thorlaksson and Birna lived [60]. If the legend is correct, Kirkjubøur (or whatever it was called then) must have been quite an important place as Birna's first husband was, as his name Thorhal the Rich shows, a wealthy man [61].

The third bishop in the roll of Faroese Bishops was Gudmundus or Gudmund [62] but there are no records to show when and by whom he was consecrated. However, he is generally taken to have come to the Faroes and to have been the first Bishop of the Faroes subsequent to 1100, so he will be dealt with in the chapter dealing with religion from 1100 to the Reformation [63].

There is no evidence available to indicate how many churches there were in existence prior to 1100, but perhaps some day archaeologists may be able to throw some light on this question.

1 See pp. 1-2 *ante.*
2 RS p. 8.
3 *Ibid.*
4 RS p. 9.
5 *Ibid.*
6 *Ibid.*
7 See p. 9. *ante.*
8 GJ pp. 272-3.
9 See p. 10. *ante.*
10 See p. 115 *post.*
11 See p. 21 *ante.*
12 RS p. 10.
13 See p. 21. *ante.*
14 See p. 20 *ante.*
15 See p. 23 *ante.*
16 SD p. 129.
17 See p. 26 *ante.*
18 SD p. 129.
19 See p. 116 *post.*
20 SD p. 129.
21 KJK p. 69. The Church has been removed to Trondheim and is now in the open-air museum at Sverresborg, see MO p. 32.
22 *Ibid.*
23 *Ibid.*
24 *Ibid.*
25 RS p. 12.

26　See p. 62 *post*.
27　See p. 118 *post*.
28　See p. 20 *ante*.
29　RS p. 11; DF p. viii.
30　RS p. 10.
31　See p. 62 *post*.
32　AB p. 94.
33　AB pp. 80, 94, 100 and 214.
34　AB p. 214.
35　AB p. 94, *n* 205.
36　AB p. 94, *n* 206.
37　AB pp. 93, 94, 183 and 214.
38　AB p. 94, *n* 207.
39　DN xviiB pp. 192 and 196.
40　DN xviiB p. 196; AB p. 93.
41　DN xviiB pp. 193 and 197. See also AB pp. 183 and 214.
42　DF p. viii.
43　DN xviiB pp.194 and 199. Nidaros was in the vicinity of Trondheim and is referred to in some documents by the latter name.
44　RDHD p. 23.
45　CM p. 237.
46　RS p. 11; DF p. viii.
47　MO p. 23.
48　AB pp. 180-3.
49　AB pp. 183 and 214.
50　AB p. 214.
51　AB pp. 33, 180 and 183; OS p. lxvii.
52　OS p. lxvii.
53　CM pp. 115 and 235. It is understood that other examples have occurred where Thorolf or Turolf has been corrupted in early manuscripts into Rolf.
54　CM p. 113, *n b*.
55　M pp. 95-6.
56　CM pp. 112-5.
57　RS pp. 10 and 11.
58　L pp. 17 and 18; see also MA p. 73.
59　RS p. 11.
60　See pp. 30-31 and chapter 6, *n* 34 *ante*.
61　See p. 30 *ante*.
62　See p. 62 *post*.
63　See chapter 11.

A rune stone from Fámjin on Suðuroy. (By courtesy of Sverri Dahl, Tórshavn.)

CHAPTER 10

1100 to 1538

As Dr. Scheel states[1], the history of the Faroes throughout the Middle Ages was very limited. This is particularly true of the twelfth century. Probably the major point of historical interest from the Faroese point of view was the creation in 1152 of the Archipiscopal see of Nidaros and the transfer to that see from Lund of the Faroese diocese which was brought about by Cardinal Nicholas Breakspear[2]. One of the Cardinal's greatest achievements was to prevail upon the chiefs in Norway to promise to attend the local things or provincial assemblies without their arms[3]. Even the king was only allowed to be accompanied by twelve armed men and that exception was conceded less to his dignity than to the need to enforce the judicial sentences[3]. It is of interest to note that Thrand suggested such a course in the Faroes about one hundred and twenty-five years previously, although his motives were probably not as pure as those of Cardinal Nicholas[4]!

In about the year 1170, an anonymous author wrote a short history of Norway in Latin[5]. The author begins with a description of Norway and the western islands[5]. He states that it is undeniable that the Faroes paid tribute to the King of Norway[5]. Payment of tribute by the Faroese is mentioned in the Saga both when Olaf Tryggvason was King of Norway[6], and in the reign of King Olaf II, the Holy[7], but, by the twelfth century, it would seem to have become a regular custom[8]. There is no evidence as to how the payment was made, but Dr. Scheel considers that it was almost certainly paid in wool for which the Faroes were famous, and that it was probably landed at Bergen[8]. Bales of wool with the name of the Faroes on them were certainly seen on the quay at Bergen at that time and they must have been either tribute or articles of trade[8]. It is interesting to recall that, when Carl of Møre went to collect the tribute for King Olaf the Holy, it was to be paid in silver, not in wool[9]. The anonymous author, however, supports Dr. Scheel's view and comments on the large number of sheep which there were in the Faroes[10].

In the latter part of the twelfth century, there came to the throne of

Norway a King with Faroese connections[11]. This was King Sverre who was born in Norway in 1151 and five years later came to the Faroes where he was brought up[11]. He returned to Norway in 1176 and became King of Norway eight years later[11].

In 1186, King Sverre gave his well-known speech in Bergen. This speech shows that the Faroes were linked with Bergen in the twelfth century and the payment of the tribute is an indication that, at that time, the islands were, in theory, a part of Norway and that the Faroese community was a section of the Norwegian community[12]: geographical conditions were not enough to give the Faroese a special position[12]. The distance from Bergen to the Faroes was no greater than that from Bergen to the middle of Hålogaland and, as Jóannes Patursson has observed, the scenery and conditions in the Faroes reminds one of those off the Nordfjord in Norway[12]. However, the facts that the Faroes came under the control of the Kings of Norway at such a late period and that the Faroese had been in the habit of running their own affairs meant that there never had been, in practice, any cause to control them as a part of Norway[12]. The Faroes were never brought into the system of Norwegian counties[12]. In addition, there was hardly any royal property in the Faroes apart from small pieces of land which reverted to the Crown as a punishment or as an unredeemed pledge for a debt[12]. The King had neither his usual representatives nor officials in the Faroes, but let the Faroese Things and chiefs control the Faroes as they wished[12].

The special position of the Faroes underwent a change during the reign of King Sverre, due in part to the fact that he was brought up there[13]. As Father Paasche put it, "the journeys over fell and fjord had, at an early age, hardened him and given him the resourcefulness and strength which the Birchlegs King should have need of." King Sverre's biblical and ecclesiastical knowledge must have been acquired in the Faroes and it is clear evidence of the good literary education of the Faroese clergy, even though they lacked a cathedral chapter with the school which would have accompanied it[13]. King Sverre had had a good background, certainly better than he would have found with the maternal side of King Sigurd II the Talkative's family[13].

It is, in fact, Sverre who tells of his youth as he took personal charge of the part of his *Saga* dealing with that period[14]. Nevertheless, there is no mention in the *Saga* of one single place in the Faroes[14] and the description is, on the whole, unreal[14]: the reason is certainly not that Sverre had a lot to hide[14]. The root fault lies in the framework of the *Saga* which was written for Icelanders and Norwegians about important events in Norway[14]. It would have been incorrect to include details about a group of islands which did not play any role whatsoever in the main act, and it is probable that he was not in a circle which would encourage him to fill his *Saga* with anecdotes about his youth[14].

Slavery was abolished in the Faroes in about 1200[15], which would have been during the reign of King Sverre as he died in 1202[16]. After the thralls or slaves were released from bondage some of them, who had saved a little money, went to remote areas and settled down there[17]. This practice was, however, severely curtailed in 1298 by the *Sheep Letter*[18].

Apart from the abolition of slavery, there is no record of anything important happening in the Faroes during the first sixty odd years of the thirteenth century. The same cannot be said of the latter part of that century. In December, 1263, Magnus VI, the Law Reformer, son of King Hakon IV and great-grandson of King Sverre, became King of Norway[19], although he does not appear to have been crowned as such until 1265[20]. During his reign and that of his elder son, Erik, the position of the Faroes underwent considerable changes.

In 1269, Canon Erlend of Bergen was consecrated as Bishop of the Faroes[21]. He was an outstanding personality who was to play a very important part, not only in Church affairs, but also in political affairs, both in the Faroes and in Norway[22].

In 1271, King Magnus VI made a decree relating to the Faroes, a translation of which is in Appendix 3[23]. The effect of this law was to extend the old Gulating law to the Faroes, except in so far as the agricultural law was concerned. It is of interest to note that, although this law was supposed to have been extended to the Faroes in about 1024[24], it would not appear to have been enforced there. The decree provided for the reduction of the amount of fines and in it the King also promised that two ships should ply between Norway and the Faroes[25]. Finally, the decree tightened up the law relating to fraud[25].

This decree shows that the King was taking over legislative powers, although it does not appear that the Faroese *Alting* was consulted[26]. The promise in the decree to provide two ships to ply between Norway and the Faroes was intended to create a royal trade monopoly for the King of Norway[27].

The 1271 decree was virtually the end of the Faroese *Alting* as a legislative body and, from then on until relatively modern times, it became, for all practical purposes, merely a court of law[28]. From the same time, the Faroese Lawmen became royal officials[28].

In 1273, King Magnus made his younger son, Hakon, then three years of age, Duke of Oppland, Oslo, the Shetlands and the Faroes, although the boy does not seem to have taken over the dukedom until his father's death in 1280[29].

In 1274, King Magnus was responsible for the enactment of the young Gulating law and it would seem that this law took effect in the Faroes between 1274 and 1276[30].

In the winter of 1277-8 Iceland's Lawman, Sturla Thordarson, who was also the author of the *Islendinga Saga,* visited the Faroes[31], but there is no evidence to show that his visit was concerned in any way with international matters.

The Faroes came on to the map by name for the first time in 1280: this was the Hereford map and on it the Faroes were called "Farei"[32]. In the same year, Archbishop John held his convocation of bishops at Bergen which was responsible for the new church law[33], which must have been the one referred to by Duke Hakon in the preamble to the *Sheep*

Letter as having been given to the Faroes by his father[34]. This was also the year in which King Magnus VI was succeeded on the throne by his elder son, Erik II, later known as "the Priest-hater"[35].

In 1294, and again in 1302, the Hanseatic merchants were prohibited by Norway from trading with the Faroes, although the prohibition did not prove to be very effectual[36]. This action would seem to have been in furtherance of the attempt to set up a royal trading monopoly between Norway and the Faroes[37].

On the 28th June, 1298. Duke Hakon enacted the famous *Sheep Letter (Seyðabraevið)* especially for the Faroes[38]. Two copies of the *Sheep Letter* are extant, one in the Royal Library in Stockholm and the other in the Library of the University of Lund. The latter is one of the most beautiful and well preserved of all Scandinavian manuscripts[39]. Copies of the translations by Michael Barnes of the two copies, together with notes on the *Sheep Letter* and a table of comparison between the two copies of the *Letter,* are contained in Appendix 4. The Stockholm copy was originally kept in the Lawman's office in the Faroes and was probably the original copy of the *Sheep Letter*[39]. On the other hand, it was believed for a long time that the Lund copy, although written by a Faroese scribe, had never been in the Faroes[39]. However, the modern view is that the Lund copy was originally in the possession of the Faroese diocese[39]: it may well have been Bishop Erlend's personal copy.

The Stockholm copy was at one time in the possession of Peder Jakobson, a farmer from Kirkjubøur, who was Lawman from 1588 to 1600 or 1601[40]. He had the *Sheep Letter* bound in a volume which also contains the Norwegian National Law and a copy of a letter from King Hans dated 14th July, 1491[40]. There are various other items written on the manuscript including the regulations relating to the payment of travelling expenses for members attending the *Løgting* and the so-called *Hundabræv* (Dog Law)[41]. This copy was in Bergen after the death of Peder Jakobson and it came into the hands of the Swedish *Antikvitetskollegium* in the 1680's from where it went to the Royal Library in Stockholm[41].

The *Sheep Letter* was a Royal Decree and, according to some authorities, the Faroese *Alting* was not consulted about it[42]. It was drafted on the advice of Bishop Erlend and of Sigurd[43], the Lawman of the Shetlands, whom Duke Hakon had sent to the Faroes to consider the deficiencies in the agricultural law[44]. Jakob Jakobsen argues that Sigurd was Lawman for both the Shetlands and the Faroes and that Bishop Erlend had had a hand in arranging that state of affairs[45]. However, the general view today does not coincide with that expressed by Jakob Jakobsen.

Duke Hakon has been criticised for not having consulted the Faroese *Alting*[46], but one could say that he had drafted his law as a result of a report made to him by a Royal Commission, which is not an unusual method these days in the United Kingdom. The criticism would be justified if it could be established that the Bishop and the Lawman had made their report without there having been adequate consultations with the Faroese people, but there is no evidence to support such an allegation.

The employment of independent persons on Commissions is commonplace today as their views tend to be more objective than those of local people who may be more open to local pressures or bias. This could justify the appointment to "the Commission" of the Lawman of the Shetlands. Bishop Erlend himself did not come from the Faroes, although he had been Bishop of the Faroese diocese since 1269[47]. He was, as has been stated, an outstanding person both in Church and State affairs[48]. Both members of "the Commission" would seem, therefore, to have been well equipped to carry out a review of the Faroese agricultural law. It is not certain how long they took over their examination of the Faroese law, but the fact that the largest part of the agricultural law contained in the *Sheep Letter* has remained unchanged for nearly seven hundred years[49] testifies to the value of their work.

The *Sheep Letter* was largely a codification of existing law and the main change in that law was in connection with the setting up of new farms. Under the *Sheep Letter*[50], a person was prohibited from establishing a new farm unless he owned three cows. The result of this was virtually to prevent any more ex-thralls from becoming crofters. Those members of the community had, in future, to become farm labourers or, if they were lucky, tenant farmers. This prohibition remained in force until 1637[51].

In 1299, King Erik II of Norway died and was succeeded by his younger brother, Duke Hakon, who became King Hakon V[52].

In the latter part of Bishop Erlend's life, complications developed between him and King Hakon V arising from complaints against the bishop and from serious accusations made against the King by Bishop Erlend and the King's ecclesiastical opponents[53]. Bishop Erlend seems, however, to have been victorious in the end, both as regards his own affairs and those of the Church[54].

During the time when Bishop Erlend was Bishop, the power of the Church increased in the Faroes as can, among other things, be seen from the fact that the Bishop was asked to advise on the improvements to the agricultural law and from the fact that he won his dispute against King Hakon V.

It is of interest to note that King Hakon V granted the Royal income from the Faroes and the Shetlands from 1312-1319 to the Mary-Church in Christiania[55] for the completion of the fabric of that church[56].

The two most important events in Faroese history during the fourteenth century were, however, the Black Death and the union of Norway and Denmark.

The Black Death probably reached the Faroes in about 1350[57] and, although there is little evidence to prove its precise effect, it may well have caused the death of about one-third of the population of the islands. At least two settlements, Húsavík in the south-east of Sandoy and Saksun in the north-west of Streymoy, seem to have been practically wiped out[58].

According to a story about Saksun, the only survivor of the Black Death in that settlement was a female servant who went to the *várting* (the local Thing) at Kollafjørður in Streymoy to claim Saksun for herself on the ground of being the only survivor[59]. The *várting* decided that the maid could succeed in her claim if she found herself a husband[59]. She then chose a young man from the island of Hestur and so returned home, not only as owner of Saksun but also with a handsome, young husband[59].

The evidence relating to Húsavík is based on sounder foundations. Húsavík was destroyed during the Black Death and was rebuilt by Gudrun, daughter of a man called Sigurd the Shetlander, and she became known as the Housewife of Húsavík[60]. Gudrun came from Bergen and had large estates in Norway and the Shetlands, as well as in the Faroes[61]. She died in 1402[62]. According to the sagas, she was the richest lady in the Faroes[63]. Certainly the documents which have survived about her estate confirm that she was a lady of considerable substance. Translations of these documents are set out in Appendix 5. These documents are not only interesting from the legal point of view[64] but are also of interest in that they show the garments which a wealthy lady of her period wore. (It must, however, be remembered that her father was a Shetlander and, to use a Manx expression, she was, so far as the Faroese were concerned, a "come-over.")

The Black Death must have caused a great change in social and other conditions in the Faroes and it is very unfortunate that there is not more information available about its effect in those islands.

In 1361, the Hanseatic League, which had its Norwegian headquarters in Bergen, obtained the same rights to trade with the Faroes as the Norwegian merchants in Bergen had[65]. This was due to the fact that the movement of goods between the Faroes and Norway was not such as to make it a very profitable concern and to the fact that the Hanseatics do not appear to have paid much attention to the restrictions which had been placed on their activities in 1294 and 1302[65].

The Black Death may have contributed in part to the decline in trade between the Faroes and Norway.

As has been mentioned[66], the second major event in the fourteenth century to affect the Faroes was the Union of Norway and Denmark under the Danish Crown. King Hakon V[67] was succeeded by his grandson, Magnus VII Erikson, who was also King of Sweden[68]. Magnus's son, King Hakon VI, who married Margaret, daughter of the King of Denmark, died in 1380 and he was succeeded by his son, Olaf IV, who had been chosen as King of Denmark at the age of five, in succession to his grandfather, Valdemar Atterdag, who died in 1275[68]. In 1280, at the age of ten, Olaf became King of Norway[68], his mother, Queen Margaret I, acting as his Regent[68]. King Olaf died in 1387 when he was about seventeen and with him the Sverre family came to an end[68]. As a result of this, the Kingdoms of Norway and Denmark became united under Queen Margaret I, a union which continued until 1814, a period of four hundred and twenty-seven years[69]. Along with Norway, the

Orkneys, the Shetlands, the Faroes, Iceland and Greenland came under the Danish Crown, but continued to be governed as provinces of Norway[70]. Sweden also elected to join the Union and brought with her large parts of Finland[71].

The first territories to leave the Union were the Orkneys and the Shetlands, which became part of Scotland in 1471 as a result of the breach of a contract of marriage entered into in 1468 between King James III of Scotland and Margaret, Princess of Denmark[72]. This meant that the nearest neighbours of the Faroes had now become Scottish, which must have had some effect on the Faroese as, although the Faroes are a small country, they became involved with other countries when the question of trade arose, and the British were great trading rivals of the Hanseatics[73].

In 1490 the Dutch were granted the same trading rights with the Faroes as those which the Hanseatics had, but there is no evidence to show how much this affected the Faroes[74].

Around 1500, the Faroes were the victims of raids by pirates from England, Ireland, France and Algeria[75], which might well indicate that the Faroes were, at that time, prosperous.

The position of the Faroes in the two decades prior to 1538 is rather confused[76]. This was due, in part, to dissension in Denmark itself which ended in civil war and the exile of King Christian II, who was King of Denmark from 1513 to 1523[76]. In or about 1520, King Christian II appointed Joachim Wullenweber of Hamburg as his bailiff in the Faroes and in 1521 gave him authority to collect outstanding monies due from those islands to the Crown[77]. In 1523 there was an uprising of the nobles against King Christian II as a result of his reform policies and the King was exiled and fled to Holland[78]. In the same year, Sweden, which had been gradually growing more powerful, left the Union[79].

Frederik, Duke of Holstein and Southern Jutland, was chosen to succeed King Christian II and became King Frederik I of Denmark[80].

After his exile to Holland, ex-King Christian II sent a Dutchman, Frederyk de Friese, to the Faroes to act as his bailiff there[81]. Joachim, however, was still in the Faroes and had taken advantage of the change of Kings to get himself well established there[81]. Frederyk, who was in the Faroes in 1524, tried to get Joachim to leave by promising him land, but Joachim did not agree and ejected Frederyk from those islands[81]. The Faroese would, however, appear to have continued to be loyal to ex-King Christian II, and Joachim would seem to have remained in the Faroes as a Hamburger and not as a representative of King Frederik I[81].

Shortly after Joachim had ejected Frederyk, Vincent Lunge, the head man in Bergen, sent an envoy, Peder Skoggard to the Faroes with a letter from King Fredrik I and at the meeting of the *Løgting* held on St. Olaf's Wake at Tinganes, King Frederik was accepted as King by the Faroese[82]. Early that year (in April), ex-King Christian II had purported to grant the Faroes in fief to Jørgen Hanssøn who was his bailiff in Bergen[83]. It would also seem, from a letter written in May, 1524, that Vincent Lunge was trying to get the Faroes out of the control of King

Frederik I and under the control of Bergen[83].

In the same year (1524), ex-King Christian II, who had become short of money, sent his Chancellor, Klaus Pederson, to King Henry VIII of England to ask for a loan[84]. In return for such a loan, ex-King Christian said he would hand over the Faroes and Iceland to King Henry[84], presumably as security for the loan. The latter, however, declined to accept the offer[84].

Between 1525 and 1529, Bergen and the Hamburgers vied for control of the Faroes and the matter was not made easier by the fact that the Lutheran movement had penetrated Denmark through Southern Jutland[85]. The Hamburgers eventually won the day and were, in practice, supported by the King of Denmark[86].

In 1529 Eske Bille replaced Vincent Lunge as the head man in Bergen and was appointed by King Frederik I to be royal bailiff of the Faroes, but he never seems to have gained control over those islands[87]. Later that year, King Frederik, who was strongly influenced by Lutheranism, granted the Faroes in fief to Thomas Kroppen, a Lutheran and a Hamburger, on condition that he shared the islands with Joachim Wullenweber who was also from Hamburg, but supported Lübeck and the Catholic Church[87]. Thomas Koppen and Wullenweber had to pay the King one hundred Lübeck marks a year, but they were given a trade monopoly with the Faroes and also the royal taxes[87]. However, Church property in the Faroes was not affected by the transaction and remained intact until the Reformation[88]. Five original letters dated 1524-31 relating to the trading activities in the Faroes of these Hamburgers can still be seen in the National Archives in Copenhagen.

Thomas Koppen and Joachim Wullenweber appear to have had opposing views so far as the Reformation was concerned and would seem to have split up before the Reformation[89].

In 1536 the Norwegian Representative Council was abolished and the Faroes, as well as Norway, were ruled as a province of Denmark[90]. In the same year, Christian, later King Christian III, who succeeded King Frederik I as King of Denmark[91], found himself in need of money as a result of the struggle with his nobles and asked King Henry VIII of England for a loan of one hundred thousand pounds and said that, if King Henry gave him the loan, he would give King Henry the Faroes and Iceland[92], presumably as security for the loan. However, once again, King Henry turned down the offer[92]. So, twice in a period of twelve years, the Faroes and Iceland escaped coming under England!

The struggle between the Catholic Church and the Lutheran Church was also a struggle between Lübeck and Hamburg[93]. Lübeck was supported by ex-King Christian II and, in the Faroes, by Joachim Wullenweber, while Hamburg received support from the other Christian (later King Christian III) and, in the Faroes, from Thomas Koppen[93]. The Lutheran Church and Hamburg subsequently gained supremacy and the Reformation came to the Faroes. The date on which this event took place in the Faroes is open to some controversy, but it would seem, on the balance of probabilities, to have occurred in or about 1538[94]. With the coming of the Reformation, King Christian III immediately confiscated two-thirds of the property of the Church in the Faroes, although it was not until 1547 that he handed that property over to his vassal, Thomas Koppen[95].

1 L p. 19.
2 See p. 63 *post* and CM pp. 171 and 172.
3 CM pp. 171 and 172.
4 See p. 29 *ante*.
5 L p. 19.
6 See p. 20 *ante*.
7 See p. 26 *ante*.
8 L p. 19.
9 See pp. 28-29 *ante*.
10 L p. 19.
11 See p. 64 *post*.
12 L pp. 19 and 20.
13 L p. 20.
14 *Ibid*.
15 RS p. 19.
16 RS p. 15.
17 RS p. 19.
18 See p. 53 *post*.
19 DF p. xviii, RS p. 15 and CM 108-111 and 223-4. See also Table I.
20 King Magnus VI's Decree of 1271 states that he was then in the eighth year of his reign, see p. 139 *post*.
21 See p. 65 *post*.
22 See pp. 65-67 *post*.
23 See Appendix 3, note 5.
24 See p. 26 *ante*.
25 See Appendix 3.
26 See pp. 140-141 *post*.
27 RS p. 17.
28 S facing page; RS p. 15. See also p. 85 *post* as regards the power of the *Løgting* to make laws of a local nature such as the *Hundabrœv*.
29 DF pp. xx and xxi. See also Appendix 1.
30 *Ibid*. p. xix.
31 Sp. 4 para iv. The statement in that paragraph that Sturla Thordarson was Iceland's first Lawman would seem at first sight, to conflict with what is stated by Gwyn Jones (GJ p. 283), but it may be that the first statement is distinguishing between a Lawspeaker (*Løgsøgumaðr*) the original Icelandic title and a Lawman (*Løgmaðr*) the name which was later given to the office.
32 S facing page.
33 See p 65 *post*. Archbishop John was John II of Nidaros.
34 See pp. 140 and 145 *post*.
35 DF pp. xx and xxi. See also Appendix 1.
36 S facing page.
37 See pp. 51 *ante* and 95 *post*.
38 See the preamble to the *Sheep Letter* at pp. 140 and 145 *post* and S p. 3 para ii.
39 JHWP p. 59.
40 S p. 3, para iii.
41 *Ibid*. For fuller details of the regulations and the *Hundabrœv*, see chapter 12.
42 RS p. 15.
43 Or Sigurd.
44 See pp. 140 and 145 *post*.
45 DF pp. xx-xxii.

46 RS p. 15.
47 See p. 65 *post*.
48 See p. 51 *ante*.
49 JHWP p. 59.
50 See Appendix 4, Part I, Art. 7 and Part II, Art.14.
51 RS p. 18.
52 See Appendix 1.
53 See Archbishop Kaltison's copybook (referred to in chapter 11 *post*) and the introduction to *"Færøske folkesagn og eventyr"*.
54 DF p. xxii.
55 Now Oslo.
56 OS p. xl, *n* 1.
57 This was the time it was ravaging Europe (RS p. 20).
58 RS pp. 19 and 20.
59 W p. 80, Article entitled *Arbeiðskonan*.
60 RS p. 19.
61 RS p. 20.
62 LZ p. 290.
63 RS p. 20.
64 See pp. 86-87 *post*.
65 RS p. 17. S facing page.
66 See p. 53 *ante*.
67 Son of King Magnus VI and grandson of King Hakon IV.
68 RS p. 15, D p. 71. See also Appendix 1.
69 D p. 73.
70 S facing page.
71 D p. 73.
72 OS p. cxxxi.
73 S facing page.
74 *Ibid*.
75 S facing page; RS pp. 17 and 19.
76 D p. 74, LZ pp. 162 and 163. See also Appendix 1.
77 LZ p. 162.
78 D p. 74, LZ pp. 162 and 163.
79 D p. 74.
80 LZ pp. 162 and 163.
81 LZ p. 163.
82 LZ pp. 163 and 164. This acceptance was confirmed by the letter of 17th August 1524 from Bishop Hilary and the Faroese *Løgting* see p. 73 *post*.
83 LZ pp. 163 and 164.
84 LZ p. 164.
85 LZ pp. 164 and 165, D p. 74.
86 LZ p. 165, D p. 74.
87 LZ pp. 13 and 165.
88 S facing page.
89 LZ p. 13.
90 S facing page.
91 See Appendix 1. There was a war of succession from 1533. From 1534, part of the Danish Council of the Realm recognised Christian as King. He may be recognised as King of Norway from 1536, but the Archbishop, the chairman of the Council, and the Northern part of the country held out against him until 1537.
92 LZ p. 178.
93 LZ p. 13.
94 S facing page, RS p. 11. See also pp. 73-74 *post*.
95 S facing page.

CHAPTER 11

RELIGION—1100 to 1538

As has been mentioned[1], the Faroes originally came under the Archbishop of Hamburg-Bremen. It is unlikely, however, that the Faroes became an independent diocese as such until after 1100[2] and it is probable that, prior to that date, the bishops were ambulatory or court bishops.

The ecclesiastical control of the Faroes was transferred from the Archbishop of Hamburg-Bremen to the Archbishop of Lund in 1104 along with Scandinavia, Iceland and Greenland, although the Faroes are not specifically named[3]. The name of Bishop Orm of the Faroes appears at the foot of a document by Archbishop Eskil of Lund made on the 8th August, 1139[4].

Some confusion appears to have arisen between references to the island of Farria (or Faria) and to the Faroes in early documents and it is proposed to deal with this point in some detail in order to try and clarify the situation.

According to Adam of Bremen, Farria was another name for Helgoland[5], which is situated in the North Sea near the mouths of the Elbe and the Weser[6]. A former Viking, called Eilbert or Egilbert[8], founded a monastery there and later became Bishop of Farria and also of Fyn[9]. He appears to have lived in Odense[10] sometime between 1061 and 1072 (the dates when both Pope Alexander II and Archbishop Adalbert were in office). Bishop Eilbert was removed from office by Pope Alexander II as a result of having refused, three years in succession, to go to Hamburg to Archbishop Adalbert despite having been summoned to do so[11]. Two documents relating to this (written as a consequence of a complaint by Archbishop Adalbert) are contained in Volume I (R II) of the *Diplomatarium Danicum,* one addressed to the Bishops of Denmark and the other to King Svend Estridsen of Denmark. It is important to note that in these documents Bishop Eilbert is referred to as "farriensis episcopus" in the Latin text of the first document and as "Farensi episcopo" in the second document. In the headnote in Danish to both documents, the Bishop is referred to as "Bishop of Farria." It is abundantly clear that these documents refer to an island under Danish jurisdiction and could not possibly refer to the Faroes which, at that period, came under Norway. These documents support the view that Adam was correct when he expressed the view that Farria was an alternative name for Helgoland [12]. Views have been expressed in certain quarters that Adam was confused when he referred to Farria and that Farria must have been the name for the Faroes. However, it is of interest to note that there does not appear to be any suggestion in the German edition of Adam of Bremen that Adam was wrong in suggesting that Helgoland and Farria were different names for the same place. Furthermore, there is no reference to any Bishop Eilbert or Egilbert in the Roll of Faroese bishops in the eleventh century or in the list of Norwegian Missionary Bishops [13].

Two documents in the twelfth century also refer to Farria. These are a papal bull by Pope Innocent II, dated the 27th May, 1133, purporting to transfer the Nordic churches back to Hamburg-Bremen from Lund and a document of the 16th March, 1158, in which Frederick Barbarossa, Holy Roman Emperor, also attempts to transfer the Nordic churches, which were at this time partly under the Archbishop of Lund and partly under the Archbishop of Nidaros [14], back to Hamburg-Bremen. In the Latin text of the first document in the *Diplomatarium Danicum* there is a reference to "episcopatus Dacie, Swedie, Norueie, Farrie, Gronlondie, Halsingaldie, Islandie, Scrideuindie, et Slauorum" although there is a footnote stating that in certain of the Latin texts the endings in "e" appear as "ae". This would be better Latin as the genitive singular ends in "ae". In the head-note in Danish, "Fariae" is translated as "Færøerne" (i.e. the Faroes) but it is submitted that this is inaccurate. The nominative singular of "Farriae" is "Farria" and it is considered that, if the writer had intended to refer to the Faroes, he would have used the genitive plural ending in "arum" and not the genitive singular. It is understood that the references in the Danish head-note to the Faroes derive from the fact that the word comes between references to "Denmark, Sweden and Norway" and a reference to Greenland. However, this word order is not conclusive evidence because between the references to Greenland and Iceland there is a reference to Helsingland, which is situated in Sweden, and after the reference to Iceland there is a reference to Skridfinnene in Norway (or possibly to Skridfinnerne in Sweden). The document concerned was issued by Pope Innocent II on the instigation of Archbishop Adalbero of Hamburg-Bremen who must have been aware that Farria (at any rate in earlier papal documents) was used as an alternative name for Helgoland. It is also relevant to note (as has been mentioned) that the 1139 document referred to Bishop Orm of the Faroes as "Faroensis episcopus" not as "Farriensis episcopus" or "Fariensis episcopus."

The document of 1158 refers to "ecclesias Danorum, Sueonum, Norwegiorum, Farrie, Grundlandonum, Halsingolandonum, Islandonum, Scredeuindonum et omnimu septentrionalium parcium metropolitanam sedem constituit". Here again, the head-note in Danish refers to "Færøerne" (i.e. the Faroes), possibly for the same reason as the headnote to the document of 1133. However, "Farrie" is also in the singular and not in the plural and once again, although "Farrie" appears between the references to the Norwegian and Greenland churches, the reference to the Halsingland churches appears between the references to those of Greenland and of Iceland, so that the word order proves nothing. This document was made in Frankfurt at the instigation of the Archbishop of Hamburg-Bremen, who was at that time Archbishop Hartvig, and he must have been aware of the earlier documents. It is submitted that the reference to Farria in the document of 1158 as well as in that of 1133 is a reference to Farria, the alternative name for Helgoland. The reason for its specific inclusion may well be on account of the island's proximity to Germany and because there was a monastery on it which would appear to have had a healthy income from Vikings and pirates [15].

It is possible that the name "Farria" was given to Helgoland because it had a lot of cattle or sheep on it. Adam of Bremen emphasizes the fact that there was a large number of cattle there [16]. There are plenty of examples of islands being called Sheep Island, apart from the Faroes. Examples of these are Fair Isle, north of Scotland, Sheep Island in the mouth of the River Roe in County Londonderry, Northern Ireland, and Fårö in the Baltic. It is also suggested that the setting out of the names Færøerne, Farensis, Faroensis, Farria and Farriensis together in the index to Vol. II (First Series) of the *Diplomatarium Danicum*[17] is obviously wrong as Farria in the two documents of 1061 to 1072 cannot possibly refer to the Faroes, and the headnotes to those documents do not suggest that it does.

However, accepting the arguments set out above as being valid, it is not suggested that the exclusion of the Faroes from the documents of 1133 and 1158 was deliberate. On the contrary, it would seem likely that the omission was due to ignorance of their existence.

The see of Lund was erected in 1104 by Pope Pascall II[18] and its first Archbishop was Archbishop Asger, who was ordained on the 8th November, 1089, and died on the 5th May, 1137[19]. He is referred to in documents of the 30th June, 1123, and the 7th January, 1133[19]. Hamburg-Bremen, however, disliked the jurisdiction of its see being reduced, and Archbishop Adalbero, who was Archbishop of Hamburg-Bremen from 1123 to 1148, and his successor, Archbishop Hartvig, who was Archbishop from 1148 to 1168, did their best to bring the northern churches back under their jurisdiction[20]. Their work must have been made considerably easier because during the period in question there was a succession of rival popes[21]. Finally, in 1133, Pope Innocent II, as a result of a visit by King Lothar of Saxony, directed that the Nordic churches should revert to the see of Hamburg-Bremen and issued five papal bulls (all dated the 27th May, 1133) to this effect, namely, to Archbishop Adalbero, (Arch)bishop Asger, King Nils of Denmark, the King of Sweden and to the Swedish bishops[22].

These papal bulls do not, however, appear to have had much effect, as, in 1139, Archbishop Asger's successor, Archbishop Eskil, seems to have been exercising his functions as Archbishop of Lund and to have held a provincial synod which was attended, among others, by Bishop Orm of the Faroes[23]. The document relating to this synod seems to be the first Church document in which the Faroes are specifically referred to.

The primary source of information regarding the Faroese bishops prior to the Reformation is the Roll of Faroese Bishops which is contained in the Latin copybook of Archbishop Henrik Kaltisen who was Archbishop of Nidaros from 1452 to 1458[24]. As has been mentioned[25], these bishops are identified by the letter "K" appearing after their names in Appendix 2. The main sources for the other bishops mentioned in that Appendix are the *Diplomatarium Færoense* and the *Diplomatarium Norvegicum*. Regard has also been had in compiling the list of Bishops of the Faroes in Appendix 2 to the list of those bishops contained in the publication *"Við Okkunugum Fólki til Kirkjubøur"* by Joánnes Patursson.

There is some confusion as to who was the author of the list subsequently transcribed by Archbishop Kaltisen of Nidaros as it begins "I, Serquirus when I came to these Islands . . .", which would indicate that Bishop Serquirus had personally made the inquiries about the earlier bishops[26]. However, the book goes on to state that there were only two men who could name all the previous bishops, which would seem unlikely if Bishop Serquirus was the person making the inquiries as he was consecrated as early as 1216[26]. Further doubt is thrown on the opening words by the fact that further down the list, when it comes to deal with Bishop John I, the German (Bishop of the Faroes from 1407 to 1430), it states "John is the one who writes (or has written) this document"[26]. This period would fit in more with only two old men knowing the earliest bishops[26]. Another possibility is that Bishop Serquirus started the list and that the list was continued by Bishop John, the German[26].

As has been mentioned[27], the first two bishops mentioned in the Roll of Faroese bishops are Bishops Bernhard and Ryngerus, who have been discussed in chapter 9, and who were missionary bishops. The first Bishop of the Faroes as such would appear to have been Bishop Gudmund who must have died before 1139 as, at that time, Bishop Orm was Bishop of the Faroes[28]. It is not possible to give the exact dates when Gudmund was Bishop of the Faroes but it is unlikely that he took office as such until the early twelfth century[29].

If legend can be believed, Bishop Gudmund was responsible for acquiring for the Church a considerable amount of property at Kirkjubøur (which became the seat of the Faroese bishops) from Gaesa, the youngest daughter of Sigurd Thorlakson and Birna[30], as a penalty for her having eaten meat during Lent[31]. Another story says that she also, as a penance, built the small church of St. Mary (of which only a few ruins remain) at St. Brandonsvík, Kirkjubøur. If there is any truth in these legends, Gaesa would seem to have been in her middle sixties at least in 1100, so it is unlikely that the incidents happened much after that date, if they did occur at all. If Bishop Gudmund was appointed, as seems likely, after 1104, when the see of Lund was erected[32], he was probably consecrated by Archbishop Asger of Lund, but there are no records available to prove this proposition.

As has been mentioned[33], Bishop Gudmund must have died before 1139. While there is no direct evidence as to the date of Bishop Gudmund's death, there is a reference in *Necrologium Lundense* to a certain Gutmundus who died on the 5th May, 1137[34]. Unlike other entries in that book, there is nothing said about whether this person was a cleric or a layman, but it is the only entry in the relevant period relating to any name resembling Gudmund and, with the Faroes coming under the see of Lund at that time, one would expect some entry to have been made in the *Necrologium Ludense* relating to his death.

Bishop Gudmund was followed as Bishop of the Faroes by Bishop Orm[35], but, apart from the fact that he attended the provincial synod in Lund in 1139[36], there is no other information extant about him.

The next event of importance in Faroese Church history occurred in 1152 when Nicholas Breakspear, Cardinal of Albano, went to Norway to erect the see of Nidaros[37]. An additional part of the Cardinal's Mission was, according to the English historian, Dugdale, to settle a dispute between the three Royal brothers, Sigurd II, Inge I and Eystein II[37], but this proposition is disputed by Norwegian historians. The visit of Cardinal Nicholas took place when Pope Eugene II was in office[38].

Cardinal Nicholas was a very remarkable individual. He was an Englishman who, at the end of 1154, became Pope as Adrian IV, in succession to Pope Anastasius IV, and he is the only Englishman who has ever attained that office. He succeeded in founding the see of Nidaros in 1152 or 1153, a see which included not only Norway (except for Jämtland, which came under the Archbishop of Uppsala in Sweden) but also Iceland, Greenland, the Faroes, the Orkneys and Shetlands and the Sudreys[39] (that is to say, the Isle of Man and the Hebrides)[40]. On the 28th November, 1154, Pope Anastasius IV, at the suggestion of Cardinal Nicholas, issued a papal bull formally confirming the erection of the Metropolitan See of Nidaros[41]. A copy of a translation of the papal bull is set out in Appendix 6. It will be noted that neither the Shetlands nor the Faroes are mentioned in the bull but the Shetlands came under the Orkneys and it is possible that the Vatican was under the mistaken impression that the Faroes were situated in Greenland and were incorporated in the expression "the Icelandic islands and Greenland". This view is supported by the fact that, under the heading "Norwegia" in folio 44 of *"liber censuum Romanae ecclesiae"* compiled by Censius Camerarius in 1192, there appears the expression *"In episcopatu Pharensi in Grotlandia"* which would seem to indicate that Rome in the twelfth century thought that the Faroes were siutated in Greenland[42]. An alternative theory is that the omission of the reference to the Faroes was due to a clerical error in transcription and reliance for this view is placed on the fact that the Faroes are mentioned in the confirmation of the erection of the see of Nidaros, and of its rights and privileges, contained in the Bull of Pope Innocent IV dated the 25th February, 1253, and published in Volume III of the *Diplomatarium Norvegicum*. The substance of the original Bull of 1154 and of the subsequent Bull is the same, but the descriptions of the dioceses concerned differ in points of detail. In particular, in the 1153 text, the word *"Insulas"* is inserted before the name of each group of islands but this is not done in the 1253 text where a different construction is used. It is suggested that the writer of the 1253 bull corrected the error in the 1153 bull by re-drafting the descriptions so as to include the Faroes.

The first Archbishop of Nidaros[14] was Jón Birgisson (Archbishop John I) who was, before that, Bishop of Stavanger in Norway[43]. He was consecrated as Archbishop in 1152[44] or 1153[45]. It would seem that the first Bishop of the Faroes to have come under this Archbishop John was Bishop Matthew (sometimes referred to as Martin) who died in 1157 [46]. There appears to have been no Bishop of the Faroes from 1157 until 1162 or, according to an Icelandic source, 1163, when Bishop Roe was consecrated[47]. This was probably due to the fact that after Archbishop John's death on the 24th February, 1157[48], there was a vacancy in the see of Nidaros until the 26th November, 1161, when Eystein Erlendsson was consecrated as Archbishop of Nidaros[14] by Pope Alexander III, although Eystein had been chosen as Archbishop by King Inge I on the 21st August, 1157[48]. The delay in consecrating the new Archbishop may have been due in part to the attempt by Emperor Frederik in 1158 to bring the Nordic churches back under Hamburg-Bremen[50]. It is of interest to note that Archbishop Eskil of Lund and a Danish Bishop had been robbed and imprisoned in West Germany in 1156, when they were on their way home from attending a papal court, on account of their opposition to the policy of Hamburg-Bremen in trying to dominate all the Nordic churches[51]. They were not released until they had been ransomed, despite pleas to the Holy Roman Emperor[51].

Bishop Roe was Bishop of the Faroes from 1162 or, possibly, 1163 until 1174[52]. One of the most important events in his episcopal career was his connection with Sverre who later became King of Norway. Shortly after the episcopal seat was established at Kirkjubøur, a school was founded there for training priests and one of Bishop Roe's student priests was Sverre, who was born in Norway in 1151 but came to the Faroes in 1156 and was brought up and educated at Kirkjubøur[53]. In 1168, Sverre went to the Orkneys on a mission for Bishop Roe, and, in 1176, he returned to Norway and became King of that country in 1184[53].

Little is known of the next two bishops, who were Sven, who died in 1212, and Olaf, who died in 1214[54]. The latter is not mentioned in Archbishop Kaltisen's notebook and it is possible that he may never, in fact, have taken up duties in the Faroes. Bishop Olaf was succeeded by Bishop Serquirus who was consecrated in 1215[54] and whose name is also mentioned in the Saga of King Hakon IV and his sons, where it states that he was present at a large meeting of leading people which was held in Bergen in 1223 and at which it was determined that King Hakon had a legal right to the Norwegian throne[56]. According to the Roll[57], Bishop

Serquirus was followed by Bishop Bergsven who died in 1243. There is some dispute as to who was the successor to Bishop Bergsven, some authorities mentioning a Bishop Nicholas and others a Bishop Peter but it is possible that they may have been the same person [58]. Bishop Peter would appear to have been consecrated Bishop of the Faroes in 1246 and translated to Bergen in 1257 [59]. Bishop Peter was followed by Bishop Gaute who was Bishop of the Faroes from 1261 or 1262 to 1268 [60] and is said to have been present at Nidaros [14] when Hakon, Bishop of Oslo, was consecrated as Archbishop of Nidaros in 1267 [61].

The next Bishop of the Faroes was the most famous of them all, namely Bishop Erlend who was consecrated as Bishop of the Faroes in January, 1269 [62]. Prior to this, he had been a canon and a teacher in Bergen [63]. He was a remarkable man and must have been outstanding as a preacher and a most intelligent person both as regards ecclesiastical and secular matters, although possibly somewhat eccentric as he is said to have gone around dressed like John the Baptist [63]. He has been described as being "bereft of faults and full of good qualities", but despite these and other beautiful words one must appreciate that Bishop Erlend, like most powerful churchmen of his period, brought everything he could, both property and taxes, under the control of the Church [63]. It was said of him that "over all his predecessors, he enriched the Faroese Church with privileges, property and secular goods", words which show the Bishop in a slightly different light to those which praise him to the skies [63].

The unfinished cathedral at Kirkjubøur, St. Magnus's, is believed to have been built during the time when Erlend was Bishop of the Faroes and as a result of his endeavours. If this is correct, it is indeed a wonderful memorial to a famous man. A detailed description of the cathedral is given later on in this book [64].

There is in Archbishop Kaltisen's copybook a note of a letter in Latin from Archbishop John II, the Red, of Nidaros [14] to Bishop Erlend dated the 4th August, 1275 [65]. In 1280 the Bishop's name appears, in red, with those of six other bishops at the foot of the church law which was made on the advice of the Convocation of Bishops held in Bergen from the 12th June to the 29th July of that year [66]. Bishop Erlend was also one of the seven bishops who witnessed the crowning of King Erik II (the elder son of King Magnus VI, the Law Reformer) and the oath which he took at that ceremony, as can be seen from the document which was executed in Bergen on the 25th July, 1280 [66]. On the 25th August, 1290, Bishop Erlend's name appears on a church law made by Archbishop Jørundur on the advice of five bishops [68]. It would seem from the preamble to the *Sheep Letter* that the 1280 law was extended to the Faroes by King Magnus VI [67], but the 1290 law does not appear to have been extended to the Faroes at the date when the *Sheep Letter* was enacted (1298) as the preamble to the *Sheep Letter* only mentions the law extended by King Magnus VI, who died in 1280 [68].

The next occasion on which Bishop Erlend's name is mentioned is in the preamble to the *Sheep Letter* where he is referred to as one of the two men who had carried out the researches into the agricultural law in the

Faroes prior to the drafting of the *Sheep Letter*[69]. He is also referred to in the preamble as the person to whom Duke Hakon's father, King Magnus VI, had presented the ecclesiastical law[69], presumably the 1280 law referred to above.

There are no other documentary references relating to Bishop Erlend until 1305, although he must have been in Nidaros[14] in 1299 when Duke Hakon was crowned as King Hakon V of Norway[70]. On the 5th December, 1305, Bishop Erlend and a Bishop Ketil assisted Archbishop Jørundur to install Canon Arne Sigurdson of Bergen, a friend of Bishop Erlend, as Bishop of Bergen, a ceremony at which both King Hakon V and Queen Euphemia of Rügen were present[70]. Bishop Erlend was one of sixteen leading dignatories and churchmen who signed their names at the foot of the document executed by King Hakon in Bergen on the 10th December of that year, in which King Hakon proclaimed that:—

(a) he had taken as the dowry which came to him, with his Queen, from Vitzlav, Prince of Rügen, three thousand silver marks (Cologne currency), two thousand of which he had lent to Valdemar, Duke of Southern Jutland; and

(b) he had given his Queen Bygdøy, which is situate in the Oslo area[70].

The signatories confirmed the document and promised to uphold it[70].

Bishop Erlend's name next appears at the foot of the law which was made on the 6th July, 1306, in Oslo by Archbishop Jørundur of Nidaros[14] and which related to monasteries and convents and their property, and to the persons who should be admitted to those institutions[71]. On the 29th September, 1306, Duke Erik of Vadstene in Sweden wrote a letter to the Norwegian church leaders and to other leading dignatories asking them to advise King Hakon V to protect his (Erik's) friends, the Danish nobles who had killed King Erik Glipping of Denmark and who had, as a result, been outlawed[71]. Bishop Erlend of the Faroes is mentioned again by name in this letter along with the other Norwegian bishops[72]. Bishop Erlend is also mentioned in a letter dated the 25th November of that year, written by the same Duke Erik, in which the Duke stated: "Erik sends the church leaders and dignatories in Norway his greetings and asks them to protect the outlawed Danes in Norway because Erik, King of Denmark" (Erik Merved) "has broken his agreement with King Hakon of Norway" (i.e. Hakon V)[72].

In an undated letter written between 1305 and 1308, probably in Bergen, Bishop Arne of Bergen gave Bishop Erlend of the Faroes authority to consecrate, on his behalf, the Royal Chapel on Tyssesøy in what is now the southern part of the Norwegian county of Bergenhus[73].

Bishop Erlend died on the 13th June, 1308, and this date is confirmed in two letters written by Bishop Arne of Bergen, Bishop Erlend's friend, on the 22nd June, 1308, one to his namesake, the Bishop of Skálholtur in Iceland, and the other to Bishop Tordur in Greenland[74]. The fact and date of Bishop Erlend's death are further confirmed by an entry in Archbishop Kaltisen's copybook[74]. This evidence completely refutes the legend that Bishop Erlend was killed at Kirkjubøur Cathedral after a battle between the inhabitants of the Northern Faroes (whom he supported) and those of the Southern Faroes (who won)[75]. It is, however, extremely likely that the Bishop was forced to leave the Faroes due to having become extremely unpopular there by reason of acquiring large amounts of property for the Church and of having increased the amount of tithes which the Faroes had to pay. Bishop Erlend is, as has been mentioned[76], credited with having been responsible for the building of the unfinished cathedral at Kirkjubøur, and this must have cost a great deal of money. Proof of Bishop Erlend's unpopularity can be seen from the fact that complaints against him were made to King Hakon V[77]. There is some corroboration of the story that he had to leave the Faroes in the fact that he appears, from the documents referred to above, to have spent a considerable amount of his latter years in Norway. According to legend, Bishop Erlend was buried in Kirkjubøur[78] and, if that is correct, it would mean that his body had been sent back to the Faroes from Norway.

As has been mentioned earlier[79], this was the period when most big Churchmen amassed property and riches for the Church. It is worthwhile comparing Bishop Erlend with one of his contemporaries in the same see, namely Bishop Mark of Sodor[80] who was bishop of that diocese from 1276 to 1299 and from 1302 until his death in about 1305[81]. He was buried at St. German on the islet of St. Patrick, Peel, which is on the west coast of the Isle of Man[81].

Bishop Mark, who came from Galloway, was nominated as Bishop of Sodor by King Alexander III of Scotland in lieu of Master Gilbert, Abbot of Rushen, who had been unanimously elected by the clergy and people of the Isle of Man[82]. The King sent Mark to Norway with a letter from himself and with other letters which he had been able to extort from the clergy[82]. As a result, Mark was consecrated as Bishop of Sodor by Archbishop John II of Nidaros at Tønsberg in southern Norway[83]. According to the *Chronicle of Man and the Sudreys*[84], Bishop Mark ruled his diocese right nobly and was a liberal and courteous man. He also seems to have been a very able and important person. He was in Norway in 1280[85] and was probably present at the Convocation of Bishops held in Bergen from the 12th June to the 29th July of that year[86] where, no doubt, he met Bishop Erlend. Bishop Mark may have gone on another mission into Norway in about 1289 as there is a charge for his expenses, in the Scottish Exchequer Rolls for that year, in respect of such a mission[87]. A possible reason for this mission would have been to attend the Convocation of Bishops which was held at Bergen in 1290[88]. In that same year, Bishop Mark was one of the guardians of Scotland and signed a letter to King Edward I of England[89].

In 1291 the Bishop held a synod at Kirk Braddan in the Isle of Man where steps were taken to increase the income of the Church and to make its discipline more severe. In all, thirty four synodal ordinances were enacted to achieve these objects. The tithes were enumerated with much greater precision than before and several new tithes were added, including a fish tithe and a tithe upon merchants and traders and upon smiths and other artificers[90]. The ordinances also provided that certain offenders should be excommunicated. These persons included all sorcerers, magicians, forgers, notorious usurers, thieves, robbers, perjurers and those defrauding the Church[91]. The duties of the archdeacon in his visitations, together with very strict rules concerning the conduct of priests and their vestments were also laid down. Laymen and clergy were prohibited from bearing arms in church and the holding of courts for the pleading of lay cases in churches or churchyards on Sundays and High Feast Days was also forbidden[92].

In 1292 Bishop Mark appeared at the Great Parliament of Berwick as one of the auditors and declared that the competitors for the Scottish Crown, Bruce and Baliol, had completed their pleadings, and that the King, presumably Edward I of England, might proceed to judgement[93]. In 1296, the Bailiff of Dumfries was ordered by King Edward I of England to bring Bishop Mark to declare his allegiance to the King[94].

In 1299 Bishop Mark appropriated the churches of St. Michael and St. Maughold to the Abbey of Furness[95]. This action seems to have been queried because the Bishop alleged that he had taken it with the consent of the clery[95]. In any event, he wrote an open letter, a translation of which is in Appendix 7. For some reason, perhaps as a result of these appropriations and of the increases which he had made in tithes and other ecclesiastical charges, Bishop Mark was expelled from the Isle of Man by the people of the Island[95]. As a result, the Island was placed under an interdict for three years[95]. At the end of that period, the Bishop was recalled and the people of the Island agreed to the imposition of a charge of one penny on every home with a fireplace[95].

As can be seen from the above, the histories of the two bishops bear striking similarities. Both were not only outstanding bishops but also took part in activities of State at a very high level and both appropriated a considerable amount of property to the Church. Both of them incurred the dislike of the inhabitants of their dioceses and had to leave them. Was all this sheer coincidence or were both bishops carrying out a policy dictated by higher authority and stemming, in the first place, from the Convocation of Bishops held in Bergen in 1280 under Archbishop John II and apparently attended by both Bishop Erlend and Bishop Mark[96]? This theory has a certain attraction.

To revert to the Faroes, there was no bishop at Kirkjubøur for four or five years after the death of Bishop Erlend[97]. This was due to a dispute between Bishop Arne of Bergen and Archbishop Jørundur as to which of them had the authority to appoint the Bishop of the Faroes[97]. Archbishop Jørundur had chosen Lodin of Borgund to be Bishop of the Faroes but Bishop Arne claimed that, by time honoured right, he and his synod had the privilege of appointing the bishops of that diocese[97]. In 1312 Archbishop Jørundur and Bishop Arne agreed, at a large church meeting in Vienna, to leave the matter to be determined by Archbishop Nikolaus of Uppsala in Sweden[97]. Archbishop Nikolaus confirmed Archbishop Jørundur's choice and as a result Lodin was consecrated as

Bishop of the Faroes, but he only lived for a short time after that as, according to the Icelandic annals, he was involved in a shipwreck and drowned at sea in 1316[97].

From 1312 to 1319, King Hakon V granted to the Mary-Kirk in Christiania[98] for the completion of the building and fabric of the Church all the King's revenues from the Shetlands and from the Faroes and decreed that this revenue would continue to be assigned in that way until the fabric of the church was fully completed, after which the revenues from the Shetlands and the Faroes would revert to the Crown[99].

The next Bishop of the Faroes was Signar who was consecrated in 1320[100]. He wrote from Nidaros[14] that year a short letter in Latin to Bishop Audfinn of Bergen, a translation of which is at Appendix 8. This letter refers to a wooden chancel which Bishop Audfinn had given to St. Mary's Church in Kirkjubøur and to a letter of authority which Bishop Audfinn had sent him. The letter also refers to certain allegations made against Bishop Audfinn by his rivals, but Bishop Signar said that the Archbishop (of Nidaros[14]) was on Bishop Audfinn's side and that he would soon (around Whitsun) be going to Bergen.

Bishop Signar appears to have been followed by Bishop Gevard[101] to whom two letters were written, the first by Archbishop Eilif on 6th May, 1329, and the second by Archbishop Paul on the 25th April, 1337 or 1339[102]. He was succeeded by Bishop Havard (1343 to 1348) who was followed by Bishop Arne Svaela[103]. This is probably the Bishop Arne to whom three petitions were granted on 21st January, 1360, by Pope Innocent VI of Avignon in France[104], the first being a request for a desk chair[105], the second concerning the confirmation of a clerk, Gerlach Speckin, as canon of Butzow in Mecklenburg and the third relating to the promotion of a Swedish priest in the diocese of Uppsala in Sweden[104]. This was at the time when the German Duke of Mecklenburg had a "foot" in Sweden. Albrecht, Duke of Mecklenburg, who was married to Euphemia, a sister of Magnus Smek, King of Sweden, had a son, Albrecht, who became King of Sweden in 1363[104]. Bishop Arne had probably known the Mecklenburgers previously, possibly (as Munch contends) when, as Clerk to King Hakon VI of Norway, he had made journeys abroad[106].

The Icelandic *Flatoyggar* annals and the annals of the *Løgmaður* state that, in 1365, Bishop Arne Svaela of the Faroes encountered bad weather at sea and had to make for Iceland[107]. The *Skálholtsannálsbrot* puts the event in the year 1363 and states that Bishop Arne spent the winter with Bishop Tórar of Skálholtur in Iceland[107]. The third reference to Bishop Arne Svaela is in a letter, dated the 19th July, 1369, written to him by Archbishop Olaf[108].

A cleric called Andrew, canon of Bergen or Nidaros[14], is said to have been *electus Farensis* in 1381 (that is to say, chosen to be Bishop of the Faroes) but it is extremely doubtful whether he ever went to the Faroes or was even consecrated as Bishop of the Faroese diocese[109]. The bishop to be named in the Roll of Bishops of the Faroes next after Arne Svaela is Bishop Arnold, but no dates are given in relation to him[110]. According to the *Diplomaticum Norvegicum,* Bishop Arnold was followed by a Bishop Richard who may have been consecrated in about 1381 and must have died before January, 1391[111]. Jóannes Patursson, on the other hand, put the date of his consecration at 1385 and goes on to say that he probably never came to the Faroes[112]. If, however, he was, at any rate in theory, Bishop of the Faroes in 1387, he would have been in office when Norway and Denmark became united, although that event does not appear to have had much effect so far as the Church in the Faroes was concerned[113].

The Faroes are mentioned from time to time in documents filed in the papal archives concerning the dues and tithes to be paid by the Norwegian Church to the Apostolic Chamber and to the College of Cardinals in Rome as can be seen in Gustave Storm's book *Afgifter fra den norske kirkeprovine til det apostoliske kammer of kardinalcollegiet 1311-1523, efter optegnesler i de pavelige arkiver,* which was published in Christiania[98] in 1897[114]. The following Faroese bishops are mentioned during the period from 1391 to 1435:—Bishop William, Bishop Vigbald, Bishop John II, the Dominican, and Bishop John III, the Chief[114]. There is a letter from Rome dated the 3rd March, 1391, concerning Bishop Vigbald (who is said to have been a German) according to which Bishop Vigbald promised to pay the main dues (33⅓ guilders) which were payable to the Apostolic See and the five lesser dues payable to the Apostolic Chamber and to the College of Cardinals[114]. The Bishop also agreed to have Lupold of Beym in Dweold, Münster, as his middleman[114]. Bishop Vigbald further undertook to pay the debts due to the Apostolic See by his predecessor, Bishop William[114]. The only documentary evidence concerning this Bishop William, who should have been a Bishop of the Faroes, is in a letter dated the 27th September, 1396, in which Pope Boniface IX gave a Bishop William (whom the previous Pope, Urban VI, had appointed and consecrated as Bishop of the Faroes), a benefice for the cure of souls because the bishop had not taken over the episcopal seat at Kirkjubøur[115]. This Bishop William may have been the Englishman, William Northbrigg, but there is doubt as to whether he ever went to the Faroes[116].

There is a receipt dated the 4th March, 1391, issued by the Vatican in Rome for all the money which Bishop Vigbald had promised to pay[117]. The next reference to Bishop Vigbald is in August, 1394, when he was present at a meeting of leading dignatories at Helsingborg (then in Denmark, but now in Sweden)[118]. Queen Margaret of Denmark had summoned this meeting, which was attended by all the Ministers of State, important men and bishops from all the northern countries[118].

There is confusion about the bishops who held office in the Faroes during the 1390's. In 1392 (between the years 1391 and 1394 when Bishop Vigbald is mentioned as Bishop of the Faroes) a certain Halgeir, at one time Bishop of Stavanger[119], is referred to as being Bishop of the Faroes[120]. This Bishop Halgeir is shown as being among the bishops who signed the decree made in Oslo on the 29th March, 1392, by Queen Margaret I, daughter of King Valdemar IV of Denmark, with the consent of the Ministers of State[120]. Bishop Vigbald must have been absent from the Faroes at this time and Bishop Halgeir must have been acting as *locum tenens:* but it is questionable whether the latter Bishop ever assumed office as Bishop of the Faroes[120].

Canon Philip Gudbrandsson of Nidaros[14] is stated to have been chosen *(electus Farensis)* to be Bishop of the Faroes in 1391, but he was never consecrated and never went to the Faroes[121]. It is uncertain how long Bishop Vigbald was Bishop of the Faroes but he was followed by Bishop John I, the German, who was selected by Pope Gregory XII in 1407, so he must have ceased to be Bishop before then[118]. The date of 1407 is supported by a papal brief dated the 9th December of that year[122]. The reference in *Diplomatarium Færoense* to the brief being signed on the 6th December, 1406[123], would appear to be inaccurate. However, he seems to have been consecrated before the 2nd May, 1408[122]. Another papal document shows that the Faroese diocese was without a bishop on the 4th May, 1431, as the result of the death of a Bishop John who is considered to be the same Bishop John[122]. John I must also have been the Bishop John who executed the document relating to Haraldur Kálvsson, Lawman, in 1412. A translation of this document is in Appendix 9, together with a translation of a certified copy of the document made on the 15th August, 1443, and a translation of a further certified copy made on the 2nd May (or 13th September), 1479.

Bishop John I and two priests are said to have exhumed the corpse of Bishop Erlend in 1420 as it was hoped to have him canonized[124]. A stone memorial tablet, written in Latin in runic script is alleged to have been discovered during the exhumation[124]. This tablet, when translated, is said to have contained a long eulogy extolling Bishop Erlend and stating, among other things, that the Bishop's church was burned down during the time of Bishop Erlend who had, as a result of this conflagration, rebuilt it in stone[124]. The tablet is also said to have stated that Bishop Erlend was the first person to have built a house of stone in the Faroes[124].

Bishop John I's successor, Bishop Severin, Bishop of Tranquilia, was appointed Bishop of the Faroes by the document of the 4th May, 1431, referred to above, but there is no evidence that he ever actually went to the Faroes[125]. Bishop Severin is also mentioned in a document made on the 2nd or 3rd May, 1434, at a convocation of all the bishops which was held at Vordinborg on Zealand in Denmark[126]. The object of the convocation was to support the complaint of the monastical community of St. Brigid which was objecting to a document which was to be laid before the Assembly of the Catholic Church to be held in Basel[126]. Bishop Severin signed this document along with the other bishops from the northern countries[126]. Bishop Severin's name also appears at the foot of a document dated the 6th July, 1434, and made at Vordingborg by the Archbishops of Lund and Nidaros[127], which provided that penitent Christians who visited St. Mary's Church in Stavanger and helped it should get forty days indulgence and absolution[127]. In *Scriptores rerum Danicarum,* Langbek contends that Bishop Severin must have been in

Fyn in 1416, Helsingør in 1427 and in Nykøbing in 1429, before going to the Faroes in 1432[127]. According to the same historian, he was buried in Roskilde on Zealand, Denmark[127]. Although Bishop Severin's nationality is not known for certain, it seems probable that he was a Dane[127].

Gustave Storm's book referred to above[128] shows that John III, the Chief, a German, was appointed Bishop of the Faroes by a papal document made at Florence in Italy on the 31st January, 1435, to succeed a Bishop John (John II, the Dominican), but there is no other reference to this Bishop except in the Roll of Bishops[129]. He may have come after Bishop Severin and been Bishop of the Faroes for only a very short time and certainly not after 1434, that is, if he ever went to the Faroes[130]. Bishop John III was probably still in Florence in November, 1435, because on the 11th November, 1435, Fransicus, Papal Vicecamerarius and Cardinal Priest of S. Clementis proclaimed that Archbishop John of Tuam (in Ireland) had consecrated John Ffere (possibly Seyre) Bishop of Man in Florence with the assistance of Bishop John of the Faroes and Bishop Andreas of Megara (in Greece).

In a short letter, dated the 14th December, 1435, Bishop John III, the Chief, promised to pay the main dues (that is those due to the Apostolic See) and also the five lesser dues to the Apostolic Chamber and to the College of Cardinals[131]. In a letter written from Rome on the 18th January, 1447, Pope Eugene IV promised Bishop John of the Faroes, who must have been Bishop John III, the Chief, a benefice because the bishop had been deprived of his diocese by "an unjust son" named Goswin[132]. This benefice would seem to have been promised to Bishop John until he was re-installed in his seat at Kirkjubøur[132]. The name Goswin (which is German or Dutch) was uncommon in the Nordic countries but, at the period in question, the Bishop of Skálholtur in the south of Iceland was called Goswin and was said to have been a zealous man, but of a hard and persevering disposition[132]. This Bishop Goswin had designs on the Church in the Faroes and wished to bring that Church under his diocese[132]. It seems, therefore, more than likely that this Bishop Goswin was the "unjust son" referred to in Pope Eugene's letter.

The next bishop of the Faroes was Bishop Hemming, who was a Dane[133] or a Swede[134], and is mentioned in a proclamation, made in Lödöse in Sweden by the Archbishop of Nidaros[14] about the letters of indulgence, dated the 7th to 9th June, 1442[133]. Bishop Hemming's name also appears in an endorsement on the document of 1412 relating to Bishop John I and Haraldur Kálvsson[135] and in the certified copy of that document dated the 15th August, 1443[136]. The Bishop's name is mentioned again in a proclamation concerning indulgences which was made in Bergen on the 4th September, 1450[133]. His name next appears in a document dated the 2nd November, 1451, and made at Innvik in what is now the northern part of the Norwegian county of Bergenhus, as a witness together with Peter Nikjalsson, parish priest of Innvik[137]. This document tells about two persons, Bardur Eiriksson and Ingibjørg, daughter of Arne, being brought before the King and the Bishop of Bergen in connection with some offence which they had committed[137].

Another Bishop John (John IV) then appears in the Roll[138]. His name is mentioned in a document made in Nidaros[13] on the 1st June, 1453, as having been among those assembled at the Archbishop's palace who testified on behalf of the Norwegian people that King Christian I of Denmark had been lawfully chosen as their King[139].

There is no further information about the Faroese Church during the remainder of the fifteenth century and the affairs of that Church during this period are enveloped in darkness. Volume XVII of the *Diplomatarium Norvegicum,* in which are published the majority of the papal documents relating to the Norwegian church in the Middle Ages, contains no details of the Faroese Church during the period in question nor does it give any information about Bishop Matthew or Bishop Chilianus[140]. Those Bishops are, however, mentioned in the *Chronicle of Bishops* by Arild Hvidtfeldt[141].

The next bishop referred to in Volume XVIIB of the *Diplomatarium Norvegicum* is Bishop Hilary[142]. According to a papal document filed in the papal archives, Pope Leo X, in a letter dated the 3rd April, 1520, asked the Bishops of Oslo and Hamar in Norway, and the Bishops of Skálholtur and Hvolung in Iceland, to send to the Archbishop of Nidaros[14] the money which their dioceses should contribute to the building of St. Peter's in Rome and that the Archbishop would transmit the money to the *Papal Nuncio* (Arcimboldus) in Germany[143]. Bishop Hilary is mentioned in the letter as Bishop of the Faroes *("Hilarius Pherensis")*[143]. This, however, conflicts with what Pastor Schrøter stated in *"Antikvarisk Tidskrift 1849-51"* page 154, namely that Bishop Hilary's gravestone indicated that he died in 1511[143]. However, the inaccuracy of Schrøter's statement is supported by the fact that there is a letter in the National Archives in Copenhagen dated the 17th August, 1524, in which Bishop Hilary of the Faroes and the Faroese Løgting swear allegiance to Frederik I, King of Denmark and Norway. Bishop Hilary was followed by Bishop Chilianus, who died before the 1st January, 1533[144].

The last Catholic Bishop of the Faroes was Amund Olafsson, whose appointment was confirmed in 1532 by the King of Denmark (Frederik I) and not, as was customary previously, by the Pope[145]. This change in the method of appointment was revolutionary and reveals the drawing to an end of papal power in Northern Europe[145]. Bishop Amund paid the King of Denmark one thousand guilders for confirming his appointment[145]. On the 1st January, 1533, Bishop Amund was appointed Bishop of the Faroes for life as a result of a petition by the Faroese[146]. There are three letters in the National Archives in Copenhagen from Bishop Amund to Eske Bille[147] in Bergen complaining about the Hamburg Merchants in the Faroes, etc.

There is some controversy as to when the Reformation actually came to the Faroes, Louis Zachariasen suggesting that it was in 1535[148], while Jakob Jakobsen placed the Reformation five years later, which would fix it in 1540[149], the same year in which the Reformation came to the Isle of Man[150]. Arild Hvidfeldt stated that Bishop Amund lost his seat in 1538[151], but this is not definite. The suggestion that the Reformation reached the Faroes in 1535 seems to be clearly wrong in view of the fact that Bishop Amund was still in office in the summer of 1536, as his servant went to Bergen in that summer and delivered to Archbishop Olaf's representatives a quantity of homespun and calves' hides[152], presumably as a due of some kind.

1538 would, however, on the balance of probabilities, seem to be the most likely date for the arrival of the Reformation in the Faroes. The Reformation came to Denmark in 1536[153] and, in 1537, the Archbishop of Nidaros vacated his see and left Norway[154]. It seems very unlikely that the Reformation should have come to the Faroes before it had worked its way north from Denmark to Nidaros. On the other hand, it seems unlikely that Bishop Amund would have remained at his episcopal post for long after his Archbishop had vacated his office. This would make 1538 a reasonable date for the Reformation to reach the Faroes as, in the following year, 1539, Bishop Amund was succeeded as leading prelate in the Faroes by Jens Riber, who was the only Evangelical Superintendent (a Lutheran post) to hold office in the Faroes[155]. 1538 is also the date which is taken by the officials in the National Archives in Denmark as being that on which the Reformation reached the Faroes. Jens Riber left the Faroes for Stavanger in Norway in 1557[156]. After his departure the Faroes came under the Lutheran Bishop of Bergen and later under the Lutheran Bishop of Zealand in Denmark[157].

The Reformation saw the finish of the Catholic Church in the Faroes and the Roman Catholic Church has never since then made any impact of note in those islands. Even today, the number of Roman Catholics in the Faroes is very small. One immediate result of the Reformation was that King Christian III confiscated two-thirds of the property of the Church in the Faroes[158].

There is very little information about the daily Christian life of members of the Church in the pre-Reformation period[159]. However, it is generally assumed that it would not have been very different from that followed during that period by Christians in other Nordic countries[159]. The language of the Church prior to the Reformation was Latin, but, when the priests preached their sermons, they would have had to speak in Faroese, which was a completely different language and not their mother tongue[159].

It would seem that the pre-Reformation clergy in the Faroes were not too faithful to their vows and that some of them were not averse to having their mistresses. It is, for example, recorded that, in 1551, King Christian III of Denmark commanded ex-Bishop Amund of the Faroes to leave his (the Bishop's) mistress[160]. Furthermore, according to stories still circulating in Suðuroy, the Faroese priests of that era used to claim the right to spend the first night with a bride[161], but there is no evidence to prove the truth of this allegation.

The relations between the Church and the Monarchy in Norway

seemed to have been more than strained on a number of occasions, which must have had some effect on the relations between the Church and the Administration in the Faroes. One example of this was the war waged between King Sverre and the Church in the latter part of the twelfth century and the beginning of the thirteenth century, which resulted in Archbishop Erik of Nidaros having to vacate the episcopal seat from 1192 to 1202 [162] and to take up his abode with the Archbishop of Lund. King Sverre's opposition to the Church must have, to a large extent, been a result of the circumstances of his birth and of his upbringing. Sverre was certainly not the legitimate son of King Sigurd II [163] and his claim to the Norwegian throne can only have been based on his mother having been a concubine of King Sigurd II. The Church was bitterly opposed to claims by bastards, a fact which must have been very much resented by Sverre despite, or possibly on account of, his ecclesiastical upbringing [164]. It is a generally accepted fact, in Britain and elsewhere, that the sons of clergymen, brought up in a strict atmosphere often turn out wild when they go to a boarding school or otherwise escape from parental control. A similar reaction could also have occurred to Sverre. His conflict with the Church ultimately resulted in his excommunication, but this did not prevent him applying for help to Archbishop Hubert of Canterbury, a step which caused Pope Innocent III to send a papal brief to the English Archbishop forbidding him to accept dogs, birds or other presents from King Sverre [165].

Another example of the conflict between the Church and the Norwegian monarchy was the dispute, about a hundred years after that of King Sverre, which took place between the Church and King Hakon V during the period when Erlend was Bishop of the Faroes [166].

1 See p. 45 *ante*.
2 Munch considered that there were no fixed dioceses in Norway or Sweden prior to 1111 (see CM p. 237), but modern historians tend to the view that at least some fixed dioceses must have existed in Norway from the second half of the eleventh century. Knud J. Krogh, however, considers that the Faroes became a fixed diocese in about 1120, see MO p. 23.
3 LW p. 172, HK p. 124. This may be due to the fact that the Faroes did not appear on any map until 1280, see p. 51 *ante*.
4 DD pp. 146-50 (vol. I) R II.
5 AB p. 193, d, see also index.
6 AB p. 188 and 193 note d.
7 DD pp. 11 to 14.
8 AB pp. 182, 188 and 189.
9 AB p. 182, DD pp. 11 to 14; SH p. 333.
10 SH p. 333.
11 DD pp. 11 to 14, SH p. 333.
12 See p. 59 *ante*.
13 See Table II and DN xviiB, pp. 189-195, 286 and 287.
14 Nidaros is situate near Trondheim in Norway.
15 AB pp.188 and 189.
16 AB p. 189.
17 DD p. 268.
18 Pope from 1099-1118.
19 NL pp. 70, 71 and 110.

20 ADJ pp. 593 to 625.
21 See Appendix 2.
22 ADJ pp. 597-8. See also DD (vol. I) R II. Nrs. 57-9 pp. 110-6.
23 See p. 59 *ante*.
24 See Appendix 2.
25 See p. 44 *ante*.
26 DF pp. viii and ix.
27 See pp. 44-45 *ante*.
28 See Appendix 2.
29 See pp. 46 and 62 *ante*.
30 See p. 43 *ante*.
31 See *"Við Okkunugum Folki til Kirkjubøur"* by Jóannes Patursson.
32 See p. 59 *ante*.
33 See p. 62 *ante*.
34 In Lund University, Sweden.
35 See Appendix 2.
36 See n. 4.
37 CM pp. 171 and 172. The brothers were the sons of Harald IV Gille.
38 CM p. 277.
39 CM p. 172, M p. 168.
40 St. p. 62.
41 CM pp. 274 to 284.
42 CM p. 258.
43 DN xviiB p. 200.
44 *Ibid.* where the date is given as August, 1152, on the assumption that Archbishop John I was consecrated shortly after the arrival of Cardinal Nicholas Breakspear in July of that year.
45 Modern historians now take the view that the See of Nidaros was erected in 1152 or 1153 and that Archbishop John I was consecrated in either 1152 or 1153.
46 DN xviiB p. 287.
47 *Ibid.*
48 DN xviiB p. 200.
49 *Ibid.*
50 See p. 60 *ante*.
51 ADJ p. 615.
52 DN xviiB p. 287, L p. 17, see also Appendix 2.
53 L p. 20 and RS p. 13.
54 See Appendix 2.
55 *Ibid.*
56 DF pp. ix and x.
57 See Appendix 2.
58 DF p. viii; DN xviiB p. 288.
59 DN xviiB p. 288.
60 See Appendix 2.
61 DF p. x.
62 DN xviiB p. 288.
63 RS pp. 11 & 12.
64 See Chapter 17.
65 DF p. ix.
66 DF p. x.
67 See pp. 140 and 145 *post*.
68 See Appendix 1.
69 See pp. 140 and 145 *post*.
70 DF p. x.
71 *Ibid.*
72 DF p. xi.

73   *Ibid.*
74   *Ibid.*
75   DB p. 54.
76   See p. 65 *ante.*
77   See p. 53 *ante.*
78   See p. 71 *post.*
79   See p. 65 *ante.*
80   Now called Sodor and Man, apparently due to an error by a legal draftsman in the seventeenth century, see M p. 178.
81   CM pp. 116, 117 and 249 to 251 & Appendix 7. Munch's suggestion that Bishop Mark died in 1299 (CM p. 251) is erroneous in that it would seem from the Chronicles (CM p. 117) that after 24 years as Bishop of Sodor he was forced to leave the Isle of Man but was later recalled to his see.
82   CM p. 250. See also Appendix 7.
83   CM pp. 249 and 250.
84   CM pp. 116-9.
85   CM pp. 249 and 250.
86   CM p. 250.
87   M p. 204.
88   See p. 65 *ante.*
89   CM p. 251.
90   M pp. 199 and 200.
91   M p. 355.
92   M p. 200.
93   CM p. 250 and M p. 204.
94   CM p. 251 amd M p. 204.
95   M pp. 204 and 205.
96   See pp. 65 and 67 *ante.*
97   DF p. xi.
98   Now Oslo.
99   OS p. xi, *n* 1.
100 DN xviiB p. 289.
101 See Appendix 2.
102 DF p. ix. The date 25th April, 1337, conflicts with DN p. 289 which places it at 25th April, 1339.
103 See Appendix 2.
104 DF p. xii.
105 Literally, "writing chair".
106 DF pp. xii and xiii.
107 DF p. xiii.
108 DF p. ix.
109 DF p. xiii.
110 See appendix 2.
111 DN xviiB p. 290. The year ended in March under the Julian Calendar.
112 See Appendix 2.
113 RS p. 15.
114 DF p. xiii.
115 DF p. xiii, note 2.
116 See DN xviiiB p. 290 and Appendix 2.
117 DF pp. xiii and xiv.
118 DF p. xiv.
119 DN xviiB p. 291.
120 DF p. xiv.
121 DF pp. vii and xiv; DN xviiB p. 291.
122 DN xviiB p. 291.
123 DF p. xiv note 1.

124 DB pp. 52 and 69.
125 DN xviiB p. 291.
126 DF pp. xiv and xv.
127 DF p. xv.
128 See p. 70 *ante*.
129 DF p. viii.
130 DF p. xv.
131 *Ibid.*
132 *Ibid.* note 1.
133 DF p. xv.
134 DN xviiB p. 292.
135 See document 1 in Appendix 9.
136 See document 2 in Appendix 9.
137 DF pp. xv and xvi.
138 See Appendix 2.
139 DF p. xvi.
140 DF p. xvi note 1, see also Appendix 2.
141 DF p. viii.
142 DF p. xvi. See also Appendix 2.
143 DF p. xvi.
144 DN xviiB p. 292.
145 DF p. xvi.
146 DF pp. xvi and xvii.
147 See p. 56 *ante*.
148 FSR Pt. 1 pp. 12 and 13.
149 DF p. xvii. The year 1540 is also supported by other authorities, see RS p. 28 and S facing page.
150 M p. 351, but the progress of the Reformation in the Isle of Man was slow, see M pp. 352-4.
151 DF p. xvii.
152 OE p. 131.
153 D p. 112.
154 DN xviiB p. 216.
155 DF p. xvii.
156 DF p. viii.
157 DF p. xvii.
158 S facing page.
159 RS p. 13.
160 DN xviiB p. 292; LZ p. 169.
161 The "*jus primi noctis*".
162 CM p. 241 note c. See also Appendix 2.
163 See Appendix 2.
164 See p. 64 *ante*.
165 DN xvii p. 200 and document No. 1233.
166 See p. 53 *ante*.

CHAPTER 12

THE LEGISLATURE, COURTS AND THE LAW

The Faroese claim that they had the first Parliament in Europe. Iceland and the Isle of Man make similar claims. The Faroese claim that their *Alting* was founded by the first landnamsmen in the ninth or tenth century before Iceland had its *Althing*[1]. The Icelandic *Althing* was founded in about 930[2] and if Manx legend were correct the Manx Tynwald (the equivalent to the *Alting)* would have been established shortly after 914[3]. However, it seems not unlikely that Manx legend is accurate and it would appear that Tynwald, as the *Alting* of the Sudreys, was established in the second half of the 970's, although there may have been a Thing place from a much earlier date.

Although it is not possible to prove beyond all reasonable doubt which of the three countries had the first National Legislature, the odds seem to be in favour of the Faroes and this view is supported by Dr. Scheel[5]. It is clear that the Faroes were settled by the landnamsmen a considerable time before Iceland was[6] and, accordingly, it would seem reasonable to assume that the Faroes had a legislature before Iceland had one.

The first written evidence of the Faroese *Alting* is contained in the *Faroese Saga* where it is stated that Einar the Sudreyan was summoned to appear before it on Streymoy[7]. The *Saga* does not state where on Streymoy the *Alting* was held, but it is logical to assume that it was held at Tinganes as that is the place where the *Alting* or, as it was later called, the *Løgting* has met since time immemorial. The meeting on Streymoy referred to above took place in about 979[8] but the *Saga* indicates that it was by that date customary for a considerable time for the *Alting* to meet on Streymoy.

Tinganes is now situated within the boundaries of Tórshavn, the capital of the Faroes, but it was probably not until long after the time of the *Saga* that Tórshavn became a sizeable town as otherwise the Faroese bishops would almost certainly have established their seat there[9]. Tórshavn was, however, on account of its situation, an ideal place for use as a central meeting place for the inhabitants of all the islands[10]. In additon, the islet of Tinganes was flat and altogether an eminently suitable site for the *Alting*[10], which may well have been the reason why it was chosen as the meeting place for the *Alting*. An alternative reason given by Dr. Scheel for Tinganes having been chosen derives from the name Tórshavn which indicates that it was a sacred place in pagan times[10]. It could, therefore, have started off as a meeting place for religious purposes and from that developed into one for the *Alting*[10].

However, whatever its origin, Tinganes seems to have been both the place where the *Alting* sat and a place where pagan religious festivals were held.

Dr. Scheel rules out the possibility that the *Alting* developed out of a local *Thing*[11]. He also points out that Tønsberg in Norway is another place which started off as a meeting place for a *Thing* and gradually developed into a trading centre[11]. This also happened in the Isle of Man and a fair is still held at St. John's in that Island on Tynwald Day (5th July).

The Faroese *Alting* was an assembly which all freemen could attend and in which they could participate directly[12]. Its functions, prior to 1271[13], were both of an executive and judicial nature[14]. According to tradition, bonfires were lit on a hill in the vicinity of Tinganes throughout the time when the *Alting* was sitting so as to inform the inhabitants of the islands that it was in session. There are cairns still in existence where other bonfires are said to have been lit for the same purpose and they are situated due north, due east, due south and due west of Tinganes. There was, up to the early nineteenth century, in the Isle of Man, a custom of lighting bonfires on the eve of Midsummer's Day, the day when Tynwald sat. At Tinganes, there is a sundial, stated to date back to possibly about 1459 as well as an earlier one which is said to go back to about five hundred years prior to that date[15]. Sámal Petersen, who has written a very interesting article on the old marks and bore holes at the ancient Thingstead at Tinganes has produced a map indicating where the *Alting* (or as it later became called, the *Løgting)* sat in its capacity as a legislature and also where it sat in its capacity as a court[16]. It is interesting to note that they did not hold their meetings at the same spot.

The *Alting,* as will be seen[17], had its main meeting around midsummer, which was the occasion in pre-Christian times of a great pagan festival. This indicates that, apart from its other functions, the *Alting* was religious in nature. This connection is of importance when it comes to considering the relationship between religion and the judicial system. It seems likely that the priests, who were probably secular priests, in the form of chiefs[18], had to supervise trials by ordeal, such as "carrying the iron"[19], to see if the accused had "passed the test". The functions of the priests after the coming of Christianity would seem to have been taken over by the clergy, who became closely involved in legal affairs. One finds in the *Faroese Saga* that, when Sigurd Thorlakson was accused of having killed Thoralf of Stóra Dímun, Sigurd elected to "carry the iron." King Olaf II, the Holy, directed that the ordeal should be supervised by the bishop[20]. It seems very likely that churches were readily used in connection with legal and judicial matters in Norse territories during the Middle Ages. In the Isle of Man, even after the Island was transferred to Scotland in 1266[21], churches were regularly used for holding lay courts as can be seen from the fact that, in 1291, Bishop Mark and his synod passed an ordinance prohibiting the use on Sundays and High Feast Days of churches, graveyards and other holy places for lay courts, particularly "blood or criminal cases"[22]. In fact, trial by prowess was not abolished in the Isle of Man until 1429[23]. Even today, the connections of the Church with legal matters can be seen in the Tynwald ceremony which is held at St. John's in the Isle of Man on the 5th July each year or, if that day is a Saturday or Sunday, on the following Monday. This ceremony commences with a church service in St. John's Church, from where the members of Tynwald process to Tynwald Hill where, among other proceedings, a précis of all Acts passed during the previous year are read out in English and Manx to the assembled populace—a relic of an ancient custom dating back to Norse times. If a précis of an Act passed during the previous year is not read out in both languages on Tynwald Hill within twelve months of its enactment, the Act will lapse[24]. After this ritual, petitions can be presented to the Tynwald Court which then retires to the Church where the certificates of promulgation are duly signed. It is also interesting to note that there are, or have been, in the Isle of Man, churches near to the mounds where the local *Things* met.

Further evidence of the use of churches in countries under Norse influence can be seen from the mortgage which was executed in 1399 by Greip Ivarsson of Hatteberg in Norway, *sysselman* (district officer) in the Faroes, in favour of Gaute Eiriksson of Norway in the church at Skien in Norway (see Appendix 10).

There is no direct evidence that churches were used as lay courts in the Faroes but it is almost certain that the practice was no different in the Faroes in this respect than in other Norse countries. This view is strongly supported by the fact that the space between the inner and outer walls of the churches[25] was formerly used in the Faroes as local prisons[26]. Two of the documents relating to the estate of Gudrun, daughter of Sigurd the Shetlander, refer to evidence taken "on a full oath on the Book"[27] which may well indicate that their testimony was taken at formal proceedings in a church. There was also, in former times, a church on Tinganes. It is of interest to note that priests were parties to three of the other documents relating to Gudrun's estate[28]. The involvement of the clergy in the proceedings may, however, have been due, at any rate in part, to the fact that, in general, the priest was, in those days, more literate than most of the members of his congregation.

Most of the written evidence about the *Alting* in the early years is contained in the *Faroese Saga*. As has been mentioned[29], all freemen were allowed to appear before the *Alting* and it would seem that, apart from deciding policies for the Faroes, for example, whether they would accept Sigmund as their ruler and whether or not they should accept Christianity[30], it also had certain, although not exclusive, judicial functions.

Examples of cases being determined by the Faroese *Alting* are the **dispute between Einar the Hebridean, represented by Brester, against Hafgrim** who appeared on behalf of Eldjarn Kamhat[31] and the trial of Thorgrim the Evil and his sons, Ormstein and Thorstein[32], and probably also the proceedings leading to the banishment of Sigurd Thorlakson, Gaut the Red and Thord the Short[33] and those relating to the banishment of Skofte[34]. All these proceedings were criminal cases and were **apparently decided by the general opinion of the people present.** The only evidence in the *Saga* of the *Alting* exercising jurisdiction in civil cases is that of the proceedings at the meeting where the people persuaded Sigmund to extend from six months to three years the time in which Thrand had to pay the blood-money[35] and that of Thrand's **counter-claim for blood-money on behalf of Leif Ossurson**[36], although these cases were really actions for compensation for criminal injuries.

The *Faroese Saga,* however, indicates that the *Alting* was not the only tribunal in the Faroes and there are three references in it to the possibility of having cases judged before "the best men in the Faroes"[37]. The first of these was in the case of Einar the Sudreyan, when Brester's suggestion that this procedure should be adopted was rejected by Hafgrim[38]. The second instance was when Sigmund Bresterson attacked Hafgrim's son, Ossur, at Skúvoy and Ossur made a similar proposal, which was rejected by Sigmund[39]. The third case was when, after the death of Sigmund and Thorer, Thrand offered a similar remedy to Sigmund's widow, Thuride, and her sons: again it was rejected[40].

The *Faroese Saga* does not state why the plaintiff in each case rejected trial by the "best men in the Faroes". It could be inferred that at such proceedings the defendant might get a fairer hearing than he might otherwise have had as "the best men in the Faroes" would have been more objective in their approach and less likely to have been blinded by oratory than, for example, a court consisting of all the freemen in the Faroes as at the *Alting* at Tinganes. It would also seem likely that proceedings before "the best men in the Faroes" were, at any rate in general, civil proceedings or arbitrations, and not criminal proceedings.

It is interesting to note that parties before the *Alting* were allowed to be represented: for example, in one matter Einar the Sudreyan was represented by Brester and Eldjarn Kamhat by Hafgrim[41], and in another matter Leif Ossurson was represented by Thrand[42]. Furthermore, Brester's representation of Einar is the first evidence in Faroese history of a party being represented by a legally trained person (Brester is stated to have been learned in the law). Moreover, Brester won the case for Einar on a point of law. He submitted that Kamhat had broken the domestic peace contrary to the ancient law of the country, in that he had struck an innocent man[43].

It is also clear that Thrand himself was no mean lawyer, as he taught Leif Ossurson's son, Sigmund, "to carry out every method of instituting suits and legal proceedings on behalf of himself and others"[44]. Further evidence of Thrand's knowledge of law is to be found in his handling of his dispute with Sigmund Bresterson when he went out of his way to try to make Sigmund judge the case himself[45], presumably with a view to getting the judgement set aside later by the *Alting* on the ground that a judgement given by a man in his own cause is contrary to natural justice. Thrand also avoided going to Norway to appear before Earl Hakon[46], again, it would appear, because he felt that *ex parte* proceedings brought by Sigmund before the Earl would be less binding on him (Thrand) than if both he and Sigmund were present when Earl Hakon heard the case. In any event, Thrand subsequently claimed before the *Alting* that blood-money should be paid by Sigmund[47] in respect of Ossur's death, although King Hakon had not penalized Sigmund, presumably because, in the King's view, the killing was justified because Ossur had taken possession of Sigmund's property[15].

It would appear that, up to the time of King Olaf II, the Holy, of Norway, the Faroese followed the old Norse law or "the ancient law of the country" which was known, at least to certain of the Faroese such as Brester[49] and presumably also by Thrand. However, King Olaf made Leif Ossurson, Gille the Lawman and Thoralf Sigmundson swear that they would uphold his laws and submit to the justice which he gave to the Faroes[50]. In order to do this, someone had to know these new laws, and it would seem logical that Gille's nickname of "the Lawman" derived from the fact that he was the person selected by King Olaf to learn these laws. Gille is certainly the first man in Faroese history who is known to have had the title of Lawman *(løgmaður)* and it is submitted that he received that title and appointment because he was the man who was given the responsibility of seeing that King Olaf's laws and justice were observed in the Faroes. It would appear, therefore, that Gille the Lawman was the first Chief Justice and Speaker of the Faroes, for that, in essence, was what the Lawman became. The law which is said to have been given to the Faroes by King Olaf II was the law of Western Norway[51] and became known as the *Gulating* law, and later as "the old *Gulating* law" so as not to be confused with the young *Gulating* law[52]. These laws received their name because of the place where the *Thing* which made them held its meetings. There is some evidence in the *Faroese Saga* that the *Alting* had also the power to make laws as Thrand, Leif Ossurson and Gille the Lawman agreed that a law should be made prohibiting the common people from coming armed to the *Alting*[53], although Thrand himself immediately flouted this law[54]. The interesting thing about this law (if it did in fact become law) is that it was passed nearly three hundred years before similar legislation was enacted in England. The English law prohibiting the carrying of arms to Parliament was contained in the *Statutu sup Aportam'* (7 Edw. 2) which was passed in 1313. It is also of interest to note that Cardinal Nicholas Breakspear is said, when in Norway in 1152[55], to have made the chiefs promise not to bring arms to meetings of the various *Things*[56].

Prior to 1293, the Lawman was Chairman of the *Alting,* both in its capacity as the highest court of justice in the Faroes and as a parliament[57]. It was his duty to know all the relevant laws by heart[57] and to explain them to the people who were present at the *Alting*. Although Gille was the first Lawman it is not clear whether he exercised all the prerogatives referred to above or whether it was at a later date that they devolved on the holder of the office of Lawman. As has been mentioned[58], the Lawman would seem to have combined the functions of Chief Justice and of Speaker of the Legislature, being responsible in the former case for summing up the law, and possibly also the facts, to the members of the *Alting*. The Lawman, at any rate prior to 1273, was, as a rule, elected by the members of the *Alting*[59].

During the period covered by the *Faroese Saga*, the *Alting* seems to have been summoned as and when required[60] although it is probable that meetings in the spring and at mid-summer were the most common, the latter being the time of year, in the Viking era, when such meetings were customary[61]. There is ample evidence in the *Saga* of meetings being held in the spring[62]. It seems likely from what is said in the *Saga* regarding the meeting of the *Alting* when Carl of Møre was murdered, that the spring meeting had by that time become a customary one[62].

Apart from the *Alting,* there were a number of local *Things* or district councils in the Faroes, although they are not referred to in the *Faroese Saga*. It is not possible to say how many local *Things* there were in the early days and it is possible that the number may have changed, as indeed the places where they were held changed with the passage of time. In later years, the local *Things* were six in number, situate in the islands of Vágar, Streymoy, Eysturoy, Borðoy, Sandoy and Suðuroy. The local *Thing* on Vágar sat at Miðvágar, that on Streymoy at Kollafjørður, that on Eysturoy at Selatrað, that on Borðoy at Vágur (now Klaksvík), that on Sandoy at Sandur and that on Suðuroy at Ørvavík off Trongisvágsfjørður. The ancient local *Thing* on Streymoy is said to have been situated on an island or islet in Kollafjørður and the ancient one on Eysturoy at Stevnuválur[63], which is between Skálabotnur and Funningsbotnur. The latter is believed to have been in tiers similar in construction to Tynwald Hill at St. John's, Isle of Man[64]. There are churches near to where, at any rate in later times, the local *Things* on Vágar and Streymoy were held, which might lend support to the view expressed earlier[65] as to the probability of courts being held in churches in the Faroes in the Middle Ages.

The name of the local *Things* in the Faroes was *várting*[66], indicating that they sat in the spring. They sat in the order of the islands mentioned above[67], beginning with Vágar where the *várting* met on the 1st March. The local *Things* were subordinate courts, whereas the *Alting* (or *Løgting* as it was re-named about 1400) was the Supreme Court of the Faroes[68]. Each district in the Faroes, of which there have been for a considerable period six in number, was represented by six members *(løgraettumen)* in the *Løgting*[68]. When the *várting* met in its own district in pre-Reformation days, it was presided over by the Lawman[68]. However, when the *Alting* or *Løgting* sat as the Supreme Court it did not, at any rate in later years, consist of all thirty-six members plus the Lawman, but was normally constituted by the Lawman sitting with either six or twelve of the *løgraettumen*[68]. It was their duty to certify the judgement of the Lawmen[68]. It may well be that the *Alting* or *Løgting,* constituted as above, exercised, among other things, the functions which were earlier within the apparent jurisdiction of the "best men in the Faroes"[69].

There is little known about the functions of the *Alting* between 1035 and 1271, particularly as regards its non-judicial functions, although the abolition of slavery about 1200[70] was probably made legal by the *Alting*.

As has been mentioned[71], the *Alting* virtually ceased to be a legislative body about 1271, at any rate so far as major legislation was concerned, but the *Løgting* did, after that date, enact certain local legislation of a minor nature. Examples of this type of legislation are the law about travelling allowances for members attending the *Løgting,* which was made by the *Løgting* between 1350 and 1400[72] and the *Hundabræv* (Dog Law), which was made about the same time[73]. A translation of the former is set out in Appendix 11. Unfortunately, the remnants of the *Hundabræv* are only fragmentary and a translation of them would serve little purpose. That law, which was to last for a year in the first instance and which was signed by the Lawman and all the members of the *Løgting,* controlled the number of dogs which could be kept in various parts of the Faroes. The probable reason for the law was to prevent sheep-worrying, but three types of dogs are mentioned in the law: sheep dogs, bird-hounds and Manx Shearwater dogs[74]. The latter two species have been extinct in the Faroes for some time and were probably of the same breed and used for catching the young Manx Shearwaters.

However, there is no doubt that the most important law relating to the Faroes during the pre-Reformation period was the *Sheep Letter* of 1298, *Seyðabraevið,*[75] the agricultural parts of which have, as has been mentioned,[76] lasted for some 700 years. The *Sheep Letter* was primarily a farming and domestic law dealing with such matters as rent for land which had been leased[77], the slaughtering of unmarked sheep[78], the maintenance of common folds,[79] penalties for taking among sheep dogs which were confirmed sheep-worriers[80], provisions in respect of uninvited guests[81] and questions of evidence[82].

As has been stated earlier[83], the *Sheep Letter* was a codification of the existing law with certain amendments, the most important of which was the restriction on the establishment of new small-holdings[84]. Possibly as a result of this restriction, begging and asking for alms were permitted[85]. However, if a person pleaded poverty in order to avoid paying damages for defamation or other forms of tort, he was, according to the Lund text of the *Sheep Letter*[86], liable to be sent to prison and to be flogged when his or her term of imprisonment was completed. According to the Stockholm text[87] the question of punishment was to be left to twelve wise men to be appointed by the judiciary.

The *Sheep Letter* is a very comprehensive and uncomplicated piece of legislation and it is not surprising that so much of it has remained unaltered for so long. The law relating to the travelling allowances of the members of the *Løgting* and the *Hundabrœv* are also simple and straightforward. One may sometimes wonder why modern legislation must be so complex and whether it would not be possible to follow the simpler styles which proved so effective in early times. Perhaps the blame must go, at any rate in part, to lawyers, including legislative draftsmen!

Apart from Gille the Lawman[88], little was known until fairly recently of the Lawmen in the Faroes prior to 1524. From that date onwards, there is a complete record of all the Lawmen up to 1816. However, a parchment scroll was discovered some years ago in the Royal Library in Stockholm which refers to a number of earlier lawmen, namely Símun, who was Lawman sometime in the fourteenth century, Dagfinnur Halvdanarson, who was Lawman about 1400, Haraldur Kálvsson, who was Lawman from 1412, and Jørundur Skógdrívsson, who was Lawman from 1479[89].

Of the Lawmen subsequent to 1524, only two are relevant to this book. Tormoður Sjúrðarson, who was Lawman from 1524 to his death (which is said to have taken place in 1531), and Andras Guttormsen (1531-1543), who is said to have been Norwegian and the son of Guttorm, a Lawman in Bergen[89]. Andras lived in Kálgarður in Sumba in the south of Suðuroy. According to one report, which is not, however, substantiated by historical evidence, he committed an offence in the Faroes as a result of which his son, Guttorm, went south to the King of Denmark in order to obtain the King's help to enable Andras to remain in office as Lawman[89].

We have so far considered the legislature, the courts and certain laws which were in force in the Faroes, but it is also of interest to consider other aspects of the law which can be ascertained from certain legal documents and from other sources.

A very informative document is the mortgage referred to earlier in this chapter[90], entered into between Greip Ivarsson and his kinsman, Gaute Eiriksson. The document is comprehensive and reveals a high standard of conveyancing although certain of its terms are so stringent that one might tend to think that the mortgagor was dealing with Shylock rather than a relative! Translations of the document and of a supplement to it are set out in Appendix 10.

As will be noticed, the transaction is in the form of a "Welsh Mortgage," in that the mortgagee is to receive the rent of the lands forming the security rather than interest on the loan itself. Similar forms of mortgage were used in the Isle of Man prior to 1704[91], a legacy from the days when the Island came under Norway[92]. The term "Welsh Mortgage" probably means "foreign mortgage", being derived from the Old English (Angl.) word *"Welisc"* meaning foreign, a term also applied by the arrogant Anglo-Saxons to the natives of England, hence "Wales" and "Welsh."

Further evidence of the high standards which existed in the Norse territories in the early fifteenth century can be seen from the documents relating to the goods and property of Gudrun, daughter of Sigurd the Shetlander[93]. These documents are not only mature in form but reveal an efficient system of administering the estate of a deceased person when the administration was disputed and further complicated by the fact that part of the deceased's property was situated in the Faroes, part in Norway and part in the Shetlands. One wonders whether it would be possible today to complete the administration of such an estate so quickly!

Another document of interest is that concerning Bishop John I, the German, of the Faroes and Haraldur Kálvsson, Lawman of the Faroes, which was executed in 1412[94]. This document indicates that, at that time, even the Lawman was chary about getting on the wrong side of the Bishop and the Church.

Finally, an interesting record of a case appears in an article by Jón Helgason. The report which is very sketchy and dates from the Middle Ages, reads as follows[95]:—

"petta var vitnat millim peira Hógni ok Margretu, at Høgni spurði Marg(re)tu ef poralf Væri mæiarmaður, hennar, en hon sagði nei viðok kvað vera (?) stórar døtur Elle(n)s, ok tók hann mdr (read moður?) mińa, en eigi Potølty: "Var Albrigt mæiarmaður Pinn?" "Nei" sagði hon ok lýsti und r vátta."

The translation of this[96] is as follows:—

"It was witnessed between Hógni and Margaret that Hógni asked Margaret if **Thoralf** had been her first lover[97] to which she said no and that her daughter and **Ellen**'s was quite big "but he made me pregnant[98] and not Thoralf." "Was Albrigt your first lover?" "No, and I can call witnesses to prove this."[99].

The material points arising from this report are that:
(a) any claim in respect of the girl would have been made by Hógni, a male member of the family, and presumably the head of the family;
(b) any such claim would have been in respect of the man who deprived the girl of her virginity;
(c) if the girl had been deprived of her virginity by some other person and a second person made the girl pregnant, no action would appear to have lain against the second person. This is shown by the fact that Margreta did not mind admitting that Ellen had filled her uterus.
(d) Hógni, the aggrieved person, could only ask if a named person had been the girl's first lover and was not allowed to ask "Who was your first lover?" Such a restriction shows a nice taste of etiquette; and
(e) hearsay evidence was admissible in such cases.

Another forum of a quasi-judicial nature which exists in the Faroes is the *grannastevna* or village council which consists of the *sysselman* (or district officer) sitting with the owners of freehold land in a *bygd* (or settlement) to decide matters of local interest[100]. There is no direct evidence to show when the *grannastevna* was first established although John F. West tends to the view that it did not come into existence until the nineteenth century[101]. However, if that were so, one would expect provision of the *grannastevna* to have been laid down by statute, but there does not appear to be any such statute enacted in the last two or three hundred years. If the *grannastevna* is not a creature of statute then it must have been a common law institution and must have been in existence for many hundreds of years, possibly dating back as far as the eleventh century.

According to entries in the *Kulturhistorisk Leksikon for Nordisk Middelalder,* the *grannastevna* or *bystevna* existed from the Middle Ages in all Nordic countries except Iceland[102].

Prior to the nineteenth century there are very few published references to the *grannastevna* in the Faroes, although there are four references to it in the eighteenth century from Suðuroy, the earliest dating back to the 14th February, 1708[103]. The absence of such records is not, however, unreasonable as the *grannastevna* generally dealt with matters of a purely local nature, such as the division of pilot whales after a *grindadráp,* deciding how many animals might be kept by a farmer, decisions relating to the repair of boundary fences and to the division of wreck etc., which had been driven ashore. These are matters on which decisions must have been required long before the nineteenth century. For example, the number of stock which could be kept had, by virtue of Article 6 of the *Sheep Letter*[104], to be agreed by all the people concerned, and the obvious forum to decide that question was the *grannastevna.*

The earliest written record of a *grannastevna* concerns the case of a person who wished to make provision for the disposal of his property on his death and was unable to go to the *várting*[105]. Here the matter was dealt with in the *grannastevna* and the contents of the notes of the proceedings were later promulgated at the *várting*[105].

The *grannastevna* is held early in the year before the *várting,* that in Suðuroy being held in February. The *sysselman* travels round his district to attend each *grannastevna* in turn and is accompanied by two "Kalsmenn" (or court messengers) whose duty (among other things) was, in the olden days, to summon people who were required to attend the *várting.* Nowadays, these officials, at any rate on Suðuroy, witness documents drawn up as a result of decisions made at a *grannastevna,* such as those relating to the persons in the *bygd* who are entitled to a share in slaughtered pilot whales. It is possible that the witnessing of the decisions of a *grannastevna* is a development of the provision in the *Rescript* of 11th May, 1775, requiring decisions relating to the number of horses which could be kept by the landowners in a *bygd* to be recorded by the *sysselman* and witnessed by "some of the best men in the *bygd*"[106].

There are references to the *grannastevna* in some of Jakob Jakobsen's folk stories[107] and although it is, of course, impossible to state the exact period from which these folk stories come, it is some evidence of the fact that those were in existence before the nineteenth century. One would expect to find more material relating to the *grannastevna* in places like Suðuroy where there is a preponderance of freeholders than in places like those around Tórshavn where most of the farmers are King's farmers and not freeholders.

It would appear that, in the early Middle Ages, the general administrative functions in the Faroes were divided as follows between the *Alting,* the various *várting* and the various *grannastevnur:—*

(a) the *Alting* dealt with matters which affected the Faroes as a whole;
(b) each *várting* dealt with matters which applied generally throughout the *syssel* (or district) in which it was situated; and
(c) each *grannastevna* dealt with matters which were of a purely local nature and applied only within the *bygd* where it was situated.

The *Alting* or *Løgting,* as is came to be called, also exercised criminal jurisdiction, but the *grannastevna* never appears to have operated as a criminal court.

In conclusion, it may be stated that, although there is very little written evidence concerning the *grannastevna* prior to the nineteenth century, it seems more than likely from what evidence there is, that it existed as far back as the Middle Ages and that it is not an institution which was created less than two hundred years ago.

The development of the *Alting* over the centuries is a matter of great interest. It would appear, primarily, to have been a meeting where the decisions were taken by all the freemen of the Faroes. During the period covered by the *Faroese Saga,* however, the freemen seemed to support the chief to whom they owed allegiance, which meant, in fact, that the decision was not that of the people but of the chief or chiefs with the largest following[108]. One is reminded of politics in England today with the "three line whip" which, in practice, tends to deprive the individual elected members of Parliament of the freedom to vote in accordance with the dictates of their consciences or of the electorate they represent!

After 1035 the constitution of the *Alting* underwent a change, and it seems probable that some time between that year and 1298 the functions previously exercised by all the freemen of the Faroes devolved on the thirty-six members selected from the six districts (the *Løgrættusmenn),* although the remaining freemen would have had access to the *Alting.*

As has been mentioned[109], the *Alting* was re-named the *Løgting* some time before 1400. The *Løgting* has had its own seal (with a sheep delineated on it) since the Middle Ages.

1 RS p. 6, GJ pp. 282 and 283.
2 GJ p. 282.
3 M p. 92.
4 See CFM.
5 L p. 14.
6 See S facing page and GJ p. 272.
7 See p. 9 *ante.*
8 *Ibid.*
9 See p. 46 *ante.* It seems reasonable to deduce that at the end of the eleventh century Kirkjubøur was more important as a town than Tórshavn.

10 L p. 16. It is interesting in this connection to note the tradition of a Thor's Temple at St. John's, Isle of Man, see David Craine: Tynwald, Symbol of an Ancient Kingdom (1961 Rev. 1976).
11 L p. 15.
12 RS p. 6.
13 See p. 51 *ante*.
14 See pp. 82-84 *post*.
15 See F pictures 1 and 2.
16 *Ibid.* map.
17 See p. 84 *post*.
18 See GJ pp. 282, 283, 324 and 325.
19 If the accused could carry the hot iron without getting burned, he was adjudged innocent.
20 See p. 27 *ante*.
21 M p. 134.
22 MSJ vol. VII p. 197.
23 MS p. 11.
24 MSR vol. X p. 31.
25 See p. 118 *post*.
26 JM p. 214, under *kirkjuskot*.
27 See Appendix 5. Documents 2 and 3.
28 *Ibid.*, Documents 4, 6 and 7.
29 See p. 80 *ante*.
30 See p. 20 *ante*.
31 See p. 9 *ante*.
32 See p. 26 *ante*.
33 See p. 29 *ante*.
34 See p. 32 *ante*.
35 See p. 16 *ante*.
36 See pp. 17 and 21 *ante*.
37 The counterpart in the Isle of Man of the "best men in the Faroes" are "the worthiest men" in the land. MS p. 6. These worthiest men later came to be called "the Keys", the lower house of the Manx Tynwald being still called the House of Keys.
38 See p. 9 *ante*.
39 See p. 15 *ante*.
40 See p. 25 *ante*.
41 See p. 9 *ante*.
42 See pp. 17 and 21 *ante*.
43 See p. 9 *ante*.
44 See p. 32 *ante*.
45 See pp. 15-16 *ante*.
46 See p. 15 and also p. 20 where Sigmund again tried to take Thrand to Norway.
47 See pp. 17 and 21 *ante*.
48 See pp. 15-16 *ante*.
49 See p. 9.
50 See p. 26 *ante*.
51 RS p. 7; FS p. 42. c. 42.
52 RS pp. 7 and 15.
53 See p. 29 *ante*.
54 *Ibid.*
55 See p. 49 *ante*.
56 CM p. 172.
57 RS pp. 7 and 8.
58 See p. 83 *ante*.
59 RS p. 8.
60 See pp. 9, 15, 21 and 26 *ante*.

61 See p. 29. This custom still prevails in the Faroes (29th July) and in the Isle of Man (5th July).
62 See pp. 16, 20 and 28 *ante*.
63 L p. 15.
64 *Ibid.*
65 See p. 81 *ante*.
66 RS p. 15.
67 See previous paragraph.
68 RS p. 15.
69 See p. 82 *ante*.
70 See p. 50 *ante*.
71 See p. 51 *ante*.
72 See p. 52.
73 *Ibid.*
74 See U VI, pp. 111-2.
75 See Appendix 4.
76 See p. 34 *ante*.
77 See Appendix 4, Part I, Art. 2 and Part II, Art. 10.
78 See *Ibid.*, Part I, Art. 4 and Part II, Art. 1.
79 See *Ibid.*, Part I, Art. 5 and Part II, Art. 3.
80 See *Ibid.*, Part I. Art. 6 and Part II, Art. 6.
81 See *Ibid.*, Part I, Art. 3 and Part II, Art. 11.
82 See *Ibid.*, Part I, Art. 12 and Part II, Art. 12.
83 See p. 53 *ante*.
84 See Appendix 4, Part I, Art. 7 and Part II, Art. 14.
85 See *Ibid.*, Part I, Art. 3 and Part II, Art. 11.
86 See *Ibid.*, Part II, Art. 11.
87 See *Ibid.*, Part I, Art. 12.
88 See pp. 26-30 *ante*.
89 RS p. 75.
90 See p. 81 *ante*.
91 MS pp. 163-177.
92 M Chapters III and IV.
93 See Appendix 6.
94 See Appendix 9.
95 See U VII, p. 104, taken from *Kongsbókin ur Føroyún*.
96 For which I owe my gratitude to harri John Davidsen of Tórshavn who has helped me both with the translation and interpretation of the record of the case.
97 The word "meiarmaður" would, despite certain learned views to the contrary, appear to mean first lover, see DN p. xii, s. 754.
98 See DN XV p. 93. Jón Helgason suggests that he not only made her pregnant but also took her virginity. This latter point is, however, open to argument.
99 The reference to witnesses here is assumed to mean witnesses to show that she had made a similar statement at an earlier time as it is most unlikely that anyone (except for the parties concerned) would have witnessed the act of intimacy itself.
100 KL, vol. II pp. 444-7 under *bystævne* and vol. X pp. 224-7 under *landsbystyre*.
101 FR b. 23 pp. 48-59, "How old is the Faroese *grannastevna?*".
102 KL, vol. X p. 224 under *landsbystyre*.
103 P, folio 69.
104 See pp. 143 and 147-8 *post*.
105 P, folio 69. See also P, folio 76 dated the 22nd January, 1709.
106 FB pp. 60 and 78.
107 JJ pp. 8-10 and 461 under *grannaskikkur* and *grannastevna*.
108 See eg. FS p. 6. c. 5 and p. 31. c. 30.
109 See p. 84 *ante*.

Above: *Múrurin*. The remains of the unfinished Cathedral of St. Magnus at Kirkjuböur on Streymoy. (By courtesy of Asmundur Poulsen, Tórshavn.)
Below: *Múrurin* and Kirkjuböur Church, with the Islands of Sandoy and Hestur in the distance. (By courtesy of Sverri Dahl, Tórshavn.)

CHAPTER 13

RELATIONS WITH THE OUTSIDE WORLD

The Faroes are situated two hundred miles North-west of the Shetlands and two hundred and forty miles south-west of Iceland but, even in early times, they were not completely isolated, having been visited from about 725, or earlier, by Irish monks[1], raided by Vikings from about 795[2] and settled by Grim Kamban about 825[3]. In addition, Floki Vilgerdason called in at the Faroes on his way to Iceland[4] as did Aud the Extremely Rich or Deep-minded[5].

There were, obviously, communications with Norway from the ninth century onwards as is exemplified from the fact that Hafgrim held half the Faroes in fief from Harald II, Greycloak, and Brester and Beiner the other half from Earl Hakon[6]. Again, Thrand's visit to Denmark and Norway after his father's death and Rafn's journey from Tønsberg to Tórshavn are examples of the way in which there were connections between Scandinavia and the Faroes in the 970's[7].

There is also evidence of communications between the Sudreys and the Faroes in the tenth century, Snæulf and Einar the Sudreyan having both come north from the Sudreys[8]. As has been mentioned[9] further evidence of Celtic connections can be found in Faroese place names such as Dímun and names beginning with Argi- and Ergi-.

One of the most important media which kept the Faroes in contact with the outside world was the Church, as all the pre-Reformation bishops were non-Faroese and came from various parts of Europe. If, in fact, Bernard the Saxon was the Bishop Bernhard who is the first bishop to be mentioned as having come to the Faroes, he must have been either German or English[10], and would seem to have been consecrated by the Pope[11]. Other Germans who became Bishops of the Faroes were Bishops Vigbald[12], John I, the German, and John III, the Chief[13]. An Englishman, William Northbrigg, was appointed Bishop of the Faroes in about 1381 or 1385, but there is some doubt as to whether he ever arrived there[14]. Bishop Hemming was a Dane or a Swede[15], but, at any rate, most of the remainder of the Bishops of the Faroes would appear to have been Norwegian. Even after the bishops took up their posts in the Faroes, they had to leave their diocese from time to time on episcopal duties, as can be seen from Chapter 11. These journeys helped to keep the Faroes in touch with the outside world. Quite apart from the bishops, it would seem that other members of the clergy came from outside the Faroes [16], despite the fact that there had been, at Kirkjubøur, a school for training priests from at least the thirteenth century [17]. These expatriate priests would also help to bring to the Faroes something of the outside world.

However, the main way in which the Faroes kept in contact with overseas countries was through trade. The most important exports from the Faroes in the Middle Ages were wool, homespun, butter and cod, with the main entrepôt port in Norway being Bergen [18]. So far as wool was concerned, the saying "wool is Faroese gold" was a by-word [19]. The *Faroese Saga* refers to wool being sold in Norway [20] while, in the twelfth century, the Germans bought wool, homespun, butter and cod from the Faroes and the Faroese bought wine, in return, from the Germans [21]. These Germans had followed the lines of the Archbishops of Hamburg-Bremen. The latter had tried to bring the Nordic countries under their ecclesiastical control [22], while the former tried to bring them under their economic control. As has been mentioned [23], the Archbishops of Hamburg-Bremen failed in their ambition, despite the efforts of Pope Innocent II and Emperor Frederik Barbarossa [23]. However, the German traders were more successful, particularly after the Hanseatic League established its headquarters in Bergen in the early 1300's [24]. Some evidence of the teutonic influence on trade in the North, even as early as the eleventh century, can be appreciated from the number of German coins which are among the Sandur "find" [25].

The *Faroese Saga* gives further information about connections between the Faroes and Scandinavia. Thrand, after his successful coup in Denmark in his young days, brought a lot of goods back to the Faroes from Norway [26], while Rafn traded between the Faroes and Southern Norway [27]. Sigmund Bresterson was constantly travelling between the Faroes and Norway [28], while further intercourse at a political level occurred as a result of King Olaf II, the Holy's, attempts to tax the Faroese [29].

Leif, son of Thorer Beinerson, was a regular trader between Norway and the Faroes [30], while the brothers, Hafgrim, Bjarngrim and Hergrim, whose cargo ship was wrecked on Suðuroy, came from the Sudreys [31] which indicates that there was commercial intercourse between the Faroes and the Hebrides in the first half of the eleventh century.

There also seems to have been a good deal of contact between the Faroes and Iceland in the Middle Ages and the visit of Sturla Thordarson to Iceland in the winter of 1277-8 has already been mentioned [32]. The connections with Iceland seem, however, to have been mainly connected with culture, a subject which will be dealt with in a later chapter [33].

The relations of the Faroes with the outside world must have been greatly curtailed in the early 1270's when King Magnus VI, the Law

Reformer, decreed that Norway should have a monopoly of trade with the Faroes[34]. The Norwegian port of call turned out to be Bergen[35]. When the King made the decree he intended that the monolpoly of the Faroese/Norwegian trade should be in his own hands[36]. As has been mentioned above[37], the Hanseatic League had moved into Norway by the early 1300's and had made their headquarters in Bergen. The fact that the King of Norway wished to keep the trade with the Faroes to himself can be seen from the prohibition on trading with the Faroes which he placed on the Hanseatic League in 1294 and again in 1302[38]. However, the movement of goods between the Faroes and Norway was not such as to make it a very profitable concern, and the Hanseatics did not pay much attention to the restrictions which had been placed on their activities[38]. As a result of this, in 1361 they acquired the same trading rights with the Faroes as the Norwegian merchants in Bergen had[39].

The fact that the Hanseatics had traded with the Faroes when forbidden to do so saw the start of the illicit trade with those islands which, especially later on, became of such importance to the Faroes[40].

Although the Faroes are a small country, they became involved with several other countries when the question of trade arose, and it was of particular importance that, at this time, both the English and the Dutch were at war with the Hanseatic League and there was keen competition in trade between the Hanseatics and the British[41].

Outsiders do not, however, seem to have had the complete monopoly of trading with the Faroes as Gudrun, the daughter of Sigurd the Shetlander, and referred to by some authorities as the Housewife of Húsavik, lived in the Faroes and must have had deep-sea-going ships. In any event, her boathouse, *"Skeiðstoftur"*, appears to have been about 60 feet long and 12 feet wide[42]. Admittedly, she originally came from Bergen and had large estates in Norway and also in the Shetlands[43].

In 1490 another trading nation, Holland, obtained the same rights to trade with the Faroes as the Hanseatic merchants had[44].

The interest which other nations had in the Faroes was due not only to what the Faroese could export[45] but also to the fact that they had to import a lot of goods. The most important of these imports was timber (as the Faroes were practically treeless), corn (as the Faroese could not grow enough for their needs) and malt[46]. Luxuries, too, would have had to have been imported from overseas.

Around 1500 the Faroese seem to have suffered from visitors of a less pleasant nature, namely pirates[47]. These pirates not only attacked merchant ships but also made raids ashore, seizing some of the Faroese and plundering their cattle[48]. The reports of the times refer to English, Irish and French pirates, but the most vicious pirates of the day were the so-called Turks who had their headquarters in the pirate kingdom of Algiers[49], although the only surviving record of such "Turkish" pirates relates to a raid made by them in 1620. On the other hand, there are records of raids by other pirates as early as 1410. Nevertheless, the Irish seemed to have been the most hated of the pirates as is indicated by the historical and secondary meaning given to the word *íri,* namely, an Irish (or Gaelic) speaking pirate[50]. These so-called Irish pirates were, in all probability, based on the Hebrides[50] which had, for a time, come under the Isle of Man. Arising from this meaning of the word *íri*, there are derived a number of derogatory words meaning Irish rabble, riff-raff or scum[50].

The influence which the Hanseatics had in the Faroes can be judged from the fact that in 1529 the King of Denmark, under whom the Faroes had come since 1387, leased the Faroes (excluding the ecclesiastic rights) to two gentlemen from Germany, Thomas Koppen and Joachim Wullenweber[51].

The Faroese themselves, however, were not allowed to leave the islands without special permission[52]. Presumably, this was to prevent the islands becoming de-populated. It is interesting to note that a similar restriction applied to the Isle of Man, apparently being in operation from the time that that Isle came under Norway[53].

1 See p. 2 *ante*.
2 *Ibid*.
3 *Ibid*.
4 *Ibid*.
5 See p. 3 *ante*.
6 See p. 6 *ante*.
7 See pp. 6 and 10 *ante*. See also MA p. 60 where it is stated that a number of the Faroese settlers came direct from Norway, from Sogn, Rogaland and Agder.
8 See p. 6 *ante*.
9 See p. 3 *ante*.
10 DN vol. XXIII pp. 193 and 219.
11 AB p. 214.
12 See p. 70 *ante*.
13 See p. 72 *ante*.
14 See Appendix 2.
15 See p. 72 *ante*.
16 See p. 74 *ante*.
17 See p. 64 *ante*.
18 L p. 19.
19 RS p. 17.
20 See p. 27 *ante*.
21 L p. 19.
22 See p. 61.
23 See pp. 60-62 *ante*.
24 RS p. 17.
25 See p. 110 *post*.
26 See p. 6 *ante* and FS p. 4 c. 3.
27 See p. 10 *ante* and FS p. 9. c. 8.
28 See ch. 4 and 5 *ante*.
29 See pp. 26-29 *ante*.
30 See p. 31 *ante*.
31 See pp. 30-31 *ante* and note 8 to this chapter.
32 See p. 51 *ante*.
33 Ch. 15.
34 See pp. 140 and 145 *ante*.
35 RS p. 17.
36 RS p. 17. See also Appendix 3.

37 See pp. 52 and 54 *ante*.
38 S facing page.
39 RS p. 17, S facing page.
40 RS p. 17.
41 RS p. 17, S facing page.
42 RS p. 21.
43 RS p. 21 see also Appendix 5.
44 S facing page.
45 See p. 100 *post*.
46 RS p. 17.
47 See p. 55 *ante*.
48 RS pp. 17 and 19.
49 RS p. 19.
50 JM p. 197.
51 See p. 56 *ante*.
52 AD p. 208 under "Sørvágur (Sørvaag)".
53 MSR vol. I, p. 5., s. 4.

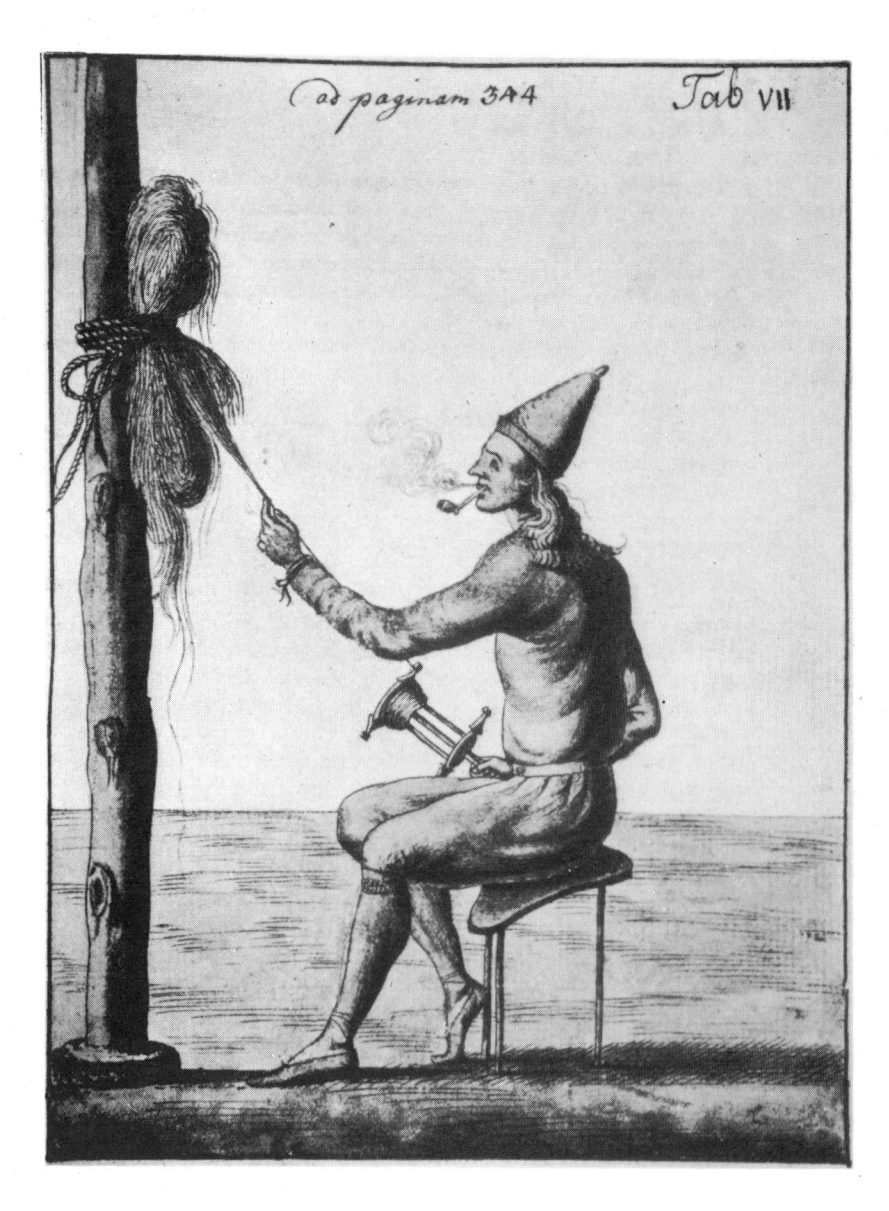

Hand spinning in the eighteenth century.

CHAPTER 14

FARMING, FISHING AND FOWLING

During the pre-Reformation period, farming was the basic means of livelihood in the Faroes, but farming has, however, never been an easy task in the Faroes because of the topography of the islands[1].

The Faroes form part of the great basalt area of the North Atlantic formed by the tertiary eruptions which extend from Scotland to Iceland and Greenland[2]. The islands consist mainly of lava flows, composed of basalt, which are up to one hundred feet thick, with thin layers of solidified volcanic ash or tuff in between them[3]. The beds are roughly horizontal and the aggregate thickness is at least thirteen thousand feet[4]. There are subsidiary sediments of sandstone, fire-clay, shale and coal[4].

Apart from the effect on the Faroes of volcanoes, the landscape is shaped in part by glacial action which has carved deep fjords into the islands and created steep-faced mountain peaks and cliffs or "hammers"[5]. The highest mountain is Slaettaratindur (2,894 feet) which is situated in the north of Eysturoy[6]. The sides of the mountains and cliffs are stepped as a result of varying resistance by the various layers which have been deposited[6].

Many of the cliffs on the coast lines are the homes of millions of sea birds which nest on the rocky ledges[6]. The guano from these birds provides luscious, but dangerous, cliff pastures for the agile sheep.

The amount of land in the Faroes suitable for agriculture is very limited[7] and most of what is available is only suitable for rough grazing. The geographical situation and climatic conditions of the Faroes, namely their northern situation and oceanic climate combined with a rainfall (63 inches) approximately double that of England, and frequent fogs, are most unfavourable for agriculture and certainly do not suit trees[8]. The temperature varies between 3.2°C in January and 10.8°C in July[8]. The vegetation consists in the main of dwarf shrubs[8], bog and grassy heath which accounts for the fact that sheep-rearing is, and always has been, the main agricultural occupation of the Faroes[8]. In fact, as has been mentioned[9], sheep and sea-birds at one time monopolized the Faroes and most of the authorities favour the view that the Faroe Islands received their name from the sheep which inhabited them[10].

At the period of the *Faroese Saga,* the principal domestic animals in the Faroes were sheep and cattle. Brester and Beiner[11], and later Sigmund and Thorer[12], made trips to Lítla Dímun to slaughter sheep, while Sigurd Thorlakson, Gaut the Red and Thord the Short are stated to have made a similar trip to another island[13]. The importance of cattle at that time can be seen from the fact that both Thrand and Svínoy-Bjarni asked for money to the value of very many cattle[14]. Cows were necessary for the milk they supplied, although it would seem from the Faroese/English dictionary[15] that, at times, sheep's milk was also used.

The *Saga* makes no mention of horses or ponies, pigs or poultry, but it would follow the normal pattern of Norse settlers if they imported them. Not only would horses or ponies be required for work on or connected with the farms, but horse meat was a delicacy of the pagan Norsemen and pork was also a favourite of theirs. Evidence of the existence of pigs and horses in the Faroes in Viking times has been discovered as a result of excavations, for example at Kvívík[16]. It is not suggested, however, that the names of two of the islands Hestur (horse) and Svínoy (pig island) indicate anything other than that their shapes have some resemblance to those animals. Dogs must also have been introduced into the Faroes at a fairly early date in order to "work" the sheep.

The *Saga* does not say much about the method of farming except that Brester and Beiner seemed to have had joint shares in the sheep on Lítla Dimun and shared the sheep which they slaughtered[17].

There is also evidence that land was leased out to tenants as Thrand let his land at rack rents before he made his trip to Denmark[18]. It is also stated that Thorgrim the Evil held his farm at Sandvík in copyhold from Thrand who lived on Eysturoy[19].

Further evidence of the fact that cows were used for domestic purposes in the Faroes in the Viking era can be found in the excavations at Kvíkvík, which revealed the existence of cowsheds adjoining the Viking-age house[20].

The importance to the Faroes of sheep and cattle in the latter part of the twelfth century can be seen from the fact that wool, homespun and butter were exported to Norway and sold to the Germans[21].

It is almost certain that turf (or peat as the English call it) was the main form of fuel used from the earliest days. It was a common form of fuel in Scandinavia and, when the Vikings settled in Ireland, they taught the Irish how to make use of it, which is the reason why it is called turf, and not peat, in Ireland. They probably also taught the Manx to use turf because it is referred to as such in the early Manx laws[22].

The real evidence of farming in the Middle Ages comes, however, from the *Sheep Letter* which laid down in 1298 the law relating to farming in the Faroes[23].

Prior to 1200 the land was held by farmers who farmed their lands with the help of thralls[24]. However, slavery was, as has been mentioned earlier[25], abolished in about that year, but when released, these persons became known as "good-for-nothings"[26]. Between 1200 and 1298, a number of the freed thralls saved half a year's supply of food and then tried to set up their own houses and small-holdings in remote areas[27]. Presumably they earned this money mainly by working as farm labourers. However, the creation of new small-holdings was virtually prohibited by the provisions in the *Sheep Letter* which required a man to own at least three cows before he could set up a house on his own[27]. The only other people allowed to set up on their own were those who were unable to find any other means of livelihood with which to support themselves. The result of the restriction on small-holdings was that people who would have started such holdings were, in general, compelled to work as farm labourers[28].

The forms of land tenure were freehold, copyhold and leasehold. The main measure of land in the Faroes is the mark *(mørk)* which is not a fixed area of land, but varies in different parts of the Faroes. It indicates a share in communal land and there are said to be two thousand, four hundred marks of land in the Faroes[29]. Today a mark of land in the Faroes is approximately two and a half statute acres[30] which would make the total area of land in the Faroes suitable for agriculture to be about six thousand statute acres. As the total area of the Faroes is about five hundred and forty square miles[31], this would indicate that only about two per cent of that area would be good for farming. Land in the Faroes has, from early times, been divided into the infield *(bøur)* which is fenced in land[32] and the outfield *(hagi)* which is used as pasture, especially for sheep and cattle[33]. References in the *Sheep Letter* to pasture or pasture land are references to the outfield.

It appears from the *Sheep Letter* that the outfield could be the subject of individual or joint ownership and that sheep could also be in individual or joint ownership[34]. Common folds were used for the sheep and the owners of the sheep had to pay for their maintenance in proportion to the number of sheep they owned[35].

It is clear from the *Sheep Letter* that dogs were used in "working" sheep, but also that they were a menace so far as sheep-worrying was concerned, and provision was made in the *Sheep Letter* requiring dogs to be kept under control[36]. Provision was also made for compensation to be paid for sheep destroyed by one's dogs[36]. The *Sheep Letter* defines a sheep worrier as a dog which harms sheep more than once or which goes off on its own into the outfield to attack sheep[36].

The number of sheep, and also of cattle and horses, which could be kept by a person on the outfield was restricted by agreement to ensure that the pasture was not "grazed out"[37]. It is interesting to note that somewhat similar legislation was enacted in the Isle of Man in 1691 (three hundred and ninety-three years after the *Sheep Letter)* in an Act, the long title to which is "An Act that Cotters and Intackholders shall not keep any more Cattle, Horses, Sheep, etc., than what they have sufficient Grass and Winter Provision for"[38]. This Act, which provided for the setting up of "fodder juries" to inquire every spring into the number of stock which crofters, etc., had so as to ensure that there was enough food for the animals for the following summer and winter, and for the sale of excess stock, has never been repealed. And now, two hundred and eighty-three years after the passing of the Manx Statute and six hundred and seventy-six years after the making of the *Sheep Letter,* circumstances in the British Islands reveal how desirable that type of legislation is.

Land could be used in the infield for growing crops. Rent for such land had to be paid by the spring or, at the latest, by St. Olaf's Day, the 29th July, and, if it was not paid by then, the landlord could take possession of the crops unless the value of the crops was greater than the amount due for rent [39]. This form of tenure bears a very close resemblance to the present-day con-acre letting in Northern Ireland.

The main crop grown at this time was corn (barley) which was sown in the autumn [39]. The climatic conditions in the Faroes were, however, unsuitable for growing corn to ripen and, accordingly, the corn was cut and threshed while it was still green, and the grain was then dried in the corn-drying house, *sornhús,* before it was ground [40].

The next most important crop was hay which was required for feeding the cattle and horses and, on occasions, sheep in the winter. Apart from manure from the animals, seaweed was also used for fertilizing the fields [41]. The main means of conveying manure, seaweed and turf was by twin creels *(leypur)* or panniers attached to pack-saddles on the backs of horses [42]. Single creels *(leypur)* were also used for carrying turf and other commodities on their backs. These creels were balanced by a head-band [43].

It seems likely that, in addition to corn and hay, white turnips were grown for human consumption in the days prior to the Reformation, as well as at the present time.

Sheep trespass in the outfield was a problem even in the time when the *Sheep Letter* was enacted and provision for compensation is provided in that law for such trespass, the measure of compensation in some cases being forty feet (ells) of homespun for each ear-marked sheep which trespassed [44]. An ell *(alin)* was two feet (see *fótur)* and a foot was about twelve inches (see *tummi* which is 2.615 cm) [45]. Stricter measures were provided in the case of sheep owners who refused to remove their sheep from another person's land after due notice had been given by the latter [46].

It is obvious from the *Sheep Letter* that the marking of sheep was an established custom [47]. The method of marking sheep in the Faroes, as in other countries inhabited by Norsemen, was by ear-marks, and that method of marking sheep is still used in the Faroes. A person who put his sheep mark over that of the owner was treated as a thief [48]. These ear-marks are very similar to those formerly used in the Isle of Man, reputedly dating back to Norse times.

Mutton was not only eaten fresh but was also dried and, when dried, could be kept for quite a long time. The main time for killing sheep was in the autumn when it was decided which sheep should be slaughtered and which should be kept as stock and for breeding purposes [49].

Apart from the flesh of the sheep, their wool was used for weaving.

In addition, the hides of the cattle and the skins of sheep were used for making shoes and other foot-wear. The hair from horses tails was used for ropes.

The *Sheep Letter* also deals with tame sheep and wild ones and makes it clear that the purpose of taming sheep was to improve them. Provision was made in that law to encourage owners who tamed their sheep[50].

Although slavery was abolished in about 1200[51], servants were tied to their masters under the *Sheep Letter* and penalties were provided for persons who put up for more than three nights servants who had run away from their masters without good cause[52].

The *Sheep Letter* also laid down a scale of charges for people who spent the winter with farmers and the scale depended on whether or not the guest took ale and, if so, whether he consumed it regularly or only on holy days and fast days. The payment was calculated in ells of homespun[53].

The lot of Faroese farmers in the pre-Reformation period must have been a lean one in view of the poor condition of the soil and of the climatic conditions[54]. Not only had they to combat these conditions but, apart from taxes to the State, they had to pay tithes to the Church which, especially through big churchmen like Bishop Erlend, brought as much land as possible under the control of the Church[55], which must not have increased the popularity of the Church!

General farming conditions in the Faroes cannot have changed a great deal between 1298 and 1540, although the *Black Death* (about 1349) must have been responsible for a considerable change in the ownership of property. Certain settlements, such as Húsavík in the south-east of Sandoy and Saksun in the North-west of Streymoy, seem to have been practically wiped out[56].

Gudrun of Húsavík was exceptionally rich and, according to the stories told about her, she was the richest woman of her time in the Faroes[57]. Her house must have been a virtual palace. The size of her brewing tub and another vessel used in brewing beer (which held about one hundred and eighty-six gallons) indicate the amount of beer which must have been consumed by her household[58]. The foundations of the farmhouse which were made of horizontal pieces of timber *(stokkahús),* can still be seen, and the house was surrounded by a yard of paved stones[58]. Although archaeological investigations have still to be carried out in connection with the farmhouse and its surrounds, it provides evidence that there were still wealthy farmers in 1400, and, in fact, it was not until the latter part of the seventeenth century that the farming community in the Faroes became, as a whole, impoverished[58].

The second most important natural resource of the Faroes in the pre-Reformation period was fishing. Fishing is not referred to in the *Faroese Saga* and the first inhabitants of the Faroes may have been farmers without any real interest in fishing: many of the farmsteads mentioned in the *Saga* (for example, Skúvoy and Lítla Dímun) are difficult to approach from the sea, which would support this view[59].

Fishing must, however, have gained importance with the spread of Christianity because the Church forbad the eating of meat on Fridays and during Lent. Excavations at Kvívík support the view that it was used for food in the Viking era[60]. By the latter part of the twelfth century[61], and possibly earlier, the Faroese were exporting cod so that, by that time, the fishing industry must have been one of considerable importance.

In addition to fishing, whaling must have been carried out in the Faroes before the Reformation as there are references in the *Sheep Letter* to making use of whales[62]. It seems likely that, from the earliest times, pilot whale hunts were carried out when schools of those mammals arrived in the vicinity of the Faroes. Whales were useful not only as food but also as a means of providing fuel for lamps. Their bones were also utilized for a number of purposes.

Another occupation in at least some of the Faroese islands was bird-catching and the collection of birds' eggs for food. There is no direct evidence concerning this occupation but the *Hundabræv*[63] refers to both bird hounds and to Manx Shearwater dogs. These two species, although now extinct, were used for catching young Manx Shearwaters (and possibly also other young birds), and the fact that they are specifically mentioned by name in the *Hundabræv* is a clear indication that bird-catching was a recognised occupation by, at least, the fourteenth century. There is no written evidence available regarding the collecting of birds' eggs in the pre-Reformation era, but it is generally accepted that this, as well as the catching of sea-birds, has, from early times, been a hazardous secondary occupation of the inhabitants of the Faroes. Egg-collecting would naturally have been only a seasonal occupation.

However, despite farming, fishing and fowling, etc., times, on occasions, were so hard in the Faroes that the Faroese had to eat seaweed in order to survive. Fortunately there are in the Faroes a number of species of edible seaweed.

1   D p. 53.
2   D pp. 30, 31 and 33.
3   D pp. 31 and 52.
4   D p. 33.
5   D pp. 31, 52 and 53.
6   D p. 53.
7   See p. 107 *post*.
8   D p. 53.
9   See p. 2 *ante*.
10 See eg. GJ p. 270 and RS p. 2.
11 See p. 10 *ante*.
12 See p. 21 *ante*.
13 See p. 32 *ante*.
14 See p. 10 *ante*.
15 See JM under "kvíggj".
16 MA p. 69.
17 See p. 10 *ante*.
18 See p. 6 *ante*.
19 See p. 22 *ante*.
20 RS p. 26.

21 L p. 19.
22 MS p. 7.
23 For translations see Parts I and II of Appendix 4.
24 RS p. 19.
25 See p. 50 *ante*.
26 RS p. 19.
27 See Appendix 4, Part I, 7 and Part II, 14.
28 RS p. 19.
29 JM p. 289.
30 AJ p. 36.
31 See p. 1 *ante*.
32 JM p. 45.
33 JM p. 130.
34 See Appendix 4, Part I, Arts. 4-6 and Part II, Arts. 1-3.
35 See Appendix B to Chapter 10, Part I, Art. 5 and Part II, Art. 3.
36 See *ibid.*, Part I, Art. 6, and Part II, Art. 6.
37 *Ibid*.
38 MS p. 148.
39 See Appendix 4, Part I, Art. 2 and Part II, Art. 10.
40 JM p. 400 under "sornur".
41 JM p. 439 under "tarabreidur" *et seg*.
42 JM p. 337 under "rossleypur". See also "klyvaross".
43 JM p. 76 under "fetil" and p. 253 under "leypur".
44 See Appendix 4, Part I, Art. 5 and Part II, Art. 3.
45 JM pp. 90 and 460.
46 See Appendix 4, Part I, Art. 10 and Part II, Art. 7.
47 See *ibid.*, Part I, Arts. 4 and 5 and Part II, Arts. 1, 3 and 5.
48 See *ibid.*, Part I, Art. 5 and Part II, Art. 5.
49 See JM p. 159 under "heystfjall" and "heystskorin".
50 See Appendix 4, Part I, Art. 5 and Part II, Art. 4.
51 See pp. 50 and 100-101 *ante*.
52 See Appendix 4, Part I, Art. 7 and Part II, Art. 15.
53 See *Ibid.*, Part I, Art. 9 and Part II, Art. 13.
54 See p. 99 *ante*.
55 RS p. 12.
56 See pp. 53-54 *ante*.
57 RS p. 20.
58 RS p. 21.
59 MA p. 63.
60 *Ibid.* p. 69.
61 See L p. 19.
62 See Appendix 4, Part I, Arts. 8 and 11 and Part II, Arts. 15 and 16.
63 See p. 85 *ante*.

Above: A Faroese ram on Mýkines. Below: Puffins on Mýkines. (By courtesy of Asmundur Poulsen, Tórshavn.)

CHAPTER 15

CULTURE

There is no evidence of a separate Faroese culture in the Viking era prior to 1000, and whatever there was must have been brought there by the Norsemen themselves and their Celtic slaves and women. The runic stone which was found at Kirkjubøur has been dated by some to the ninth century (probably about 865) but other authorities date it at about 1000[1].

The Church brought with it to the Faroes its ecclesiastical culture and teaching. The standard of teaching at the clerical school at Kirkjubøur must have been extremely high because King Sverre of Norway, who was educated there[2], had a very high reputation for his knowledge and learning. Part of the culture which the Church brought to the Faroes was music and the only pre-Reformation music which has survived is ecclesiastical music.

The present-day so-called Faroese ring dance is Western European and not Faroese in origin, and probably came from France or from countries near to France from where it spread throughout Western Europe and thence to the Faroes[3].

The Faroese language, as distinct from the old Norse language, emerged sometime in the Middle Ages, and was certainly established as a separate language prior to the Reformation[4], although it was not until the middle of the nineteenth century that it developed into a true written language. However, it is fortunate for the Faroese that King Henry VIII of England did not accept the Faroes and Iceland in return for giving ex-King Christian II, or King Christian III, of Denmark a loan[5] as otherwise it is extremely unlikely that the Faroese language would be in such a strong position as it is today, because the English have always been far keener on making the inhabitants of their dependent territories learn English than on themselves learning the language of those territories. Examples of countries where the native languages have suffered in this way can be found in, for example, Scotland, Ireland and the Isle of Man. The preservation of a country's native language goes a very long way to the country preserving its national integrity, even in times of severe adversity.

As has been mentioned[6], Sturla Thordarson, one of Iceland's Lawmen and the author of the *Íslandinga Saga,* visited the Faroes in the winter of 1277-8. He was the nephew of Snorri Sturluson, the famous Icelandic saga-writer, and the brother of Olafr hvítaskáld[7]. It seems likely that Sturla's visit to the Faroes would have exercised some influence on literary life there[7]. In addition, there is clear evidence in the Faroese ballads of literary connections with Iceland, although it seems very probable that the Faroese borrowed much more than they gave[7].

The Faroese ballads are the first Faroese literary works and they date back to the fourteenth century[8]. These ballads were sung at dances, especially those which were held between Christmas and Lent[8].

The remote situation of the Faroes, the physical nature of the country, the hard life which the inhabitants had to live and the smallness of their population (probably only about three to four thousand people in the period being dealt with in this book) have been responsible for giving the Faroese special traits and have also had an effect on Faroese culture[9]. It is, perhaps, symptomatic of the conditions in the Faroes that the Faroese ballads are sung unaccompanied, without the assistance of musical instruments.

The *Faroese Saga* is not an original Faroese work but a collection of relevant pieces from Icelandic Sagas. However, the stories from the Sagas and other folk tales and legends must, during the period prior to the Reformation, have been told round the fireside by story-tellers and the telling of those stories and legends is of considerable value, as it has preserved them for posterity. The world would have lost a great deal without this oral tradition.

As will be seen from what is stated above, it would not be unfair to say that, prior to the Reformation, Faroese culture was only in its formative stage.

1   RS p. 25; MA p. 63.
2   See p. 64 *ante.*
3   RS pp. 21 and 22.
4   RS p. 21.
5   See p. 56 *ante.*
6   See p. 51 *ante.*
7   S p. 7, para. IV.
8   RS p. 21.
9   RS p. 22.

CHAPTER 16

COINAGE

There is no mention of coinage in the *Faroese Saga,* though there is a reference to silver in relation to the payment of tribute[1]. There is no silver in the Faroes and it must, therefore, have been imported and "worked" in the Faroes. When Carl of Møre came to the Faroes, he was given three grades of silver, the first, from the Northern Islands, of a very poor quality, the second of better quality and the third of good quality[2]. The implication is that the pure silver had been mixed with other metals.

The first evidence of coinage in the Faroes came from a find in the churchyard at Sandur on Sandoy which was unearthed in 1863[3]. This "find" consisted of 98 silver coins from England, Ireland, Denmark, Norway, Germany and Hungary[4]. It was considered that the coins had been buried between 1070 and 1080[5].

There were twenty-four English coins made up as follows[6]: —
3 from the reign of Ethelred II (978 to 1013 and from 1014 to 1016);
9 from the reign of Canute the Great (1016 to 1035), but one of these was a forged coin;
3 from the reign of Harald Harefoot (1035 to 1040);
8 from the reign of Edward the Confessor (1042 to 1066);
1 forged coin;

One Irish coin was found, but it has not been dated exactly[7], although Michael Dolley[8] has expressed the view that it was minted about 1050. There were five Danish coins, including one from the reign of Hardicanute (1035 to 1042), one from somewhere between 1050 and 1095 and two forged coins[9].

There were seventeen Norwegian coins made up as follows[10]: —
  1 from the joint reign of Magnus I, the Good, and Harald IV, the Ruthless, (1046 to 1047);
  2 from the solo reign of Harald IV, the Ruthless, (1046 to 1066);
  4 from the joint reign of Magnus II Haraldsson and Olaf III, the Quiet, (1066 to 1069);

10 of uncertain date, either from the joint reign of Magnus II and Olaf III (1066 to 1069) or from the beginning of the solo reign of Olaf III (i.e. 1069 to 1093);

There were fifty coins of German origin, namely[11]:—
1 from the reign of Emperor Conrad II (1024 to 1039);
2 issued by Count Bruno III of Braunschweig (1038 to 1057);
1 issued by Duke Theoderik of Lothringen (959 to 1032);
1 issued by Bishop Eberhard of Augsburg (with the name of Emperor Conrad II on it);
1 issued by Bishop Bernold of Utrecht (1027 to 1054);
1 coin of uncertain origin but of the same type;
1 coin possibly from Breisach;
1 coin from Celle;
1 coin from Deventer;
1 coin from Duisberg;
1 coin from Gosler;
1 coin from Hoy;
1 coin from Magdeburg;
1 coin from Remagen;
4 coins from Speier;
1 coin from Thiel;
1 coin from Würzburg;
29 coins whose origins are undetermined.

Finally, there was one Hungarian coin from the reign of Stephan I (1000 to 1038)[12].

There is no evidence to show how the coins came to be where they were found and their metal value is not very great[13].

Herbst was informed that the place where the find was made was under the altar of the old church[14]. This, however, does not fit in with Krogh's findings, which indicate that each church was built on top of its predecessor[15]. Recent excavations have revealed the remains of a farm house near the church. It is now felt that the original church was probably a private one attached to the farm. If this is so, the hoard may well have belonged to the owner of the farm.

The great variety of coins in the "find" could give great scope for one's imagination if it were not for the fact that, at the time they were buried, coinage in the northern lands depended for its value on its silver content rather than where it was minted. Accepting this and the fact that German coins have been found in Norwegian hoards of approximately the same period, the contents of the Sandur "find" do not appear so strange. However, it is impossible to say from where the owner of the coins obtained them and why he buried them, although it would not be unreasonable to suggest that, if he was of sufficient standing as a farmer to have his private church, he obtained the coins for goods, such as wool, which he had sold abroad or to traders from outside the Faroes.

The "find" at Sandur does not, however, mean that coinage was in general use in the Faroes in the latter part of the eleventh century. The opposite would seem to have been the case, although it is uncertain when coinage came to be used widely in the Faroes. There are references in the *Sheep Letter* to marks and ører of silver[16], but these amounts may well have been paid in their equivalent value in local produce such as cows, sheep, homespun or butter. This view is supported by the fact that there were local equivalents to the mark of mint silver[17]: —

1 mark mint silver = 1 *kúgildi*[18] (the approximate value of 1 cow)

= 1 *hunðrað vaðmala* (approximately 120 ells of homespun)

= 3 creels *(leypur)* of butter, each creel containing 18 kg.

The mark of mint silver is also stated to have been equivalent to six (or in certain circumstances) eight sheep.

The use of the word *"hunðrað"* here in relation to homespun is a reference to the "long hundred" or "great hundred" (in Faroese, *Stórthundrað),* which in countries under Norse influence indicated not one hundred but one hundred and twenty[19]. The use of the "long hundred" is still (or, at any rate, until very recently has been) used for counting herring in the area around Kilkeel, Co. Down, Northern Ireland, a legacy of the days when part of Northern Ireland was under the Norsemen. For the same historic reason, the "long hundred" was used, within living memory, in the Isle of Man for counting herring and also in connection with the length of rope. In the latter case, if one purchased one hundred fathoms of rope one obtained one hundred and twenty fathoms of rope. In addition, eggs were counted in the Isle of Man by the "great hundred" (i.e. one hundred and twenty) as late as the 1930's as can be seen from the Third Schedule to the Isle of Man (Customs) Act 1933 (an Act of the Parliament of the United Kingdom). The fact that statutory recognition was given in the twentieth century to an ancient Norse custom is of considerable interest. Today, however, the custom appears to have died out in the Isle of Man.

Under the *Sheep Letter,* which was enacted in 1298[20], rents[21] and alimentation[22] were fixed in terms of homespun.

Travelling allowances to the members of the *Løgting* in the latter part of the fourteenth century were also paid in homespun and not in cash[23]. Greip Ivarsson's mortgage (made in 1399) refers to two hundred marks in cash, two skins for each mark, and to homespun[24] but it was drawn up in Norway where coins had been minted from the eleventh century[25].

One of the Gudrun documents[26] refers to rents being payable in creels *(leypur)* of butter, but the properties concerned were situated in Norway. Although the Faroese word for this type of rent *(leypabol* or *leypsbol)*[27] does not appear in the second edition of the Faroese/Danish Dictionary or in the recently published Supplement to that dictionary there was, as has been mentioned[28], a butter equivalent in the Faroes to the mark reckoned at the rate of three creels (each containing eighteen kilogrammes) to the mark of mint silver.

It is interesting to note that while the Gudrun document mentioned above[29] refers to payment of rents in Norway being paid by so many creels of butter, references in that and another document[30] to rents payable in the Shetlands are to rents payable in shillings or English pounds. This was probably due to the fact that the Shetlands were close to Great Britain where coins had been minted for many centuries before the period in which the Gudrun documents were made[31].

The Norwegians and Danes were unfamiliar with coins when they first arrived in the British Islands and learnt from England the art of minting coins[32]. As can be seen from the *Sheep Letter*[33], the basis of coinage in the Norwegian Empire was silver, the original basic coin being the mark. Originally, the mark was a measure, one mark of silver weighing 215.8 grammes[34]. However, in due course, a silver mint mark was produced which was equivalent to approximately one third of a mark of pure silver[34]. As time went on, the mint mark became equivalent to one quarter, one fifth and then still smaller proportions of a mark of pure silver[34].

In the reign of King Hakon IV Hakonsson[35], the mark became subdivided into two hundred and forty pennies, and a penny was divided into two half-pennies and four quarter pennies[36], which bears a striking resemblance to the former British monetary system. One øre was equivalent to thirty pennies (or one eighth of a mark)[35]. The following is a table showing the comparative value of Scandinavian coinage between the Middle Ages and 1911[37]:—

	Silver Value	Butter Value	1911 Value
1 mark silver mint	10.66 kroner	54.00 kg.	100.00 kroner
½ mark silver mint	5.33 kroner	27.00 kg.	50.00 kroner
3 øre	4.00 kroner	20.25 kg.	37.50 kroner
2 øre	2.66 kroner	13.50 kg.	25.00 kroner
1 øre	1.33 kroner	6.75 kg.	12.50 kroner

The mark silver subsequently became further sub-divided as follows:—

1 mark silver mint	. . 2 guilders and 8 skinns[38].
1 guilder	. . 20 skinns
¼ guilder (copper)	. . 5 skinns
1 øre silver	. . 6 skinns
1 ørtug silver	. . 2 skinns

The following Table may serve as a guide so far as the Norse, Scandinavian and Faroese coins compares with old English currency. The Table is based on the premise that one Danish skilling was worth about a farthing[39] and one Faroese skinn was equivalent to four Danish skillings.

1 Faroese skinn	=	approx. 1 penny (old English currency)
1 Norse penny	=	approx. 1/5 penny (old English currency)

1 ell of wool	=	approx. 2/5 penny (old English currency)
1 ørtug	=	approx. 2 pennies (old English currency)
1 silver øre	=	approx. sixpence (old English currency)
1 guilder	=	approx. 1 shilling (old English currency)
1 mark silver mint	=	approx. 4 shillings (old English currency)

It is interesting to compare the value of the Scandinavian mark with that of the English mark. The latter was, according to the Shorter Oxford Dictionary, worth two thirds of an English pound or thirteen shillings and four pennies (old English currency)[40], whereas the Scandinavian mark was equivalent to approximately one fifth of an English pound. One also finds a similar disparity between the value of the Danish crown *(krone)* and the English crown, the former being worth formerly approximately one shilling (old English currency) and the latter five shillings in that currency.

It is very difficult to express the equivalent in present-day British currency to the value of the silver mint mark, but a fair guide would be to base it on the current price in 1974 of fifty-four kilogrammes of butter. This would give the mark an approximate value of £27 and an øre the approximate value of £3.50. Allowance must be made, however, for subsequent inflation. Applying this very rough and ready test, the fines in the *Sheep Letter* become more intelligible[41].

1 See pp. 28-29 *ante.*
2 See p. 29 *ante.*
3 H p. 2.
4 H pp. 3 to 17.
5 H p. 18.
6 H pp. 3 to 5. The dates of Harold Harefoot and Edward the Confessor have been adjusted to their correct dates.
7 H. p. 5.
8 MRIA Reader in Modern History, the Queen's University of Belfast.
9 H pp. 5 and 6. One coin originally considered to be Norwegian from the reign of Magnus I the Good has now been identified as being of Danish origin.
10 H pp. 6 to 13.
11 H pp. 13 to 17.
12 H p. 17.
13 H p. 2.
14 H pp. 2 and 3.
15 KJK pp. 70 to 71.
16 See Appendix 4, Part I, Arts. 1 to 3, 5, 7, 10 and 12 and Part II, Arts. 2, 4, 5, 8 and 10 to 12.
17 FB p. 14.
18 Also called *kýrlag* and *kýrverd*, see FB p. 14.
19 FB p. 16.
20 See p. 52 *ante.*
21 See Appendix 4, Part I, Art. 5 and Part II, Art. 3.
22 See *Ibid.,* Part I, Art. 9 and Part II, Art. 13.
23 See Appendix 10.
24 See Appendix 11.
25 See p. 109 *ante.*
26 See Appendix 5, document 2.

27 See DF p. 28, footnote.
28 See above.
29 Appendix 5, document 2.
30 *Ibid.*, document 3.
31 1403.
32 MD p. 10.
33 See Appendix 4, Parts I and II.
34 FB p. 13.
35 1217-1263 see Appendix 1.
36 FB p. 13.
37 FB p. 14.
38 The skinn was the only purely Faroese coin and it is uncertain when it was first minted.
39 DEO vol. II, p. 329 under "skilling".
40 See Shorter Oxford Dictionary under "mark".
41 See Appendix 4.

CHAPTER 17

HISTORIC REMAINS

There are few historic remains in the Faroes from the pre-Reformation era to assist in formulating the history of that period[1]. Excavation for historic purposes is of only comparatively recent origin in the Faroes, the first known excavation having been carried out a mere two hundred years or so ago. However, it is only in very modern times that the excavation of historic remains has begun in earnest[1]. A very great deal of the credit for this work must go to Sverre Dahl, until recently Curator of the Faroese Museum, Tórshavn.

The *Faroese Saga* states[2] that Hafgrim, Brester and Beiner were buried according to ancient custom, which would mean that they were buried in barrows. These burials took place before Christianity came to the Faroes. There is still at Hov on Suðuroy a place called "Hafgrim's Grave" which is supposed to be the grave of the Hafgrim referred to in the *Saga*. This grave was excavated in 1834 or 1835 at the request of hr. Pløyen who was at that time Governor of the Faroes[4]. Unfortunately, the persons who carried out the excavation were not experts. Governor Pløyen described the grave as follows:—

"It was 24 feet long and 4 feet broad consisting of loose, rich soil . . . Around the grave there was a type of stonework of loose stones which were of the kind which is found on the beach and not on mountains and must have been carried from the shore up to the grave and that, with some difficulty, as the grave is situated high up. Hafgrim's grave was opened by Farmer Ole Mortensen of Hov. According to the account of that person the stonework came to an end when one dug a bit deeper."

As a result of the excavation, some small pieces of iron and bones were found and also, possibly, a small whetstone but that is not entirely clear[4].

The first time, however, that a pre-Christian era grave was excavated in the Faroes by experts was in 1956 at the village of Tjørnuvík in the extreme north-west of Streymoy[5]. This was a chance find in a village which had no ancient history[5]. However, one day in 1955 some boys were playing in a sandy place and one of them found what appeared to be human bones[5]. As a result, excavations were carried out in the following year and human remains, including a skull and a thigh bone, were discovered[5]. As a result of a medical examination by Dr. J. Balslev Jørgensen it was decided that among the remains were those of a grown woman of about 155 cms. height[5]. The body faced East-North-East to West-South-West with the head facing East-North-East[5]. This form of burial most resembled that of the pagan Norwegians from the Viking era, but the grave itself was nearly the same as that of the Norse graves in neighbouring islands. The only archaeological object from the Viking age found at the site was a Scottish Celtic ring pin of the type used in that era by both men and women for holding their cloaks together[6]. This ring pin is further evidence of the connections which the Celts had with the Faroes. Sverri Dahl dates the burial find to the tenth century[7].

During excavations on Skúvoy, crude Celtic crosses have been found which have been dated by P. M. C. Kermode, an archaeologist from the Isle of Man, as having been made about 1000, although it is possible that they might have been made by Irish monks between 725 and 825[8]. If Kermode is correct they could have come from the Church which is said to have been built on Skúvoy in the time of Sigmund Bresterson[9]. Another reminder of Sigmund is to be found in the impressive stone known as *Sigmundarsteinur,* which is in Ólansgarður on Skúvoy and has a Roman Cross cut into it[10].

After the arrival of Christianity, people were buried in consecrated soil in churchyards[11] and, as has been stated previously[12], the first church to be built in the Faroes would appear to be that referred to in the preceding paragraph. In the porch of the parish church on Svínoy there is a stone which is said to be the tombstone of Svínoy-Bjarni[13]. The stone was originally buried under the floor of the church but, when the church was replaced in 1828, the stone was dug up and left outside for many years before it was brought into the porch of the church. According to oral tradition, the stone, which is extremely old, had been known as *Bjarnasteinur* from long before the time it was dug up[14]. It is, of course, impossible to prove that this was the stone which was placed over Svínoy-Bjarni's grave, but it could well be and, if the *Faroese Saga* can be relied on, Bjarni, like the other Faroese, became a Christian[15]. The measurements of the stone are one hundred centimetres by thirty-five centimetres and there is a simple cross on the upper part of it, while, below the cross, are two sets of five strokes which intersect each other diagonally[16]. The stone is broader at the top than at the bottom with the sides tapering down[16].

Three runic stones have been found in the Faroes, one at Kirkjubøur, the second at Sandavágur in the island of Vágar and the third at Fámjin on the west coast of Suðuroy[17].

As has been mentioned[18], there is a difference of opinion among the authorities as to the date of the Kirkjubøur runic stone, some stating that it is ninth century and others that it dates from about 1000.

The runic stone found at Sandavágur dates from about 1200 and is in memory of Torkil Onundarson, while that at Famjin is of a younger vintage, dating from the 1500's[19].

Five excavations carried out in connection with ancient Faroese houses prior to 1960 have been "written up." The first excavation was carried out during the Second World War at Kvívík on the west coast of Streymoy, the second in 1950 at Syðragøta[20] on the east coast of Eysturoy and the third in 1958 at Fuglafjørður, which is only a few miles away from Syðragøta[21].

The excavation at Kvívík was once again one which was carried out at a place which had no historic background, but the results of the excavation were invaluable[22]. Investigations of the site revealed that there were in fact two houses, one built above the other, and that there was a layer about half a metre thick between them[22]. Below the ruins, there was a hall which ran North- South and was twenty-one to twenty-two metres in length, being broadest in the centre, and becoming narrower towards each end[23]. There was a fireplace several metres long in the centre of the hall and there had, no doubt, been benches or seats along the walls[23]. It has been said by the people carrying out the investigation:—

"The most thrilling moment during the whole operation was when the hall was swept and the fireplace cleaned. Everything was so untouched and so familiar that it felt as if one had dropped in on people who had not been at home for a short period, but had gone out on an errand and had intended that the fire would not have burned out by the time they returned"[23].

There were cowsheds on the same level as the hall which, from the size of the bones of cattle and horses which have been found there, could have housed at least three animals on either side of the groop (the ditch for draining the dung)[24]. The partitions between the stalls were, no doubt, made of large flat stones[24].

The ruins at the lower level can, from their remains and from the objects which have been found there, be dated definitely to the Viking era, while the ruins from the upper level date back undoubtedly to the Middle Ages[24]. Evidence to support this was found in a shoe which resembles shoes found on a number of occasions in Norway and Sweden, which have been dated to the twelfth century[25].

Although the ruins found at Syðragøta differ from those at Kvívík, the objects discovered at Syðragøta indicate that these ruins also date from the Viking era[26]. The excavations at Fuglafjørður, like those at Kvívík and Tjørnuvík, were made without any historic background[26]. The remains are those of an ancient building which, together with the objects which were found there, are considered to date back to the early Middle Ages, that is to shortly after 1035[26]. As a matter of fact, the various levels at the site at Fuglafjørður, reveal the existence of a series of buildings right up to the present day[26]. Several of the objects found during the excavation contained ribbon motifs, in all probability originally Celto—Norse, which resemble the ribbon motif on the ring-pin found at Tjørnuvík[27]. Furthermore, the earliest of the houses, which is of the 'Hall' type, is almost identical with that excavated at Kvívík[27]. Sverri Dahl has expressed the view[27] that the motifs and the type of house indicate contact with the British Isles or direct settling from there[27].

The fourth excavation was carried out in 1956 at a place called *i Eingjartoftum* at Sandavágar on the island of Vágar, close to where the runic stone of Torkil Onundarson referred to above was discovered in 1917[28]. The excavation revealed the existence of two houses dating from different periods[28]. The earlier house was probably built in the early Middle Ages as can be seen from the method of construction and from the earthen vessels which were found on the site[25]. The later house would seem to date from a period prior to the sixteenth century[25]. It would appear likely that the earlier house belonged to Torkil Onundarson, who seems to have been the founder of the settlement at Eingjartoftum[28].

The fifth excavation was carried out in 1957, also on Vágar, near a stream called *við Hanusá* at Seyrvágur[29]. The site was situated high up in the infield and had been subjected to a lot of disturbance, partly due to cultivation and partly due to the erection of buildings in recent years[26]. The earliest of the buildings revealed by the excavation are considered to date back to the Viking era, but it also seems as if they had been inhabited during the Middle Ages[29].

In the first half of the 1960's, a bishop's grave was discovered under the bishop's church at Kirkjubøur but, as yet, it is not known which bishop was buried there[30].

Between 1969 and 1972, excavations were carried out at the request of the Faroese Museum and with the co-operation of the Faroes Department of Antiquities by Knud J. Krogh, Curator of the National Museum of Denmark, in the parish church at Sandur on the island of Sandoy. It now appears that the present church is the sixth to be built since the eleventh century on the same site[31]. The first church was built in the eleventh century and the second in the twelfth or thirteenth century[31]. The first church would seem to be best described as a small Norwegian stave church about twenty-seven feet long with a nave that narrowed into a choir towards the west[31]. Hr. Krogh has expressed the view that the original church at Sandur must have looked very much like the stave church at Holtålen in Norway[31].

The second church at Sandur was a little larger than the first: it also had a nave but a somewhat narrower choir, the main difference between these two churches being that the second one had an outer wall of stones, constructed without mortar, with a space between it and the main wooden wall which it protected[32]. This would mean that less strong boards than would otherwise have been necessary could be used for the main wall, which was important because all wood in the Faroes, except driftwood, had to be imported[33]. The space between the walls would seem to be that referred to earlier[34] as being used as a local prison.

The habit of building on the site of existing ruins has hampered excavation of Viking-age sites both in Scandinavia and in other places where the Norsemen lived. The reason for building on previous remains is logical because the site would, as a rule, have been a good one and it is a help to build on existing foundations. It is, however, a bane to archaeologists.

The most important relic in the Faroes is, undoubtedly, the unfinished cathedral at Kirkjubøur, whose remains are known as "Mururin"[35]. It is believed that the Cathedral was built in about 1300[36] under the directions of Bishop Erlend of the Faroes[37] who, although he died in Norway[38], is said to have been buried at Kirkjubøur[39].

Although the cathedral itself was never completed, the building, or at least part of it, was probably used for religious services. This assertion is supported by the fact that the cathedral did possess "holy relics", and it is most unusual for such relics to be found in a cathedral which has not been consecrated. On the east wall of the cathedral, about six feet above the ground, there is a plaque on which there is, in high relief, Christ on the Cross between Mary and Mary Magdalene and below it there is an inscription in Latin which indicates that there are[40] among the relics of the cathedral a piece of our Lord's Cross and bones of "the blessed martyr Magnus" (believed to refer to Saint Magnus, Earl of the Orkneys[41]) and of Bishop Torlak Torhalleson, who was Bishop of Skálholtur in Iceland from 1178 to 1193[42]. The Cathedral at Kirkjubøur is dedicated to that same St. Magnus[43].

In 1905 an architect, L. Koefoed-Jensen, who was carrying out repair work on the exterior of the east wall, found in a recess of the wall seven small packets in a leather container on which there were several letters and the word "Maria"[44]. The contents of these packets, which were in excellent condition, appeared to correspond to the relics referred to in the Latin inscription[44].

The architect returned the packets to the recess after the repair work had been completed[44]. A number of years later, the recess was opened by an archaeologist only to find that the contents of the packets had disintegrated in the meantime. It seems almost unbelievable that the contents should have survived without harm for over six centuries and then disintegrated within a few decades: whoever wrapped the articles originally must have had some special formula for preserving the contents.

There is no evidence to show why the cathedral was never completed, but it is not unreasonable to consider that this was, at any rate in part, due to the same circumstances which forced its founder, Bishop Erlend, to leave the Faroes[45]. The position, as regards the cathedral, must have been made worse by the fact that the Faroes did not have a bishop for four or five years after the death of Bishop Erlend[46].

The following is a description of the cathedral based on that given by Daniel Bruun in *Far de Færøske Bygder*[47]:—

"The cathedral ruins consist of a nave with a chancel eighty-four feet long, seventeen feet broad and twenty-eight feet high, and with a chapel, about thirty-one by nine feet, on the northern side. The cathedral is built of stone. There is only one window on the north of the cathedral and it is high up in the nave with a flat Gothic arch. A door leads from this wall to the sacristy. There is a Gothic-arched window on the east or chancel gable, while there are five windows on the south wall. Three of these windows are in the nave and the other two, which are small ones, high up in the chancel, which indicates that it had been decided to erect something higher up. In addition, there are two entrances in the south wall.

There is a large Gothic-arched entrance in the west wall which is, to a great extent, characteristic of the cathedral. At this end of the cathedral, one can also see that it has been intended to erect a tower, but no evidence has been found that any work had ever been begun on it.

The windows on the south wall are beautifully decorated with roses, but, unfortunately, some of them have been badly damaged.

The chancel is separated from the nave of the cathedral by two richly-decorated pillars.

There are four openings in the walls of the chapel, of which one is a doorway leading in from the chancel. On the east there is a very low window, while on the north side there is a doorway leading to spiral stairs which have been started but never completed. It seems as if there was a round window on the west wall, shaped as a rose, but, unfortunately, only three stones remain to establish its existence. The east window is also badly damaged and the whole of the north-east corner has fallen down and been re-built.

It can be stated with certainty that the chancel and nave were never arched. On the other hand, it is extremely probable that the cross-vaulting over the chapel was completed. Clear evidence of this is still visible, such as the rabbets of the vaulting and part of the vaulting itself. According to legend, the vaulting was carried away by heavy falls of snow."

However, despite all the ravages of time, *"Mururin"* still exists as a historic relic of which the Faroese have every justification to be proud.

1 RS p. 22.
2 See p. 10 *ante*.
3 RS p. 22.
4 SD p.126. Pløyen was Amptman of the Faroes, the equivalent, in the Faroese context, to the Governor of a British dependency.
5 RS p. 23. See also FR b. 5, pp. 153-68 *Víkingaaldargrøv í Tjørnuvík* by Sverri Dahl and Jóannes Rasmussen.
6 *Ibid.* The neighbouring islands were probably the Shetlands.
7 FR b. 5, pp. 166-7.
8 MA.
9 See p. 21 *ante*.
10 T vol. XIII, *Fortidsminder* by Sverri Dahl p. 192.
11 RS p. 22.
12 See p. 21 *ante*.
13 See p. 42 *ante*.
14 TBL, Part II, p. 16.
15 See p. 20 *ante*.
16 TBL, Part II, p. 16.
17 RS pp. 24-6.
18 See p. 107 *ante*.
19 RS pp. 25 and 26.
20 T vol. XIII, *Fortidsminder* by Sverri Dahl p. 196.
21 *Toftarannsóknir í Fuglafirði* by Sverri Dahl. FR b. 7, pp. 118-146.
22 *Ibid.* See also V b. 29, pp. 65-96, *Fornar toftir í Kvívík* by Sverri Dahl. AIF pp. 137-9.
23 *Ibid.*
24 *Ibid.*

25 *Ibid.*
26 *Ibid.*
27 FR b. 7, pp. 118-46 *Toftarannsóknir í Fuglafirði* by Sverri Dahl.
28 FR b. 10, pp. 53-76. *Bústaður i Eingjartoftum, Sandavági* by Sverri Dahl.
29 FR b. 14, pp. 9-23 *Vikingabústaður í Seyrvági* by Sverri Dahl.
30 RS pp. 26 and 27. KJK p. 67.
31 KJK p. 69. See also ch. 9. n. 22.
32 KJK pp. 69 and 71.
33 KJK p. 71.
34 See p. 81 *ante.*
35 RS p. 12.
36 KJK p. 67.
37 See p. 65.
38 See p. 66 *ante.*
39 See pp. 67 and 71 *ante.*
40 DB p. 62.
41 *Ibid.* pp. 64-6.
42 DB p. 67.
43 MA p. 73.
44 DB pp. 62-6.
45 See p. 68 *ante.*
46 See Appendix 2.
47 DB pp. 58-60.

Above: The interior of Kirkjuböur Church. Below: A ram's head on the farmhouse at Kirkjuböur. (By courtesy of Asmundur Poulsen, Tórshavn.)

122

APPENDIX 1

Scandinavian Monarchs connected with the Faroes prior to the Reformation

PART I

Period	Monarch	Remarks
c.885-945	Harald I, Fairhair	
c.945-47	Erik I, Bloodaxe	
c.947-60	Hakon I, the Good	
c.960-70	Harald II, Greycloak	
c.970-95	Earl Hakon	Never had control of eastern Norway during his reign. Harald Bluetooth of Denmark ruled over that area of Norway from 970-85.
c.995-1000	Olaf I Tryggvason	
c.1000-16	Earls Erik and Sven Hakonarson	? Came to power in 999 or 1002. They were sons of Earl Hakon.
1016-28	Olaf II the Holy Haraldsson	Son of Harald II.
1028-30	Canute the Great	A Dane, Norway being under Denmark from 1028-35 see ch. 6 n. 33.
1030-35	Sven	Son of Canute the Great and Canute's Mistress Aelgifu. He ruled Norway under Canute.
1035-46	Magnus I, the Good	
1046-47	Magnus I & Harald the Ruthless	
1047-66	Harald III, the Ruthless	Killed at Stamford Bridge, England.
1066-69	Magnus II and Olaf III, the Quiet	Sons of Harald III.
1069-93	Olaf III, the Quiet	
1093-1103	Magnus III, Barelegs	Killed and buried near Downpatrick, Co. Down, Northern Ireland.
1103-22	Eystein I, Magnusson	Sons of Magnus III.
1103-15	Olaf	He died in his teens and is not entitled to any number.

Period	Monarch	Remarks
1103-30	Sigurd I, the Crusader	He was absent on Crusades for a period commencing in 1107.
1130-35	Magnus IV, the Blind	
1130-36	Harald IV, Gille	Son of Magnus III by a concubine. Hence the Celtic nick-name "Gille" — the servant (of Christ).
1136-61	Inge I, the Hunchback	
1136-55	Sigurd II, the Talkative	Sons of Harald IV. See p. 63 for background.
1136-57	Eystein II	
1161-62	Hakon II, with the Broad Shoulders	
1163-84	Magnus V, Erlingsson	
1184-1202	Sverre	Son of King Sigurd II.
1202-4	Hakon III, Sverresson	Son of King Sverre.
1204	Gutorm	
1204-7	Inge II, Bardasson	
1207-17	Inge II and Philip	
1217-63	Hakon IV, Hakonsson	Son of Hakon III.
1263-80	Magnus VI, the Law Reformer	Son of Hakon IV.
1280-99	Erik II	Son of Magnus VI. Later nick-named the Priest-hater.
1299-1319	Hakon V	Son of Magnus VI. Prior to Becoming King, he was Duke Hakon.
1319-55	Magnus VII, Eriksson	Son of Erik II and grandson of Hakon V. He was also King of Sweden and continued as such after 1355.
1355-80	Hakon VI, Magnusson	Elected as King in 1343 but did not start to reign until 1355. Married Margaret daughter of the King of Denmark.
1380-87	Olaf IV, Hakonsson	Son of Hakon VI. His mother, Margaret II acted as Regent during his reign because of his youth.

PART II

SOVEREIGN OF NORWAY & DENMARK

| 1387-97 | Margaret I | She had acted as Regent of Norway from 1380-87. |

PART III

SOVEREIGNS OF THE SCANDINAVIAN UNION

1387-1412	Margaret I	See Appendix, note (4).
1412-42	Erik III of Pomerania	See Appendix, note (14).
1442-48	Christopher of Bayern	
1449-50	Karl Knutsson of Sweden	
1450-81	Christian I	
1481-1513	Hans	

Period	Sovereign	Remarks
1513-23	Christian II	Deposed as a result of an uprising of the nobles in 1523. 1523 was also the year in which Sweden left the Scandinavian Union.

PART IV

DANISH MONARCHS

Period	Sovereign	Remarks
1523-33	Frederick I	Previously Duke of Holstein and Southern Jutland.
1533-36		War of Succession, see Chapter 10, note 91.
1536-59	Christian III	Was responsible for the Reformation taking place in Denmark in 1536.

APPENDIX 2

ECCLESIASTICAL HIERACHY AFFECTING THE FAROES

Key:
A = Pope of Avignon
H-B = Hamburg-Bremen (in the case of Archbishops)
K = Faroese bishop referred to in Archbishop Kaltisen's copybook
L = Lund (in the case of Archbishops)
M = Missionary Bishop (in the case of Bishops)
N = Nidaros (in the case of Archbishops)
P = Pisa (in the case of Popes elected by Council of P)

Period	Pope	Rival Pope	Archbishop
988-1013	—	—	Lievizo the Elder H-B
996-999	Gregory VI	—	—
997-998	—	John XVI	—
999-1003	Sylvester II	—	—
1003	John XVII	—	—
1003-09	John XVIII	—	—
1009-12	Sergius IV	—	—
1012	—	Gregory VI	—
1012-24	Benedict VIII	—	—
1013-29	—	—	Unwan H-B
1024-32	John XIX	—	—
1029-32	—	—	Lievizo the Younger H-B
1032-45	Benedict IX	—	—
1032-35	—	—	Hermann H-B
1035-43	—	—	Bezelin *alias* Alebrand H-B
1043-72	—	—	Adalbert H-B
1045-46	Gregory VI	Sylvester III	—
1046-47	Clement II	—	—
1047-48	Damascus II	Benedict IX	—
1047-67	—	—	—
1049-54	Leo IX	—	—
1055-57	Victor II	—	—
1057-58	Stephen IX	—	—
1058-61	Nicholas II	—	—
1059	—	Benedict X	—
1061-73	Alexander II	—	—
1061-64	—	Honorius II	—
1072-1101	—	—	Liemar H-B
1073-85	Gregory VII	—	—
1080-1100	—	Clement III (Vibertus)	—
1086-87	Victor III	—	—
1088-99	Urban II	—	—

Rival Archbishop	Bishop of Faroes	Remarks
—	—	—
—	—	—
—	—	—
—	—	—
—	—	—
—	—	—
—	—	—
—	—	—
—	—	—
—	—	—
—	—	—
—	—	—
—	—	—
—	—	—
—	—	—
—	—	—
—	—	Benedict IX doubtful
—	—	—
—	Bernhard the Saxon M K	Doubtful, but see pp. 44-45 for arguments
—	—	—
—	—	—
—	—	—
—	—	—
—	—	—
—	—	—
—	—	Commencing date doubtful
—	—	—
—	—	—

Period	Pope	Rival Pope	Archbishop
Last quarter of 11th century	—	—	—
1099-1118	Pascall II	—	—
1100-02	—	Theodericus	—
c. 1100-37	—	—	—
1101-04	—	—	Humbert H-B
1102	—	Albertus	—
1104-37	—	—	Asker L
1105-1111	—	Sylvester IV	—
1118-19	Gelasius II	—	—
1119-24	Calixtus II	—	—
1119-21	—	Gregory VIII	—
1124-29	Honorius II	—	—
1124	—	Celestine II	—
1130-43	Innocent II	—	—
1130-38	—	Anacletus II	—
1133-48	—	—	—
[1138-?]	—	Victor IV]	—
1138-52	—	—	Eskil L
[1138-?]	—	—	—
1143-44	Celestine II	—	—
1144-45	Lucius II	—	—
1145-53	Eugene II	—	—
1157	—	—	—
1152/3-57	—	—	John I N
1153-54	Anastasius IV	—	—
1154-59	Adrian IV	—	—
1157-61/2	—	—	*Vacant*
1158-68	—	—	—
1158-62	—	—	—
1159-81	Alexander III	—	—
1159-64	—	Victor IV	—
1161-88	—	—	Eystein N

Rival Archbishop	Bishop of Faroes	Remarks
—	Ryngerus M, K or Ragnar M	Doubtful, but see p. 45 for arguments.
—	—	—
—	Gudmund K	Period doubtful, but see pp. for arguments.
—	—	Knud J. Krogh considers that the Faroes did not become a fixed Diocese until about 1120— so 1100 may be too early.
—	—	—
—	—	Became Archbishop on erection of see of Lund
—	—	—
—	—	—
—	—	—
—	—	—
—	—	—
—	—	—
Adelbero H-B	—	Became Archbishop of H-B in 1123. See p. 60 for background
—	—	Doubtful
—	—	The Faroes came under Nidaros on erection of that See in 1152 or 1153 see p. 63. Eskil remained Archbishop of Lund until 1171.
—	Orm K	—
—	—	—
—	—	—
—	Matthew I K	Doubtful when he succeeded Orm.
—	—	First Archbishop of Nidaros see p. 64.
—	—	—
—	—	Adrian IV (previously Cardinal Nicholas Breakspear) was the only Englishman ever to become Pope See p. 64 for explanation.
Hartvig H-B	—	Became Archbishop of H-B in 1148. See pp. 60-61 for background. See. p. 64 for explanation.
—	Vacant	
—	—	—
—	—	Chosen as Archbishop in 1157 but not consecrated until 1161. See p. 64.

Period	Pope	Rival Pope	Archbishop
1162-74	—	—	—
1164-68	—	Pascall III	—
1168-77	—	Calixtus III	—
?-1212	—	—	—
1179-80	—	Innocent III	—
1181-85	Lucius III	—	—
1185-87	Urban III	—	—
1187	Gregory VIII	—	—
1187-91	Clement III	—	—
1189-1205	—	—	Erik N
1191-98	Celestine III	—	—
1198-1216	Innocent III	—	—
1206-14	—	—	Thorer I N
[1212]-14	—	—	—
1215-24	—	—	Gudthorm N
1215	—	—	—
1216-27	Honorious III	—	—
1216-[37]	—	—	—
1225-26	—	—	Peter N
1227-41	Gregory IX	—	—
1227-30	—	—	Thorer II N
1231-52	—	—	Sigurd the Miserable N
?-1243	—	—	—
1241	Celestine IV	—	—
1242	*Vacant*	—	—
1243-54	Innocent IV	—	—
[c. 1245	—	—	—
1246-57	—	—	—
1253-54	—	—	Sorle N
1254-61	Alexander IV	—	—
1255-63	—	—	Einar Butterback N
1258-60/1	—	—	—
1261/2	—	—	—
1261-64	Urban IV	—	—
1264-66	—	—	*Vacant*
1265-68	*Clement IV*	—	—

130

Rival Archbishop	Bishop of Faroes	Remarks
—	Roe K	Possibly consecrated in 1163. See p. 64.
—	—	—
—	—	—
—	Sven K	Date of consecration uncertain, but it must have been before 1174. See under Bishop Roe.
—	—	—
—	—	—
—	—	—
—	—	—
—	—	Was forced to leave his seat as a result of a dispute with King Sverre. Recalled by King Hakon III in 1202 but resigned in 1205. Died in 1213
—	—	—
—	—	—
—	Olaf	Date of consecration uncertain
—	—	—
—	*Vacant*	—
—	—	—
—	Serquirus K	According to Joannes Patursson he died in 1232.
—	—	—
—	—	—
—	—	—
—	Bergsven K	Date of consecration uncertain
—	—	—
—	—	—
—	Nicholas]	Doubtful. Possibly the same person as Bishop Peter, see p. 65.
—	Peter K	—
—	—	—
—	—	—
—	*Vacant*	—
—	Gaute K	D.F. says he became bishop in 1257 but this is doubtful
—	—	—
—	—	—
—	—	—

Period	Pope	Rival Pope	Archbishop
1267	—	—	Hakon N
1268-82	—	—	John II the Red N
1269-70	*Vacant*	—	—
1269-1308	—	—	—
1271-76	Gregory X	—	—
1276	Innocent V	—	—
1276	Adrian V	—	—
1276-77	John XXI	—	—
1277-80	Nicholas III	—	—
1281-85	Martin IV	—	—
1283-87	—	—	*Vacant*
1285-87	Honorius IV	—	—
1288-92	Nicholas IV	—	—
1288-1309	—	—	Jørunder N
1293	*Vacant*	—	—
1294	Celestine V	—	—
1294-1303	Boniface VIII	—	—
1303-04	Benedict XI	—	—
1305-14	Clement V A	—	—
1309-12	—	—	—
1310	—	—	*Vacant*
1311-32	—	—	Eilif [?the Short] N
[1313]-16	—	—	—
1316-34	John XXII A	—	—
1317-19	—	—	—
1320-[?]	—	—	—
1328-30	—	Nicholas I	—
?	—	—	—
1333-46	—	—	Paul N
1334-42	Benedict XII A	—	—
1342-52	Clement VI	—	—
1343-48	—	—	—
1346-49	—	—	Arne N
[1347-49]	—	—	—
1356-70	—	—	Olaf I N
[1350]-59	—	—	—
1352-62	Innocent VI A	—	—
1359-69	—	—	—
1362-70	Urban V A	—	—
1370-78	Gregory XI A	—	—
1371-81	—	—	Thrand N
[?]	—	—	—

Rival Archbishop	Bishop of Faroes	Remarks
—	—	—
—	—	—
—	—	—
—	Erlend K	—
—	—	—
—	—	—
—	—	—
—	—	—
—	—	—
—	—	—
—	—	—
—	—	—
—	—	—
—	—	—
—	—	—
—	—	—
—	—	—
—	—	—
—	—	—
—	*Vacant*	See pp. 68-69 for reasons
—	—	—
—	—	—
—	Lodin K	Date of consecration uncertain
—	—	—
—	*Vacant*	—
—	Signar K	Date of death or ceasing to be Bishop of Faroes uncertain, but was alive in 1321
—	—	—
—	Gevard K	Mentioned in 1329 and in 1337 or 1339
—	—	—
—	—	—
—	—	—
—	Havard K	—
—	—	—
—	*Vacant*	Dates doubtful
—	—	—
—	Arne I K	Date of consecration or translation uncertain
—	—	—
—	Arne II Svaela K	—
—	—	—
—	—	—
—	—	—
—	Arnold K	Doubtful

Period	Pope	Rival Pope	Archbishop
1373-89	Urban VI	—	—
1378-94	Clement VII A	—	A
[1381]	—	—	—
1382-86	—	—	Nicholas Finkenoge (? the Drunkard)
1385-?	—	—	—
1387-1402	—	—	Vinald N
[?]	—	—	—
1389-1404	Boniface IX	—	—
[1392]	—	—	—
1394-1417/24	—	Benedict XIII A	—
1403	—	—	*Vacant*
1404-06	Innocent VII	—	—
1404-26	—	—	Eskil N
1406-15	Gregory XII	—	—
1408-[30]	—	—	—
1409-10	—	Alexander V P	—
1410-15	—	John XXIII P	—
1416	*Vacant*	—	—
1417-31	Martin V	—	—
1424-29	—	Clement VIII	—
1429	—	—	*Vacant*
1430-50	—	—	Aslak Bolt N
1431-47	Eugene IV	—	—
1431-34	—	—	—
[1434]	—	—	—
1434-[?]	—	—	—
1439-49	—	Felix V	—

Rival Archbishop	Bishop of Faroes	Remarks
—	—	—
—	—	—
—	Richard	Jóannes Patursson places him in 1385 and states that he probably never came to the Faroes
—	—	—
—	William Northbrigg	An Englishman. Jóannes Petursson places him in 1385 and states that he probably never came to the Faroes.
—	Vigbald or Vigbold K	Dates uncertain. Mentioned as in office in 1391 and 1394.
—	Halgeir	Possibly never consecrated. His date conflicts with that of Bishop Vigbald, see pp. 70-71. Final date doubtful
—	—	—
—	—	—
—	John I the German K	He died before May, 1431
—	—	—
—	—	—
—	—	—
—	—	Although Aslak Bolt was in Nidaros from 1428 his appointment was not confirmed until 1430
—	—	
—	Severin K	Doubt is expressed as to whether he ever went to the Faroes, see DN Vol. XVII B at p. 291
—	John II the Dominican K	Jóannes Patursson dates him from 1430.
—	John III The Chief	According to Jóannes Patursson he was bishop of the Faroes until 1447, but this conflicts with other evidence (see p. 105) and with the dates of Bishop **Hemming**.
—	—	—

135

Period	Pope	Rival Pope	Archbishop
[1441/2-51]	—	—	—
1447-55	Nicholas V	—	—
1451	—	—	*Vacant*
1452-58	—	—	Henrik Kaltisen N
[1452-53]	—	—	—
[1453-?]	—	—	—
[?]	—	—	—
1455-58	Calixtus III	—	—
1458-64	Pius II	—	—
1459-74	—	—	Olaf II N
1464-71	Paul II	—	—
1471-84	Sixtus IV	—	—
1475-1510	—	—	Gaute N
1484-92	Innocent VIII	—	—
[1486-1520]	—	—	—
1492-1503	Alexander VI	—	—
1503	Pius III	—	—
1503-13	Julius II	—	—
1510-22	—	—	Erik Valkendorf N
1513-21	Leo X	—	—
[?]-[1532]	—	—	—
1522-23	Adrian VI	—	—
1523-34	Clement VII	—	—
1523-37	—	—	Olaf III N
[1532-38]	—	—	—
1534-39	Paul III	—	—

Rival Archbishop	Bishop of Faroes	Remarks
—	Hemming K	Dates uncertain. Mentioned as in office in 1442, 1443, 1450 and 1451. According to Jóannes Patursson he was Bishop of Faroes from 1442 to 1451
—	—	—
—	—	—
—	—	Allowed to retire on pension. Died in 1464
—	*Vacant*	Dates uncertain
—	John IV	Dates uncertain
—	Matthew II	Dates uncertain
—	—	—
—	—	—
—	—	—
—	—	—
—	—	—
—	—	—
Hilary	—	Dates uncertain
—	—	—
—	—	—
—	—	—
—	—	—
—	Chilianus	Date of consecration uncertain. He died in or before 1532
—	—	—
—	—	—
—	—	Fled from Norway in 1537 and died in 1538
—	Amund	The exact dates when Amund was appointed and when he relinquished his office are uncertain
—	—	—

Above: A Faroese bird-catcher on Mykines. Below: Typical weather near Eiði on Eysturoy. (By courtesy of Asmundur Poulsen, Tórshavn.)

APPENDIX 3

THE DECREE OF KING MAGNUS VI THE LAW REFORMER, SON OF HAKON, MADE FOR THE FAROES IN THE SPRING OF 1271

Magnus, by the mercy of God, King of Norway, son of King Hakon, sends to all God's friends in the Faroes God's greetings and his own.

By the mercy of God and because of the obedience which our subjects have shown to us here as in other places around our Kingdom, we have to consider what matters are essential for our subjects, and it is our wish that all men should know that we have agreed to confirm[1], according to your petition and the advice of all the best men[2], all the laws which run through the community of the *Gulating*[3] except the agricultural law, which should remain the same as previously set out in your own law book.

We do not want a district officer[4] to have more than two officials. It is our wish to give you this decree, for our salvation and that of our forefathers, that, if anyone is fined, two thirds of the fine should be waived, but that the remainder of what is stated in the book should stand confirmed. We have also promised you that two ships which are most advantageous for you should ply between Norway and the Faroes. We have further been told that there are many men who cheat men of money and property by lies and for that reason it is our will that all men should know that whoever is found guilty of telling a man such a thing and has not proved it with witnesses shall surely know that if he is convicted of the offence, he shall owe that same amount to the person from whom he has taken the money or property. This law was enacted at Tønsberg in the eighth year of our reign[5]. Chancellor Aki put his seal on this document but Bødvar the Clerk has written it.

1 Viz, as law in the Faroes.
2 See p. 82 *ante*.
3 See p. 83 *ante*.
4 The *Syslamaður*.
5 King Magnus VI came to the throne in 1263, so this decree, which was enacted in the eighth year of his reign, must have been made in 1271, not in 1273 as is mentioned in DF and in R vol. I p. 114 and in S, facing page.

APPENDIX 4

THE SHEEP LETTER

PART I

TRANSLATION OF STOCKHOLM COPY
BY MICHAEL BARNES, M.A.

Hákon, by the grace of God, Duke of Norway[1], son of King Magnus the Crowned, sends God's greetings and his own to all men in the Faroes who see or hear this document. Our spiritual father and dearest friend, Erlendr[2], bishop of the Faroes, and Sidurðr[3], lawman from Shetland, whom we had sent to you, pointed out to us on behalf of the inhabitants of the islands those things which seemed to them to be deficient in the agricultural law. We therefore caused to be drawn up on these four pages the ordinance we have made in counsel with the best men, in accordance with what we trust will be of greatest benefit to the people. But with regard to the ecclesiastical law we are unable to make any changes at the present. Let it remain as the noble lord, our father the King, had it fashioned and presented it to Bishop Erlendr[2], as the National Law[4] itself testifies. Our whole command and true desire is that both these laws be kept well and carefully, saving the honour of the Crown and of our successors, until such time as we decide to make a new law in counsel with the wisest men, in accordance with our knowledge and the understanding given us by God of what would be most beneficial to the people. In confirmation we had our seal placed on this ordinance which was issued in Oslo on the Saturday after the feast of St. John the Baptist (28 June) in the year of Our Lord 1298, in the nineteenth year of our dukedom[5]. It was sealed by Aki, the chancellor, and written by Teitr, the priest. Bárðr Pétrsson, our scribe, wrote the letter.

1. The next thing is that the following items are those which my lord, the Duke, has granted us, and which are most beneficial to our country although they do not appear in the law code which our noble

lord, King Magnus the Crowned, gave us and which was accepted at the General Assembly[6]. If a man goes into another man's pasture and drives away his livestock, doing half a *mork's*[7] worth of damage, he is to make a personal atonement to the man who owns the livestock, according to his situation, and pay half a *mork* of silver[8] to the king, and he is to provide the owner with fresh livestock as good as he had before. But if a man accuses another of having been in his pasture with dogs and of having inflicted damage on him in that way, he is to make atonement in accordance with a lawful judgement, provided there are witnesses. But if he denies the charge, he is to make his denial in accordance with the law, and those who own sheep or pasture land jointly (with him) are to be informed and summoned to a meeting at their common fold with three days' notice. But anyone who refuses to come to the meeting without a lawful excuse is to pay a fine of two *aurar* of silver[9] to the king. But wherever men own sheep or pasture land jointly, there are not to be more dogs than all sensible men are agreed on, and all the dogs are to be equally available to them all.

2. But if a man leases land from another and the rent is not paid before he leaves the land, the landlord is to take possession of the crops. But if a man leases land from another and has not the money to pay his rent when he leaves the land in the spring, he is to have paid it all by Ólafsvaka[10] (29th July), or the landlord is to take possession of his crops, unless their value is less than that of the rent. Now a tenant leaves his land and another man takes over. Each of them is to work on the land he used to farm in such a way that the new tenant suffers no loss. But if men leave the land they are on during the winter and move so far away that they are unable to attend to their corn or look after it themselves, then the new tenant must fence it in and look after it, reap it and thresh it, and by doing so gain a quarter of the corn and the straw. But if the corn is spoilt, he is to make good corn damage to the owner of the land, to be fixed by judgement, and pay two *aurar* of silver[9] to the king.

3. Then there are those men who force themselves upon others for no good reason and stay with them for five nights or longer. They are to pay a fine of three *aurar*[11] to the king, except in cases where household servants might go to take up a new position, or are sent on business by their master. All the poor may go and ask for alms with impunity. Then there are also those whom householders take in; if they do so, they are to pay a fine of three *aurar* of silver[12] to the king and another three *aurar*[12] to you(?).

4. We have also heard about the bad custom concerning sheep and their young which has been more prevalent in this country than it ought, and about which it does not befit us to remain silent any longer; rather we should take steps to put an end to it so that every man may enjoy what is his by law. If two men or more put their sheep to graze on the same land, and both want to slaughter their animals—first of all those which are unmarked, whether they be lambs or sheep—then, with the help of his dog or by some other means, each takes all the unmarked ones he can get, whether he owns them or not. Now since it seems to us and to wise

men that it cannot accord with our dignity that lawlessness break out in the country or wrongfully prosper, we hereby issue that decree and ordinance: if a man wishes to take his lambs or those of his sheep (for slaughter) which are unmarked, he is to produce the testimony of two trustworthy men to the effect that they are his sheep and that they (the men) know the dam. But if this testimony fails, he is to make such amends as if the animals were not his property.

5. Now if pastures lie adjacent outside the home-fields, and two men each have their own piece of pasture land, and the sheep belonging to one of the men invade the pasture of the other and graze there constantly and the owner of the pasture objects, then the owner of the sheep is to move them all back into his pasture. Now these sheep go back into the same pasture from which they were removed and do this a second and a third time; they may then be taken without compensation being paid to their owner, unless the owner of the pasture is willing to accept rent for the use of his land—twenty ells[13] of *vaðmál*[14] for each *sheep mork*[15]. But if he will not have rent then the owner of the sheep is to offer to sell him half of them. Now if he will neither buy, nor take any rent, then the owner of the sheep is to remove them from the pasture at his own convenience, and they are to be removed within a year. Now the owner of the sheep refuses either to offer rent or to sell to the owner of the pasture; the sheep may then be taken with impunity as before. Sheep are to be driven down from the pasture where they normally graze and each man is to maintain the (common) folds according to the number of sheep he owns. But if men act in any other way, they are to pay a fine of three *aurar* of silver[12] to the king and compensation as prescribed by the law to any sheep owner if damage occurs. Now if men are at a common fold and there are many who own sheep there, each is to mark lambs according to the number of ewes he owns and to take note of how many ewes have twins. Similarly if strange sheep get into the fold, the shepherds are to take note of how many of the ewes have lambs and to mark a lamb for every ewe that is not barren. But if anyone incorrectly marks sheep in this fold, as soon as they are recognised they are to be returned to their rightful owner, if he is able to prove his ownership, or he is to have other sheep of equal value. But the man who incorrectly marked sheep in a common fold is not liable to any penalty. Now several men graze (their sheep) together on one pasture and one or more of them wishes to tame his sheep, while others do not. In that case the man who wishes to tame his sheep and improve them is to have his way, and not the one who would spoil them. Now a man who owns tame sheep drives them into a fold and wild sheep get in amongst them: he is to quieten them down and not to drive them in among the tame sheep. But if he drives his wild sheep in among another man's tame sheep, causing him loss and damage, he is to pay him a personal atonement for the damage and compensation for malice as the law prescribes. He is further to pay three *aurar* of silver[12] to the king and to tame those of his sheep which remain on that pasture land. Now if men walk alone through pasture land without letting anyone who has sheep there know and (one of them)

wrongly puts his mark on a lamb belonging to one of those who share the pasture without informing him, and the lambs were previously unmarked, then he has marked in secret and is to pay compensation to the owner to be fixed by judgement. He is also to pay three *merkr*[11] to the king if it is valued at one *eyrir*. If it is worth less, it is a case of pilfering. But if he marks sheep which are already marked and puts his mark over that of the owner, he is a thief.

6. Now if men take dogs which are confirmed sheep worriers into pasture land and they attack the sheep, the owner is to be compensated with sheep as good as those he owned before; and if the dog attacks sheep again, the owner is to pay the same compensation he would pay if he had slaughtered them himself. But if the dogs which men have agreed are to be used in the pastures harm any sheep, then the man the dog follows is to compensate the owner with sheep as good as those he had before and so be warned to keep his dog under control. A dog is a sheep worrier if it harms sheep more than once or goes off into a pasture of its own accord to attack sheep. The number of sheep to be kept on an area of pasture land shall be the same as it was in previous times, unless men see that it can accommodate more. In that case they are to have as many sheep as they agree on, and each man is to keep a flock proportionate to the size of his pasture. The same applies to other forms of livestock, cattle or horses. No-one is to keep a greater number than has previously been agreed upon by everyone. And no-one is to keep animals in any man's pasture but his own; but if he does, he is to answer for it as the law prescribes.

7. Something must also be said about men who set up house in some poor croft as soon as they have sufficient food for half a year. Now from now on no man who owns less than three cows[17] is to set up house on his own; but if anyone provides a man who owns less with land, both of them are to pay a fine of an *eyrir*[18] to the king. And no other men are to set up on their own except those who are unable to find any (other) means of livelihood with which to support themselves. Similarly, with regard to servants who run away from their masters without good reason, no-one is to keep them for more than three nights, but if they do keep them longer, they are to make such payments as the National Law[14] stipulates for men who take away another's servants.

8. Now if a farmer's servants find a whale out at sea and cut off sufficient to make a boatload, they are to have a seventh of it; but if they bring a whale ashore uncut, they are to have the amount stipulated by the National Law[4]. Now men drive a whale ashore, kill it and get it safe above high water mark, but do not themselves own the land above the shore; they are to have a quarter share. The same applies to driftwood. But if men find cattle or sheep or any other animal out at sea and bring it ashore, they are (also) to have a quarter share.

9. And then concerning men who stay here over the winter whom farmers invite to live with them, there is the question of how much farmers are to take for keeping them for a year. Those who do not have ale, but the same food as the farmer are to pay three hundred and sixty ells[20]

of *vaðmál*[4]. But a man who has ale with his meals on holy days and fast days is to pay four hundred and eighty ells of *vaðmál,* and one who has ale every day six hundred ells[21].

10. The next matter is that if a man fills another man's pasture with his sheep and refuses to remove them in spite of the owner's objections, the owner is to give him notice to clear his pasture within a given period. The first period is to run from Ólafsvaka[10] to the feast of St. Andrew (30th November). But if the sheep have not been removed by the end of this period and no reasonable excuse is offered, the owner of the pasture gains possession of a third of the sheep. The second period runs from the feast of St. Andrew to the beginning of Lent. But if the sheep have not been removed by the end of this period and no reasonable excuse is offered, the owner of the pasture gains possession of two-thirds of the sheep. The third period runs from Lent to Ólafsvaka[10]. But if the sheep have still not been removed by the end of this period, the owner of the pasture gains possession of all the sheep, unless their removal was prevented by genuine difficulties which their owner's neighbours know about and which wise men consider a reasonable excuse. Now if it is considered that genuine difficulties have prevented the owner from removing his sheep, although he wished to do so, he is to receive payment for all those of his sheep which remain in the other man's pasture. It is also laid down that the only sheep which are constant grazers in another man's pasture are those which graze there through the winter and lamb there in the spring. But where men's pastures share a boundary line and their sheep visit each other, the man who wishes to go to the boundary line is to send word to the owner of the adjacent pasture, and they are both to go together. But if either of them refuses to go, then the man who sent for the other is to go into his own pasture, but not into the other's without lawful witnesses. Now if he goes across the boundary line into the other man's pasture, he is to answer for it as though he had not sent the other man word. But if no word is sent and he goes (across) all the same, he is liable to answer any charge the man who remained at home cares to make and (is liable for) all the damage which resulted from his trip up to the pasture on that day and (to pay) such compensation for malice as the National Law[4] prescribes, and three *aurar* of silver[12] to the king. But if men own pasture land jointly and have wild sheep and some wish to tame them while others do not, then the man who wishes to tame them and improve his sheep is to have his way, and not the man who is causing them both damage. But otherwise the man who refuses to bring them in is to take responsibility for any damage that is caused by his neighbour's sheep, unless there is some good reason why he could not do so.

11. We have also decided that those pieces of whale which we call "killer cuts", or pieces which have been drifting for so long that they cannot be salted, are to be given to the person who owns the land where they drift ashore. This is for the sake of God and of our father and mother, to bring us peace and prosperity, and is to be done in the following way; it (the whale) is first to be shown to two witnesses, and

they are to reach some decision about it—unless our successors feel that this is against the interests of the Crown.

12. Then there are those who harm good men in word or deed and rely on their poverty, having nothing with which to pay compensation. They are to have such punishment as twelve wise men lawfully appointed by the justiciary shall decide [22]. Now if a man is present at a quarrel, or when men strike a bargain, and he refuses to give testimony about it when lawfully summoned, he is to pay a *mork* of silver [23] to the king for each refusal, until such time as he gives the testimony [24].

PART II

TRANSLATION OF THE LUND COPY BY MICHAEL BARNES, M.A.

The rettarbœtr of the noble lord, King Hákon

Hákon, by the grace of God, Duke of Norway [1], son of King Magnús the Crowned, sends God's greetings and his own to all men in the Faroes who see or hear this document. Our spiritual father and dearest friend, Erlendr [2], bishop of the Faroes, and Sigurðr [3], lawman from Shetland, whom we have sent to you, pointed out to us on behalf of the inhabitants of the islands those things which seemed to them to be deficient in the agricultural law. We therefore caused to be drawn up on these four pages the ordinance we have made in counsel with the best men, in accordance with what we trust will be of greatest benefit to the people. But with regard to the ecclesiastical law we are unable to make any changes at present. Let it remain as our noble lord and father, the King, had it fashioned and presented it to Bishop Erlendr [2], as the National Law [4] itself testifies. Our whole command and true desire is that both these laws be kept well and carefully, saving the honour of the Crown and of our successors, until such time as we decide to make a new law in counsel with the wisest men, in accordance with our knowledge and the understanding given us by God of what will be most beneficial to the people. In confirmation we placed our seal on this ordinance which was issued in Oslo on the Saturday after the feast of St. John the Baptist (28th June) in the year of Our Lord 1298, in the nineteenth year of our dukedom [5]. It was sealed by Aki, the chancellor, and Teitr, the priest, wrote the text, Bárðr Pétrsson, our scribe, wrote the letter.

Here begin the rettarboetr of King Hákon, son of King Magnus.

1. We have also heard about the bad custom concerning sheep which has been more prevalent in the country than it ought, and which it does not befit us to allow to continue, so that everyone may have what is his. Now if two men or more put their sheep to graze on the same land,

and both want to slaughter their animals—first of all those which are unmarked, whether they be lambs or sheep—then, with the help of his dog or by some other means, each takes all the sheep he can get whether he owns them or not. Now since it seems to us and to other wise men that it does not accord with our dignity that lawlessness break out in the country, we hereby issue our decree: if a man wishes to take any lambs or those of his sheep that are unmarked (for slaughter), he is to produce the testimony of two trustworthy men to the effect that they are his sheep and that they (the men) know the dam. But if their testimony fails, he is to make amends for what was not legally his.

Concerning going into pasture land and accusations.

2. If a man goes into another man's pasture and drives away his livestock, doing half a *mork's*[7] worth of damage, he is to make a personal atonement to the man who owned the livestock, according to his situation, and pay half a *mork* of silver[8] to the king, and he is to provide the owner with livestock as good as he had before. But if a man accuses another of having been in his pasture with dogs and of having inflicted damage on him, he is to make atonement in accordance with a lawful judgement, provided there are witnesses. Otherwise he is to make a denial which amounts to what sensible men consider lawful, and the man who owns sheep or pasture land jointly (with him) is to be informed and summoned to a meeting at their common fold with three days' notice. But anyone who fails to come to the meeting without a lawful excuse is to pay two *aurar* of silver[9] to the king. Now wherever men own sheep or pasture land jointly, there are not to be more dogs than all the most sensible men are agreed on, and they are to be equally available to them all.

If sheep should invade another man's pasture, and concerning the driving of sheep down from pastures.

3. Now if pastures lie adjacent outside the homefields, and two men each have their own piece of pasture land, and the sheep belonging to one of the men invade the pasture of the other and graze there constantly and the owner of the pasture objects, then the owner of the sheep is to move them back into his pasture. Now these sheep go back into the same pasture a second time and a third; they may then be taken without compensation being paid to their owner, unless the owner of the pasture is willing to accept rent for the use of his land—twenty ells[13] of *vaðmál*[14] for each *sheep mork*[15]. If he will not have rent, then the owner of the sheep is to offer to sell him half of them. Now he will neither buy, nor take any rent; then the owner of the sheep is to remove them from the pasture at his own convenience, and they are to be removed within a year. Now the owner of the sheep refuses either to offer rent or to sell half the sheep to the owner of the pasture; the sheep may then be taken with impunity. Sheep are to be driven down from the pasture where they normally graze and each man is to maintain the (common) folds according to the number of sheep he owns. But if men act in any other way they are to pay three *aurar* to the king[25] and compensation as

prescribed by the law to any sheep owner if damage occurs. Now men are at common folds; each man is to mark lambs according to the number of ewes he owns and to take note of how many ewes have twins. And if strange sheep get into the fold, the shepherds are to take note of how many of the ewes have lambs and to mark a lamb for every ewe that is not barren. Now someone incorrectly marks sheep in a common fold; as soon as they are recognised they are to be returned to their rightful owner, if he is able to prove his ownership, or he is to have other sheep of equal value. But a man who incorrectly marks sheep in a common fold is not liable to any penalty.

Concerning the taming of sheep.
    4. Now many men graze their sheep together on one pasture, and one or some of them wish to tame their sheep while others do not. In that case the man who wishes to tame his sheep and improve them (is to) have his way, and not the one who would spoil them. Now a man who owns tame sheep drives them (into a fold) and wild sheep get in amongst them; he is to quieten them down and not to drive them in among the tame sheep. Now he drives wild sheep in among another man's tame sheep, causing him damage; he is to pay the man a personal atonement and compensation for malice as the law prescribes. He is also to pay a fine of three *aurar* of silver to the king and to tame those of his sheep which remain on that pasture land.

Concerning sheep—(?)
    5. Now men walk alone through pasture land without letting anyone who has sheep there know and (one of them) wrongly puts his mark on a lamb belonging to one of those who share the pasture without informing him—and the sheep were previously unmarked; in that case he has marked in secret and is to pay compensation to the owner to be fixed by judgement. He is also to pay three *aurar* of silver [26] to the king, if it is valued at one *eyrir* [18]. If it is worth less, it is a case of pilfering. Now he marks sheep which are already marked and puts his mark over that of the owner; in that case he is a thief.

Concerning sheep worriers and the number of sheep to be kept on an area of pasture land.
    6. But if men take dogs which are confirmed sheep worriers into pasture land and they attack the sheep, the owner is to be compensated with sheep of equal value. If the dog attacks sheep again, the owner is to pay the same compensation he would pay if he had slaughtered them himself. If the dogs which men have agreed are to be used in the pastures harm any sheep, the man the dog follows is to compensate the owner with sheep as good as those he had before, and so be warned to keep it under control. Dogs are sheep worriers if they harm sheep more than once or if one goes off into a pasture of its own accord to attack sheep. The number of sheep to be kept on an area of pasture land shall be the same as it was in previous times, unless men see that it can accommodate more. In that case they are to have as many sheep as they agree on. But

they are not to fill the pasture with more cattle or sheep than their proper share—the number which has previously been agreed by everyone. And no-one is to keep animals in any man's pasture but his own, or he is to answer for it as the law prescribes.

Concerning notice to remove sheep.
7. But if a man fills another man's pasture with his sheep and refuses to remove them in spite of the owner's objections, the owner is to give him notice to clear his pasture within given periods. The first period is to run from Ólafsvaka [10] (29th July) to the feast of St. Andrew (30th November). If the sheep have not been removed by the end of this period and no reasonable excuse is offered, the owner of the pasture gains possession of a third of the sheep. The second period runs from the feast of St. Andrew to the beginning of Lent. If the sheep have not been removed by the end of this period and no reasonable excuse is offered, the owner of the pasture gains possession of two-thirds of the sheep. The third period runs from Lent up to Ólafsvaka [10]. If the sheep have not been removed by the end of this period and no reasonable excuse is offered, the owner of the pasture gains possession of all the sheep, unless their removal was prevented by genuine difficulties which their owner's neighbours know about and which men consider a reasonable excuse. [Now if it is considered that genuine difficulties [27]] have prevented the owner from removing his sheep, although he wished to do so, he is to receive payment for all those of his sheep which remain in the other man's pasture. It is also laid down that the only sheep which are constant grazers in another man's pasture are those which lamb there and graze there all through the winter.

8. Now where men's pastures are contiguous and their sheep visit each other, the man who wishes to go to the boundary line is to send word to the owners of the adjacent pasture, and they (are) both (to) go together. If either of them refuses to go, then the one who sent for the other is to go into his own pasture, but not into the other's. Now he goes across the boundary line into the other man's pasture; he is to answer for it as though he had not sent him word. Now no word is sent and he goes (across) all the same; he is liable to answer any charge the man who remained at home cares to make and (is liable for) all the damage which resulted from his trip up to the pasture on that day and (to pay) such compensation for malice as the National Law prescribes, and three *aurar* of silver to the king.

Concerning the taming of sheep.
9. Now if men own pasture land jointly and have wild sheep and some wish to tame them while others do not, then the man who wishes to tame them is to have his way; otherwise the man who refuses to bring them in is to take responsibility for all the resulting damage to the other man's sheep, unless there is some good reason why he could not do so.

Concerning rent.
10. If a man leases land from another and the rent is not paid

before he leaves the land, the landlord gains possession of the crops. But if a man leases land from another and has not the money to pay his rent when he leaves the land in the spring, he is to have paid it all by Ólafsvaka, or the landlord is to take possession of the crops and receive the rent as well. Now a tenant leaves his land and another man takes it over. Each of them is to work on the land he used to farm in such a way that the new tenant suffers no loss. But if men leave the land they have been on during the winter and move so far that they are unable to attend to their corn or look after it, then the new tenant must fence it in and look after it, reap it and thresh it, and by doing so gain a quarter of the corn and the straw. But if the corn is spoilt, he is to make good corn damage to the man who owned the land, to be fixed by judgement, and pay two *aurar* of silver [9] to the king.

Concerning householders.

11. Then there are those men who force themselves upon others for no good reason and stay with them for five nights or longer. They are to pay three *aurar* [11] to the king, except in cases where household servants go to take up a new position, or are sent on business by their master. All the poor may go and ask for food and alms with impunity. Then there are also those whom householders take in; if they do so, they are to pay three *aurar* [12] to the king and another three to you [12]. Then there are those who harm good men in word or deed and rely on their poverty (i.e. to avoid payment of compensation). They are to have such punishment as wise men think fit, and are to go into jail and remain there as long as the seriousness of their crime dictates. They are also to be flogged on leaving jail, since the Duke does not wish people who do that sort of thing to go without punishment, neither men nor women [28].

Concerning testimony.

12. If a man is present at a quarrel, or when men strike a bargain, and he refuses to give testimony about it when lawfully called upon to do so, he is to pay a *mork* of silver [21] to the king for each refusal, until such time as he gives the testimony. Now if men are present when bargains are struck or where there is some matter about which people disagree, and they afterwards side with either of the parties, they are not to give testimony even though called upon to do so, unless no other witnesses can be found who are impartial and more trustworthy [29].

Concerning payment for alimentation.

13. And then there are men who stay here over the winter whom farmers invite to live with them. There is the question of how much farmers are to take for keeping them for a year. Those who do not have ale, but the same food as the farmer, are to pay three hundred and sixty ells [19] of *vaðmál* [14]. But a man who has ale with his meals on holy days and fast days is to pay four hundred and eighty ells [20] of *vaðmál* [14], and one who has ale every day six hundred ells [21].

Concerning households.

14. And then there are men who set up house in some poor croft as

soon as they have half a year's supply of food. But from now on no man who owns less than three cows[17] is to set up (house) on his own; but if anyone provides a man who owns less with land, he is to pay an *eyrir* of silver[18]. And no other men are to set up on their own except those who are unable to find any (other) employment with which to support themselves. Similarly, with regard to servants who run away from their master without good reason, no-one is to keep them for more than three nights, or they are to make such payments as the National Law[4] stipulates for men who take away another man's servants.

Concerning the finding of (dead) whales.

15. If a farmer's servants find a whale out at sea and cut off sufficient to make a boatload, they are to have a seventh of it. Now they bring a whale ashore uncut; they are to have the amount stipulated by the National Law[4]. Now men drive a whale ashore and get it safe above high water mark, but do not themselves own the land above the shore; they are to have a quarter share. The same applies to drift-wood, cattle or sheep or any other animal; if men find these things out at sea and bring them ashore, they are to have a quarter share.

Concerning flotsam.

16. We have decided that those pieces of whale which we call "killer cuts" are to be given to the people who own the land where they drift ashore. This is for the sake of God and of the soul of our father, to bring us peace and prosperity, and is to be done in the following way: it (the whale) is first to be shown to two trustworthy men, and they are to reach a decision about it—unless our successors feel that this is in some way against the interests of the Crown.

PART III

NOTES ON THE SHEEP LETTER

1. In fact, Hákon was the Duke of Oppland, Oslo, the Shetlands and the Faroes, and not the Duke of the whole of Norway, see p. 51 *ante*.
2. Referred to in the body of the book as Erlend.
3. Referred to in the body of the book as Sigurd.
4. The *Gulating law*, see p. 51 *ante*.
5. Hákon got the title "Duke" in 1273 (see p. 51 *ante*) when he was three years old, although the *Sheep Letter* seems to indicate that he became Duke on his father's death, i.e. in 1280.
6. The Faroese Thing held at Tinganes.
7. i.e. half a mark. It is assumed that the references in the Sheep Letter to a mark and to a mark silver and also to an øre and to an øre of silver are to mint silver and not to pure silver. Applying the "butter test" (See p. 111 *ante*) half a mark would be worth £14 today.

8   See note 7 above. Here, however, are the additional words "of silver".
9   i.e. two ører. Applying the test mentioned in note 7 above the fine would be £7 at present-day values.
10 Otherwise *Olafsøka* or St. Olaf's Day or Wake.
11 i.e. three ører. Applying the test mentioned in note 7 above the fine would be £10.50 at present-day values.
12 See note 11 above. Here, however, the words "of silver" are added in the first reference and would also appear to apply to the second one.
13 One ell equals about 0.6277m or about 2 feet.
14 Homespun. The width of a piece of the material is about 36 inches. The value of 360 ells of homespun would have been 3 marks mint silver, see p. 111 *ante*.
15 There is some doubt as to what this exactly means. It possibly means 20 ells of homespun as rent for every 6 (or, on occasions 8) sheep which used the land, see FB p. 16 and p. 111 *ante*. The value of 20 ells of homespun would have been 1/6 mark or 8 *skinns*, see pp. 111-112 *ante*.
16 i.e. three marks. Applying the test mentioned in note 7 above the fine would be £84 but see note 24 below on para. 5 of the Lund Copy which deals with the same offence.
17 The equivalent money value of 3 cows would have been 3 marks of mint silver, see p. 111 *ante*.
18 i.e. one øre. Applying the test mentioned in note 7 above the present-day value would be £3.50.
19 About 720 feet, value 3 marks mint silver, see p. 111 *post*.
20 About 960 feet, value 4 marks mint silver, see p. 111 *post*.
21 About 1200 feet, value 5 marks mint silver, see p. 111 *post*.
22 The penalty in the second sentence differs substantially from the corresponding one in the last two sentences of Article 11 of the Lund Copy.
23 i.e. a mark. Applying the test mentioned in note 7 above this amount would be £28 today.
24 See Article 12 of the Lund Copy which contains an extra sentence.
25 The words "a fine" which appear in Article 4 of the Stockholm Copy are omitted here and the words "of silver" appear here and not in the Stockholm Copy.
26 i.e. three ører. In applying the test mentioned in note 7 above, the amount would be £10.50. This amount differs from the Stockholm Copy, see note 16 above.
27 Taken from A, see S, p. 56, column 3, note 1.
28 The reference to flogging does not appear in the Stockholm Copy, see Part 1, Article 12.
29 There is no provision in the Stockholm Copy corresponding to the second sentence of this Article.

PART IV

TABLE OF COMPARISON BETWEEN STOCKHOLM AND LUND COPIES

Stockholm copy		Subject matter	Lund copy		Remarks
Preamble		Preamble	Preamble		—
Article 1	First sentence	Introductory	—		—
	Remainder	Driving away another person's livestock	Article 2		—
Article 2		Rented land and crops on such land	Article 10		—
Article 3		Uninvited guests, authorised begging and restriction on taking people in	Article 11	First four sentences	Minor difference.
Article 4		Unmarked sheep	Article 1		—
Article 5	First ten sentences	Sheep straying into adjoining owner's pasture, common folds and marking lambs	Article 3		Minor differences.
	Next five sentences	Tame and wild sheep	Article 4		—
	Remainder	Illegally marking sheep, pilfering and stealing sheep	Article 5		Substantial difference in penalties, the Stockholm copy referring to "*merkr*", and the Lund copy to "*aurar*".
Article 6		Sheep worrying dogs and stocking of pastures	Article 6		Certain differences in later sentences.
Article 7		Prohibition of small crofters and restrictions on housing run-away servants	Article 14		—
Article 8		Shares in whales, driftwood, cattle and other things swept in by the sea	Article 15		—
Article 9		Scale of charges for winter lodgers	Article 13		—
Article 10	First eight sentences	Provision relating to a person who puts his sheep on another owner's pasture and fails to remove them after notice	Article 7		—

Stockholm copy		Subject matter	Lund copy		Remarks
	Next four sentences	About trespassing without notice on wrong side of common boundary, etc.	Article	8	Certain differences.
	Remainder	Taming sheep on common pasture	Article	9	—
Article 11		Dead whales as flotsam	Article	16	Certain differences.
Article 12	First two sentences	Punishment for defamation or committing torts, having no money to pay compensation	Article 11	Fifth sentence to end	Considerable differences in penalties.
	Remainder	Penalty for refusing to testify, having witnessed a quarrel, or the striking of a bargain	Article 12	First sentence	—
		Witnesses to the striking of a bargain or a matter in dispute who side with one of the parties not to testify	Article 12	Remainder	—

153

A fine portrait study of a weather-beaten Faroese fisherman in traditional dress. (By courtesy of Asmundur Poulsen, Tórshavn.)

APPENDIX 5

TRANSLATION OF DOCUMENT ABOUT GOODS AND PROPERTY (INCLUDING HEREDITARY PROPERTY) OF GUDRUN, DAUGHTER OF SIGURD

1403—1407

DOCUMENT 1 dated 22nd AUGUST, 1403

To all men who see or hear this document we, Ketil Kristiansson, Andreas Summaldason and Ari Albriktsson, send God's greetings and our own, making known that we were present and heard Tróndur Dagfinnsson after judgement was delivered against Magnus Erlingsson concerning the Húsavík property, to which the document testifies, ask the afore-mentioned Magnus whether he had any more evidence or had the hope of any, but the afore-mentioned Magnus said that he had no more evidence and did not know of any[1] and we heard the afore-mentioned Tróndur then ask the oft-named Magnus if he saw any fault in the representation which he Tróndur had delivered in respect of Ellindur Filipsson and Magnus Erlingsson, but the said Magnus said that he did not know of any, and gave the oft-mentioned Tróndur complete quittance and release both on his own behalf and on behalf of Ellindur, and further gave the oft-named Tróndur every right of action which could come to him or his heirs in relation to the afore-mentioned Húsavík property for the pains he had taken and for the goodwill which he had had from him, everything included and without any reservations; and to signify to the truth thereof we have set our seals with the seal of Magnus on the document which was made in Tórshavn on the Wednesday before St. Bartholomew's Day in the year of our Lord 1403[2].

1 i.e. he saw no hope of obtaining any further evidence.
2 24th May.

DOCUMENT 2 dated 7th SEPTEMBER, 1403

To all men who see or hear this document we, Sjurður Birgisson and Dagfinnur Nikulasson, send God's greetings and our own, making known that we were present and heard Ingirid Oyvindardottir first testify and then swear a full oath on the Book[1] that she knew that Gudrun, Sigurd's daughter of Finngård[2], wife of Arnbjørn Gudleiksson of Húsavík, owned this property in the estate of the afore-named Arnbjørn. There was first all of Finngård[2] which contained fifteeen houses and sixty-eight rooms AND she also owned two lots of land in Brattan[3] but she *(the deponent)* did not know how many houses there were on it, AND THEN *(she owned)* three farms at Rossalandsstrand[4], one called Løfall the second Myre and the third Leitet AND THEN property in Rogalandsfylke[5] the rent for which amounted to ten creels[6] of butter a year[7], AND THEN *(she owned)* in the Shetlands, as much land as yielded forty-six shillings[8] in rent every year; AND *(she also owned)* six beds with pillows which had good fringes[9] and there went with them eiderdowns of goose-feathers and pillow-cases with good ticking[10] around all of them; THEN there was a head decoration (diadem) valued at thirteen ører[11] AND a rosary of pearls and silver[12] AND three gold finger-rings AND a "sheild-dress"[13], two silver beakers and a silver beaker with a foot or stem, three cloaks[14] with skins and kirtles[15] going with them and a surcoat[16] AND two sets of household furniture, one for the (main) room and the other for the sea room[17], with woven curtains and glittering under-curtains[19], together with fringed curtains[20], a kettle which holds six barrels, and all the beer vessels, to say nothing of jugs, dishes, pots and other cooking utensils, the number of which she did not remember, AND a large silver buckle *(or clasp)*; AND she had then taken the "full Book oath"[i] and said that she knew that the afore-mentioned Gudrun . . ."[21] hangings[22] of red and green silk AND that she had heard it said that the oft-mentioned Gudrun had owned land in Sogn[23] the rent for which amounted to ten creels[6] of butter a year[7] but she said Ingirid said that she did not dare swear on oath that she knew it; AND, to testify to the truth of above, we have placed our seals on this document which was made at Viðareiði on the Eve of the later Feast of St. Mary[24].

1 i.e. she swore on the Bible.
2 & 3 These places are on the Bryggen in Bergen in Western Norway.
4 Rossalandsstrand is believed to be in Western Norway although the modern names of the three farms cannot be traced. In the old Norse text their names are given as "a Myri", "Leiti" and "Laudu fall". Rossalandsstrand is referred to in that text as "Hrossa lands strand".
5 A county in Western Norway.
6 i.e. a Faroese *"leypur"*. The rent was based on a *"leypabol"* or *"leypsbol"* i.e. the amount of land which would produce a creel of butter in a year, see DF p. 38 footnote.
7 One creel of butter means, in this context, a creel containing about 18 kg. and would be worth 1/3 mark of mint silver, see p. 111 *ante*.
8 The value of this shilling is uncertain — possibly 1/3 or 1/4 of a mark of mint silver, see DF p. 39 note 1 and p. 113 *ante*.

9   See DF p. 39, note 2.
10 See DF p. 39, note 3.
11 A silver *øre* was worth 1/8th of a mark of mint silver, see DF p. 39, note 4.
12 See DF p. 39, note 5.
13 A type of dress with shields worked into it superimposed on a kirtle, see DF p. 39, note 6. This was probably a dress which the deceased had brought with her from Norway.
14 A cloak hung around the shoulders and worn outside the kirtle.
15 A type of woman's gown or outer petticoat.
16 An outer coat or garment, commonly of rich material, worn by people of rank of both sexes.
17 A building or room whose foundations were at sea-level or projected to some degree over the sea.
18-20 See DF p. 40, notes 1 to 3 respectively.
21 There is a hole in the original parchment which leaves a gap in the text.
22 Curtains or draperies which hang in front of a bed, see DF p. 40, note 4.
23 A place in Norway.
24 8th September, see DF p. 40, note 5.

DOCUMENT 3 dated 7th OCTOBER, 1403

To all men who see or hear this document *(we)* Joán Binarsson, priest, and Joán Nikulsson send God's greetings and our own, making known that we were present and heard Arnora, Arnbjørn's daughter, first testify and then swear a full oath on the Book[1] that Gudrun, Sigurd's daughter, who had been the lawful wife of Arnbjørn Gudleiksson, owned all of Finngård[2] and half of Brattan[3] AND *(had)* a head-decoration (diadem) valued at thirteen or fourteen *ører*[4] AND a "shield dress"[5], *(which was)* so big that the kirtle[6] covered her completely down to the waist and then went across down around her loins, AND a rosary of pearls, silver and coral[7] and under it a buckle *(or clasp)* of silver with gilt or gold AND ALSO a finger ring and two silver beakers—although she *(the deponent)* was not certain if she *(Gudrun)* owned them, but she had heard it said that she did, AND *(she had)* two cloaks[8] with accompanying kirtles, one with hooks or the like and the other with another type of hooks[9], hangings of red and green, all glittering[10], AND *(she, the deponent, said)* that she *(Gudrun)* had other headbands without ornaments[11] for use on Fridays[12], but she did not remember how many there were when she was with her, AND *(she had)* five or six eiderdowns and pillows with pillow cases with ticking[13], AND THEN *(she had)* a varnished[14] chest, ALSO washing vessels and water jars[15], vessels of tin[16] and other dishes, jars, pots and kettles *(of such a number)* that she *(the deponent)* did not know how many there were, but she *(Gudrun)* had no lack of them AND (she had) two sets of furniture with woven curtains[17] and glittering under-curtains[18] and fringed curtains[19], AND she *(the deponent)* knew that she *(Gudrun)* had land rents from the Shetlands but she *(the deponent)* did not remember how many English pounds she *(Gudrun)* received each year in respect of the said land rents, AND, to testify to the truth of the above we have placed our seals on this document at Húsar on the Sunday before the Feast of St. Dionysius[20] in the year of our Lord 1403, and *(to confirm)* that the oft-mentioned Gudrun owned all the above-named property in the estate of her husband, Arnbjørn.

1-3 See document 2 *ante* notes 1 to 3.
4 See document 2 *ante*, note 11.
5 See document 2 *ante*, note 13.
6 See document 2 *ante*, note 15.
7 See document 2 *ante*, note 12.
8 See document 2 *ante*, note 14.
9 See DF p. 42, note 1.
10 See DF p. 42, note 2.
11 See DF p. 42, note 3.
12 The day for fasting.
13 See DF p. 39, notes 2 and 3.
14 See DF p. 42, note 5.
15 See DF p. 42, note 6.
16 The word "tuifot" in the old Norse text in DF p. 42 should read "tinfot".
17-19 See DF p. 40, notes 1 to 3 respectively.
20 9th October.

DOCUMENT 4 dated 22nd MARCH, 1404

To all men who see or hear this document *(we)* Brynjolvur Torbegsson, priest of Sandoy, Jóan Olavsson and Svein Magnusson, members of the Løgting[1] from Sandoy aforesaid send God's greetings and (our) own, making known that Arnbjørn Gudleiksson, who had Gudrun, daughter of Sigurd the Shetlander, of Finngärd[2] as his lawful wife, owned Húsavík and so much of Skarvanes and Sandur as came under Húsavík AND that the above-named Arnbjørn had a legitimate son and a legitimate daughter by the aforementioned Gudrun AND that he *(the son)* was called Sigurd AND that he succeeded to the property of his father, the said Arnbjørn, AND that Sigurd's legitimate sister inherited *(that property)* from her brother, but she died AND THEN the oft-mentioned Gudrun was the next in line of inheritance after her legitimate daughter, AND, before God, we have no knowledge of anything else being the truth; AND to testify to the truth of this we have placed our seals on this document which was made at Viðareiði on the Saturday before the Feast of St. Benedict[3].

1 See Chapter 12 *ante*.
2 A place in Norway.
3 21st March.

DOCUMENT 5 dated 13th OCTOBER, 1405

To all men who see or hear this document *(we)* Joán Nikulasson and Dunaldur Haraldsson send God's greetings and *(our)* own, making known that we have been to Setr[1] in the Shetlands and heard Ragnhild Hávarðsdóttir admit that she had given her son Magnus full, legal representation over all the property which was kept by Gudrun, daughter of Sigurd, in Húsavík. We further heard Tróndur Dagfinnson tell her *(Ragnhild)* there that her son Magnus had left him and his heirs, as their property for all time, all rights of action which he could bring forward over the property which *(was left)* in the Faroes by Gudrun, Sigurd's daughter, of Húsavík, *(and)* that they were both present, she and her son, the above-named Magnus, and had both been represented there and prior to that occasion. The oft-mentioned Magnus then admitted that he had done as the above-mentioned Tróndur had testified while both were present. Then the oft-named Tróndur asked the oft-named Ragnhild if she would continually abide by the decision which her son had made, and the said Ragnhild took the above-named Tróndur by the hand and said that she would willingly abide by it and would not wish to break it after all the written testimony and proof which the oft-mentioned Tróndur had *(produced to the effect)* that Magnus had mortgaged it *(the property)* to him. This decision of theirs was given in the presence of the said Magnus, and, to testify to the truth of the above, we, the above-mentioned men, have placed over seals on this document which was made at Vindasur[3] on the last Tuesday in the summer[4] in the year of our Lord 1405.

1 Now called Setter.
2 See document 1 *ante*.
3 Now called Windos or Windus.
4 13th October (the day before the winter half of the year begins — see DF p. 46, note 2).

DOCUMENT 6 dated 9th NOVEMBER, 1405

To all men who see or hear this document *(we)* Gudbrandur Magnusson, parish priest of Jala[1] in the Shetlands, Svein Markusson, Lawman of the same country, and Joán Haraldsson, member of the Shetland's court of law, send God's greetings and our own, making known that **Ragnhild Hávarðsdóttir had not handed over the property,** but managed it herself, when Tróndur Dagfinnson came to Vindasur[2] and that she lived there *(i.e. in that house),* and to testify to the truth of this, we have placed our seals on this document, which was made at Papil[3] on the Monday before St. Martin's Day[4] in the year of our Lord 1405.

1 Now called Yell.
2 See document 5, note 3.
3 In the North-east of the island of Yell: probably the place now called Papilness.
4 11th November.

DOCUMENT 7 dated 3rd JULY, 1407

Certified Transcript of Documents 1 to 6 above

To all men who see or hear this document *(we)* Halvan, priest, son of Eirik, Tormoður Andresson, sysselman[1] in Suðuroy, and Símun Albriktsson send God's greetings and *(our)* own, making known that we saw and examined, and read over carefully, six open documents, whose seals were complete and intact and which, word for word, state as follows:—*(Here follows a transcript of documents 1, 5, 4, 6, 3 and 2 above)* And, to testify to the truth hereof, we have placed our seals on this transcript, which was made at Tórshavn on the first Sunday after St. Swithin's Day in the year of our Lord 1407.

1 District officer.
2 2nd July.

APPENDIX 6

Erecting the See of Nidaros

Papal Bull of Pope Anastasius IV

(Copied from Volume II of the *Chronicle of Man and the Sudreys*)

To all whom these presents shall come, Sweyn Dean, Ulph Archdeacon of the Church of Drontheim[1] Ingewald Prior of the Canons Regular of St. Augustine of the Holy See (Cathedral) at Drontheim[1], and Peter Prior of the Friars Preachers of the same place.

Know ye that we have seen and carefully perused the subjoined letters of the Lord Pope, Anastasius IV, of happy memory, in which there is nothing cancelled, nothing erased, nor anything in any part vitiated, guaranteed by the brown silk threads, with the leaden seal, and the signatures of the said Supreme Pontiff Anastasius, and of the Cardinals. Their tenor, together with the signatures, omitting however, here, the seals which are affixed to the document, is word for word as follows:—

Anastasius, Bishop, Servant of the servants of God, to our venerable brother John, Archbishop of Drontheim[1], and to his successors hereafter canonically appointed; in perpetual memory of the transaction. Albeit, the same power of loosing and binding was granted to all the disciples; albeit, one and the same precept of preaching the Gospel to every creature extended to all; nevertheless a certain distinction, as it were, of dignity, was observed amongst them, and the charge of the Lord's flock, which pressed equally upon all, was in a special manner received by one, the Lord saying unto him, "Peter, lovest thou me? Feed my sheep." He also, amongst all the apostles, obtained the title of prince, and received a special command from the Lord to confirm his brethren. Whereby future generations were given to understand that although many should be ordained to govern the church, yet should one exclusively be placed above all, in the position of the highest dignity, and he alone preside over all, vested with supreme jurisdiction, and charged with universal government. And hence, after this pattern, a distinction of dignities has been preserved in the Church. And as in the human body there are various members according to the diversity of the functions to be discharged, so in the structure of the Church diverse persons are placed in diverse orders, for the performance of various ministrations. For while some are appointed to regulate and govern particular churches, some particular cities, others are constituted over particular provinces, whose decision holds the first place amongst their brethren, and to whose examination are to be referred all questions and matters regarding the persons subject to them. But the Roman Pontiff, like to Noah in the Ark, is acknowledged to hold the first place above all. He, by virtue of the privilege granted to him from above in the person of the prince of the apostles, judges and decides the causes of all, never ceasing to confirm in the solidity of the Christian faith, the children of the Church throughout the world, and constantly standing forth as one who seems to have heard the voice of the Lord, saying, "And thou being once converted, confirm thy brethren." And, to conclude, the apostolic men, who after the blessed Peter, have in successive ages arisen to administer the government of the Apostolic See, have with unremitting zeal endeavoured to fulfil this injunction, and throughout the whole world, either in person or through their legates, have strenuously laboured to correct what was amiss, and provide by salutary enactments for the general welfare. Following in their footsteps, Pope Eugenius, Our predecessor of happy memory, unable, by reason of the charge which he had of the universal Church, to fulfil in person the duty of amending such things as seemed to require correction in the kingdom of Norway, and of sowing there the word of faith, performed it through his legate, our venerable brother Nicholas, Bishop of Albano, who, going into those parts in obedience to the command he had received from the father of the family, placed out at interest the talent confided to his care, and as a faithful and prudent servant laboured to return it with suitable increase. Amongst other things, which he there performed to the glory of God's name and to the commendation of his own ministry, he, in accordance with instructions he had received from Our said predecessor, conferred the pallium on thee Brother. And that the province of Norway might not ever afterwards be deprived of the care of a metropolitan, he constituted the city of Drontheim[1], which is under thy charge, perpetual metropolis of the said province, and ordained that the bishoprics of Oslo, Hamar, Bergen, Stavanger, the Orkneys[2] the Sudreys, the Icelandic Islands, and Greenland[3], should be in all future times subject to it, as to their metropolis, and that the bishops of those sees should obey thee and thy successors as their metropolitan. Wherefore, in order that no one may ever attempt to violate this constitution, we confirm it by apostolic authority, and strengthen it by the present instrument, ordaining that the city of Drontheim[1] shall in all future times be held to be the metropolis of the above mentioned cities, and that their bishops shall owe obedience to thee and to thy successors as to their metropolitans, and shall seek at thine and their hands the grace of consecration. But as to thy successors, they shall have recourse to the Roman Pontiff alone for the gift of consecration, and shall for ever be subject to him only, and to the Roman Church. And as for the pallium which has been granted to thee, and in which lies the fulness of the pontifical office, thou, brother shall wear it only in the church at the solemn office of mass on the following days: Christmas Day, the Epiphany, Maunday Thursday, Easter Sunday, Acension Day, Whitsunday, the Solemnities of the blessed Mary, Mother of God, ever a virgin, the Feast of the blessed apostles Peter and Paul, the Nativity of St. John the Baptist, the Feast of blessed John the Evangelist, the Commemoration of All Saints, at the consecration of churches or of bishops, the blessing of abbots, the ordination of priests, the day of the dedication of thy church, the Feasts of the Holy Trinity and of St. Olave, and the anniversary day of thy consecration. Wherefore, Brother, seeing that thou has received the fulness of so great a dignity, endeavour to act in all things with such earnestness that the adornments of thy good actions may be in keeping with it. Let thy life be an example to thy subjects, that from it they may learn what to seek after, and what to avoid. Be foremost in prudence, clean of heart, pure in action, discreet in thy silence, useful in thy speech; be more anxious to do good to men than to preside over them. The quality of thy nature, not the authority of thy Order, should occupy thy thoughts. See that thy life forsake not learning, nor that thy teaching, on the other hand, be in contradiction to thy life. Remember that the governing of souls is the art of arts. Let it be thy endeavour, above all things, firmly to observe the decrees of the Apostolic See, and humbly to obey her as thy mother and mistress. Behold, dearest Brother in Christ, these, amongst many others, are the duties which belong to the pallium and to the priesthood, all of which thou mayest, with the help of Christ, easily fulfill, if thou hast the mistress of all virtues charity, and humility; and if what thou outwardly showest thou possessest in thy heart. We decree thereupon that it shall not be lawful for any man rashly to disturb this same Church, or take away its possessions, or retain them when taken, or diminish them, or disturb them in any way, but let them be preserved whole and entire, for the advantage of those for whose government and support they were given, saving always the authority of the Apostolic See. Wherefore, if any ecclesiastical, or lay person, having knowledge of this our Constitution, shall rashly attempt to contravene it, and after a second or third admonition shall not make amends for his presumption by proper satisfaction, let him be deprived of whatsoever place of power and honour he may hold; and let him know that he is guilty before the divine judgement of an unjust deed; and let him not partake of the most holy Body and Blood of our God and Lord Jesus Christ, our Redeemer; and let him be amenable to severe vengeance at the last judgement. But to all those who shall preserve to this place its rights, may the peace of our Lord Jesus Christ be granted, so that they may receive here the fruit of their good actions, and may meet hereafter at the hands of the just Judge the rewards of eternal peace.   Amen.   Amen.

I Anastasius, Bishop of the Catholic Church.

I Imarus, Bishop of Tusculum.

I Nicholas, Bishop of Albano.

I Hugh, Bishop of Ostia.

I Cencius, Bishop of Porto and St. Rufina.

I Gregory, Bishop of Sabina.

I Guido, Cardinal Priest of St. Chrysogonus.

I Manfred, Cardinal Priest of St. Sabina.

I Aribertus, Cardinal Priest of St. Anastasia.

I Astaldus, Cardinal Priest of St. Prisca.

I John, Cardinal Priest of S.S. John and Paul.

I Henry, Cardinal Priest of S.S. Nereus and Achileus.

I Guido, Cardinal Deacon of St. Mary in Porticu.

I John, Cardinal Deacon of S.S. Sergius and Bacchus.

I Odo, Cardinal Deacon of St. Nicholas at the Tullian prison.

Given at the Lateran, by the hand of Roland, Cardinal Priest and Chancellor of the Holy Roman Church, on the first(?) of December, in the third indication, in the year from the Incarnation of our Lord 1154, in the second year of the pontificate of our Lord Pope Anastasius IV.

Moreover, we, the aforesaid Dean, Archdeacon, and Priors, have seen also other six Letters Apostolic, viz.—of Adrian IV, Clement III, Innocent III, Gregory IX, Innocent IV, and Clement IV, with the leaden seals therefrom suspended, altogether above suspicion, in the same tenor of words, containing the same grants in all respects made to the above named Church of Drontheim[1], similarly signed and sealed by the sovereign Pontiffs, and the cardinals.

In faith and testimony of all which as aforesaid, we have thought it right to attach our seals to the present letters.

Given at Drontheim[1], on the 26th June, in the year of our Lord, 1429.

1 Or Nidaros, now Trondheim.
2 This included the Shetlands.
3 These included the Faroes.

APPENDIX 7

OPEN LETTER FROM BISHOP MARK OF SODOR DATED 1299.

To all the faithful of Christ, who shall see or hear these present letters, Marc, by divine permission Bishop of Soder, greeting in the Lord. Since it is holy to resist gainsayers by the testimony of truth, and to stop the mouths of those speaking unjustly. We therefore protest at the appropriation of the churches of St. Michael and St. Michaldus in Man, in our diocese, to the abbots and monks of Furness by us, with the consent of our clergy, according to the tenor of these presents made, confirmed and ratified, without compulsion or exaction made or to be made, or even fear of the said Abbot, although at the time of the appropriation he had the custody of the Isle of Man; or of any others, but out of our entire and free will, for the honour of God and the blessed virgin, and for the sake of our soul, and those of our parents and friends, and especially for the soul of the Lord Richard of pious memory, our predecessor, who is buried in the basilica of the aforesaid monastery. We, by our own wish, properly and entirely, without a retention of the third part of the aforesaid churches, truly protest it, on the word of God, to be done. In the testimony whereof we have affixed our seal to the present letters. Given in the Abbey of Russyn, on the morrow of the circumcision of our Lord, in the year of our Lord 1299, and 23rd of our consecration.

APPENDIX 8

TRANSLATION OF A LETTER FROM BISHOP SIGNAR OF THE FAROES TO BISHOP AUDFINN OF BERGEN
Dated 1320
(Translated by Miss M. Gawne of Peel, Isle of Man)

To (my) honourable father in Christ and Lord, Audfinn, Bishop of Bergen, by the grace of God[1] your brother Signar by the same grace (Bishop of the Faroes): I myself have undivided concern for everything and honour for your letter of authority which recently came to me—it was most pleasing and welcome and I discerned in it what I desired. Your friendship is sufficient for myself and my family but, ever and above this, you assembled a wooden chancel which you, to its honour, consecrated at the Blessed Church of the Virgin at Kirkjubøur: AND, just as I know that you are arranging for it *(the chancel)* to be set aside for Her worship, so may the Church itself by its works and prayers place you in the Choir of Angels. However, I *(have)* discovered that certain of your rivals *(and)* in particular Finn and Búi are writing many things against you on divers matters, but I also *(have)* perceived that His Lordship, the Archbishop[1], is your true friend, and, although they *(may)* say in the presence of other prelates that they were influenced against you for good cause, nevertheless, you will not have to be afraid of this but you will have to expand your Church and its doctrines. I *(have)* indeed heard it said that F and B[2] are not only striving to harm you but also to acquire for themselves by evil methods the benefactions of our[3] Church. Our Lord, the Archbishop[1], is directing his attention towards preparing himself for (a journey to Bergen) so that he can come with all speed to the Feast of Pentecost[4]: then all will be well. May your authority extend for a very long time[5].

1 The Archbishop of Nidaros (now Trondheim).
2 i.e. Finn and Búi.
3 Above the Latin word meaning "our" is written the Latin word meaning "your".
4 Whitsun.
5 Literally "for longer times".

APPENDIX 9

DOCUMENT 1

TRANSLATION OF DOCUMENTS ABOUT JOHN, BISHOP IN KIRKJUBOUR, AND HARALDUR KALVSSON, LAWMAN

DOCUMENT 1, dated 1412 *(No day or month stated)*

WE, John,[1] by the Grace of God Bishop of the Faroes, acknowledge by this document that WE have come to an agreement with the honourable Haraldur, Lawman of the Faroes, over four and a half marks[2] of land which is situate at Sandur on Sandoy and called Nikkajarðir, *(being)* land which Haraldur Siggasson, priest, had unlawfully mortgaged, AND, because the afore-mentioned Haraldur the Lawman did not seek to take legal action concerning the land against Holy Church and US *(WE have agreed that)* he and his heirs and successors should have all the out-field appurtenant to the afore-mentioned land together with the holm[3] and home pasture for cattle and byres in Brekkar, on the outskirts of Sandur, *(both)* above and below, BUT *(the land)* out towards Kleivgarður and Seyvágar[4] will belong to US and Holy Church, AND WE and Holy Church shall hold all the other rights to the afore-mentioned lands. WE have written this document at Kirkjubøur under our seal in the year of our Lord 1412 [and, for further confirmation hereof, WE, Bishop Hemming, consent to this settlement with the above-named Haraldur the Lawman][5].

1 This would appear to be written by Bishop John I the German, see p. 71 *ante*.
2 See p. 101 *ante*.
3 A small island.
4 See DF p. 50, note 1.
5 The words in square brackets relate to the transcript contained in document 2 below. It is obviously not part of the original document of 1412, but merely an endorsement thereon by Bishop Hemming.

DOCUMENT 2, dated the 15th AUGUST, 1443

Certified transcript of Document 1 above

We, Hemming[1], by the grace of God Bishop of the Faroes, and brother Janus Niklasson make it known to all men that we read an open document made by worthy father Bishop John, and with his seal thereon intact, which, word for word, states as follows:— *(Here follows a transcript of Document 1 above.)* And to testify to the truth hereof, WE, Bishop Hemming, append our seal and brother John *(his seal)* and this transcript which was written in Tórshavn in the year of our Lord 1443 on the Day of the Ascension of our Holy and Dearly Beloved Virgin Mary[2].

1 See p. 72 *ante*.
2 15th August.

DOCUMENT 3, dated MAY, 1479

Certified transcripts of Documents 2 and 1 above

We, Jørundur Skógdrívsson, Lawman of the Faroes, Búi (alias Búgvi) Patursson, Royal Official *(and)* Jóan Olavsson, sworn member of the *Løgting*[1], of the same place set out in this our open document the documents which, word for word, state as follows: *(Here follows a transcript of Document 2 above and then of Document 1 above).* And, to testify to the truth hereof, we, the above-written men, Jørundur Skogdrívsson, Búi Patursson and Jóan Olavsson, have appended our seals to this document which was made in Tórshavn on the Eve of the Holy Cross[1] in the year of our Lord 1479.

1 It is uncertain whether this refers to the 2nd May or the 13th September, see DF p. 52, note 1.

APPENDIX 10

MORTGAGE ETC. BY GREIP IVARSSON IN FAVOUR OF GAUTE EIRIKSSON

DOCUMENT 1, dated the 12th MAY, 1399

I, Greip Ivarsson, acknowledge by this my deed, that I have bought from an honourable man and my dear kinsman, Master Gaute Eiriksson, for two hundred marks[1] in cash, two skins[2] for each mark, and twenty-four packages[3] of homespun, a ship which I will, with God's help, sail to the Faroes. I, or my heirs or successors, shall pay to the above-mentioned Gaute Eiriksson, or his heirs or successors, this debt in Bergen without hindrance or objection as soon as God shall permit my property to come from the Faroes; (and for the further assurance of this payment), I[4], Greip Ivarsson have pledged as security to the oft-mentioned Gaute Eiriksson as security for the afore-mentioned two hundred marks and twenty-four packages[3] of the Faroese homespun the land herein mentioned (that is to say) land, the work of four men[5], in Hatteberg[6] which is situate in Sunnhordaland in the parish of Skåle[6], AND land, the work of three men[5], in Hause[6], AND land situate in the parish of Kinsarvik[6] in Hardanger[6] capable of producing food[7] for seven and a half men in a year, together with all the rights and interests which are or have been appurtenant thereto, both old and new, and the amount of the rent in respect of that land shall not reduce the amount of the money due. I, Greip, would like Master Gaute to have all the rights which I have in Aga[6] and Jastad[6] which are situate in the parish of Ullensvang[6] in Hardanger[6] and the rights which I have in Kjaerland[6] which is situate in the parish of Skåle to the same extent as I have them[8] with all the rights of action which the absolute owner of the freehold has. If I should die before these moneys are paid, then, the oft-mentioned Master Gaute Eiriksson shall hold the afore-mentioned lands in perpetuity, he and his heirs, both freehold and freed freehold[9], and all the rights which I have in respect of the oft-mentioned lands, namely, Hatteberg[6], Hause[6], Aga[6], Jåstad[6] and Kjaerland.[6] ALSO all the property which I possess in the Faroes AND all the property which I can appropriate in the Shetlands shall be his, if I die before the oft-mentioned moneys are paid, until the day when my heirs free it (the property) again for two hundred marks and twenty-four packages[3] of homespun, without reduction being made in respect of rent received therefrom. And to testify to the truth of this and for further confirmation hereof these good men who were present when we made our bargain[10] have affixed their seals, together with my seal and "yes" and a handshake, their names being Harald Hakonsson, Lawman of the district[11] of Skien[12], Hinze (alias Henze) from Jutland, Gunnulv Audason, Svein Vigleiksson, Olaf Olafsson, Herbrand Ketilsson, Holm Sigurdsson, members of the Law Thing of the same place, and Gunnlaug Gudmundarson have affixed their seals to this document which was executed in the church in the town of Skien[12] on the Monday before St. Halvard's Day[13] in the tenth year of the reign of our worthy Lord, Erik[14], by the Grace of God King of Norway and of the Swedes, Danes and Goths[15] and Duke of Pomerania.

1 See pp. 111-113 *ante*.
2 This would indicate that in 1399 a sheepskin was worth half a mark whereas the coin "a Skinn" was worth only one forty-eighth of a mark, see p. 113 *ante*.
3 It is uncertain how much homespun was contained in such a packet. This is unfortunate because, if it were known how many ells of homespun there were in such a package, it would be possible to calculate the value of the 24 packages and thereby arrive at the total cost of the ship since one ell of homespun was worth 2 Norse pennies (see pp. 111-113 *ante*.). The cost would seem to have been 200 marks, or £40 (old English currency) (see p. 113 *ante*.) plus the value of the 24 packages of homespun.
4 The word "and" (Ok) in the original has been omitted in translation as superfluous.
5 As much land as the number of men mentioned can cultivate and look after in a day.
6 These places are all in Western Norway.
7 Especially flour and butter.
8 Certain words cannot be read as there is a hole in the parchment.
9 Presumably entailed land which has been freed from the entail.
10 Literally "agreed purchase".
11 Sysselman.
12 In Southern Norway.
13 15th May.
14 Erik of Pomerania (see Table I). Erik was born in about 1382 and died in 1459. He was King of Norway from 1389 to 1442, King of Sweden from 1396 to 1439 and King of Denmark from 1412 to 1439. He was crowned King of the Scandinavian Union in 1397 at Kalmar and recognised as such in 1401, although he did not, in fact, take over until 1412 when Queen Margaret I died. See GL vol. I, p. 278.
15 It would seem that in fact he was, or may have been, King of the people, but not of the countries concerned.

DOCUMENT 2
PARCHMENT NOTE SUPPLEMENTARY TO DOCUMENT 1

I, the oft-mentioned Greip Ivarsson, also confirm that I have received from the oft-mentioned Master Gaute Eiriksson one ship's anchor which weighs twelve lispund[1] and one ship's rope which weighs sixteen lispund[1], and that I owe for these in addition to the two hundred marks[2] and twenty-four packages[2] which are set out in the document to which is annexed this piece of parchment which was written on Gimsøy[3] on St. Halvard's Eve[4] in the year which is mentioned previously in the document under my seal.

1 One lispund 8 kilogram.
2 See p. 168 *ante*.
3 Near to Skien in Southern Norway.
4 15th May.

APPENDIX 11

The Law about Travelling Allowances for members attending the *Løgting* (written between 1350 and 1400). DF 27 & 28

It was then the law of the *Løgting* that each member[1] for Suðuroy should have twenty ells[2] of homespun if he represented the area south of the Manna pass but fifteen ells[3] if he represented the area north of that pass. The representative from Skúvoy should have twelve ells[4]. Each member for Sandoy should have ten ells. Each member for Mykines should have fifteen ells. Each member for Vágar should have twelve ells[4] if he represented the area beyond the lake[5], but if he represented Eastern Vágar[6] he should have ten ells[2]. For Koltur the rate was eight ells[7]. The rate for each member[1] for Kvívík and Vestmanna was eight ells[7], and eight was the rate for the member for Saksun. Each member[1] for Kollafjørður, Strendur and Nólsoy was to have five ells[8]. Each member for Funningur was to have twelve ells[4]. Each member[1] for Oyndarfjørður, Fuglafjørður and both Gøtas was to have ten ells[9]. Each member[1] for the Northern Islands was to have fifteen ells[3], if he represented the area north of the mountain, and twelve ells[4] if he represented the area[10] south of the mountain.

1 The members were those sent to the *Løgting* each year by the people they represented and were called *løgrættumenn*. There were in all 36 of them. (see pp. 84-85 *ante*.).
2 An ell is approximately 2 feet in length and an ell of homespun is 36 inches in width. It was at the relevant period, worth 1/1120th of a mark or 2 Norse pence (see pp. 112-113 *ante*.). 20 ells of homespun would, therefore, have been worth 40 Norse pence or 8 skinns (see pp. 112-113 *ante*.).
3 15 ells of homespun would have been worth 30 Norse pence or 6 skinns (see note 2 above).
4 12 ells of homespun would have been worth 24 Norse pence (see note 2 above).
5 West of Sørvágsvatn (see DF p. 27, note 2).
6 East of Sørvágsvatn (see DF p. 27, note 3).
7 8 ells of homespun would have been worth 16 Norse pence (see note 2 above).

8   5 ells of homespun would have been worth 10 Norse pence or 2 skinns (see note 2 above).
9   10 ells of homespun would have been worth 20 Norse pence or 4 skinns (see note 2 above).
10 This shows a division in the Northern Islands (see p. 28 *ante*). The reference to the mountain in this document must be to the mountain ridge which runs from Borðoy north-east to Múlin (see DF p. 28, note 2).

APPENDIX 12

IMPORTANT EVENTS IN, OR AFFECTING, THE FAROES

c. 725 (or possibly up to 75 years earlier)	Irish monks first go to the Faroes.
c.795	Irish monks driven westwards to Iceland by the Vikings.
825	Dicuil states that the Faroes are uninhabited apart from sheep and sea birds.
c.825	Grim Kamban colonizes the Faroes.
c.885-90	Further settlements of Faroes from Norway consequent on King Harald I Fairhair's tyranny in Norway.
c.900	Establishment of Faroese *Alting* at Tinganes on Streymoy.
c.999	Sigmund, son of Brester, converts the Faroes to Christianity on the directions of Olaf I Tryggvason of Norway, against the wishes of Thrand and many of the Faroese farmers.
c.1000-5	Feud arises between Thrand and Sigmund ending with Sigmund's death.
c.1026	King Olaf II the Holy of Norway tries to impose Norwegian laws and taxes in the Faroes.
c.1028	Killing of Carl of Møre ends the attempt to collect taxes from the Faroes.
c.1035	Thrand's nephews, Sigurd, Gaut the Red, and Thord the Short are killed by Leif the son of Ossur. Thrand himself dies and with him the rule of the Chiefs in the Faroes wanes. Leif becomes sole ruler of the Faroes and holds them in fief from King Magnus I the Good. From 1035 onwards the power of the Norwegian Kings over the Faroes increases. The end of the Viking era and the beginning of the Middle Ages.

1066	King Harald III the Ruthless of Norway is killed at the battle of Stamford Bridge in England.
c.1100	The Faroes become a separate diocese with its seat at Kirkjubøur on Streymoy.
c.1104	The Faroes are transferred from the Archbishopric of Hamburg-Bremen to that of Lund.
1133	Pope Innocent II tries to bring all the Nordic churches back into the see of Hamburg-Bremen, but apparently without success.
1152/3	The see of Nidaros is erected by Cardinal Nicholas Breakspear and the Faroes are transferred to it.
1156	Sverre, son of King Sigurd II the Mouth of Norway, comes to the Faroes at the age of five and is brought up at Kirkjubøur.
1158	Holy Roman Emperor Frederik Barbarossa tries to bring all the Nordic churches back into the see of Hamburg-Bremen but without success.
1176	Sverre returns to Norway and becomes King of Norway eight years later.
c.1200	Slavery is abolished in the Faroes.
1269	Canon Erlend of Bergen becomes Bishop of the Faroes.
1271	King Magnus VI the Law Reformer enacts a Decree relating to the Faroes and extends the old *Gulating* law to the Faroes. From this time onwards, the Faroese *Alting*, ceases to exercise legislative functions except in relation to a few local matters. The Decree also sets up a trade monopoly with the Faroes.
1273	King Magnus VI makes his younger son, Hakon, Duke of Oppland, Oslo, the Shetlands and the Faroes.
1274	King Magnus VI enacts the young *Gulating* Law which is extended to the Faroes between 1274 and 1276.
1280	The Faroes are first mentioned on a map, the Hereford Map. They are called the "farei".
1294	The Hanseatic traders are prohibited from coming to the Faroes.
1298	Duke Hakon enacts the famous *Sheep Letter* for the Faroes, acting on the advice of Bishop Erlend of the Faroes and of Sigurd Lawman of the Shetlands: the Faroese *Alting* is not consulted.
c.1300	The building of St. Magnus' Cathedral at Kirkjubøur is commenced, but is never finished.
1302	The Hanseatics are again prohibited from trading with the Faroes.

c.1303	Bishop Erlend is forced to leave the Faroes.
1308	Bishop Erlend dies in Norway, but buried at Kirkjubøur.
c.1349	The Black Death comes to the Faroes.
1361	The Hanseatics acquire the same trading rights with the Faroes as the Norwegian traders in Bergen have.
1387	The Faroes come under Denmark with the Union of Denmark, Norway and Sweden, but continue to be ruled as a province of Norway.
c.1400	The Faroese *Alting* is re-named the *Løgting*.
c.1447	Bishop Goswin of Skálholtur in Iceland tries to bring the Faroes into his diocese, but does not succeed.
1490	Dutch merchants receive the same trading rights in the Faroes as the Hanseatic traders.
c.1500	The Faroes are raided by pirates from Britain, Ireland and France.
c.1520	King Christian II of Denmark appoints Joachim Wellenweber of Hamburg as his bailiff in the Faroes.
1523	King Christian II is exiled.
1524	Ex-King Christian II purports to grant the Faroes in fief to Jørgen Hannssøn his bailiff in Bergen. He then offers the Faroes and Iceland to King Henry VIII of England in exchange for a loan, but the offer is refused.
1529	King Frederik I grants the Faroes in fief to Thomas Koppen (a Lutheran from Hamburg) and to Joachim Wellenweber.
1532	Amund Olafsson (last Catholic Bishop of the Faroes) has his appointment confirmed by King Frederik I of Denmark, and not by the Pope, showing that papal power in the North is drawing to an end.
1533	King Frederik I of Denmark dies and from 1533 to 1536 there is a war of succession in Denmark.
1536	Christian III King elect of Denmark asks King Henry VIII of England for a loan of £100,000, and offers him the Faroes and Iceland as security, but again King Henry declines the offer. In the same year Christian becomes accepted as King by all except the Archbishop. The Reformation takes over in Denmark. The Norwegian Representative Council is abolished, with the result that the Faroes as well as Norway are ruled as a province of Denmark.
1537	The Reformation moves north to Trondheim and the Archbishop of Nidaros leaves Norway.

1538   The Reformation reaches the Faroes.
1539   Evangelical Superintendant Jens Riber comes to the Faroes: King Christian III of Denmark confiscates two-thirds of the Church's property in the Faroes.

Acknowledgements

I should like to express my sincere thanks to the very many people who have assisted me with their advice and help and, in particular and without prejudice to the generality of the foregoing, to the following:—

Arnbjørn Mortensen of Tórshavn for having read through the typescript of the book and for his very helpful comments; **John Davidsen of Tórshavn** for his very helpful advice, comments and criticism and, in particular, for his assistance in relation to the *grannastevna*; **Michael Barnes M.A., of University College, London** for permitting me to reproduce his translations of the Lund and Stockholm copies of the early Sheep Letter; **Føroya Frødskaparfelag of Tórshavn** for permitting me to reproduce the plates of the Sheep Letter; **Sverri Dahl, formerly State Antiquary of the Faroe Islands** for his help and advice in all matters relating to antiquities in the Faroes, and for allowing me to reproduce some of his photographs; **Erik Gunnes, Dr. Philos., of Oslo University** for his help and advice, particularly in relation to the Kings, Archbishops and Bishops of Norway; **Førstekonservator Kolbjørn Skaare** of **Universitetets Myntkabinett, Oslo,** for his help and advice in relation to the coin find at Sandur; **Carl-E. Normann, Professor of Church History, Lund University, Sweden** for his help and advice in relation to the early Church history of the Faroes; **Asmundur Poulsen of Tórshavn** for providing photographs for the illustration of the book; **Miss C. R. Clewer, B.A., of University College, London** for the map of the Faroes; **Mrs. Marinda Faragher (née Gawne)** for having translated Appendix 8 from Latin into English; **Arthur Bawden of Peel** for his very helpful comments and suggestions, particularly on those parts of the book which refer to the Isle of Man.

G.V.C.Y.

INDEX OF NAMES OF PERSONS AND PLACES

"A"

Abingdon (In England) 44.
Adalbero (Archbishop of Hamburg-Bremen) 60-1.
Adalbert (Archbishop of Hamburg-Bremen) 44-5, 59.
Adam of Bremen 44, 59-61.
Adrian IV (Pope) *see* Breakspear.
Aga (In the parish of Ullensvang, Hardangar, Western Norway) 168.
Agder (In Western Norway) ch. 13 n. 7.
Áki (Norwegian Chancellor) 139-40, 145.
Albano (In Italy) 63, 161, 163.
Albrecht (Duke of Mecklenburg) 69.
Albrecht (Son of Duke of Mecklenburg and later King of Sweden) 69.
Albrigt (Man in Middle Ages' report) 87.
Alexander II (Pope) 59.
Alexander III (King of Scotland) 67.
Alexander III (Pope) 66.
Algiers 55, 95.
Amund Olafsson (Bishop of the Faroes) 73-4.
Anastasius IV (Pope) 63, 160, 163.
Andras Guttormsen (Lawman of the Faroes) 86.
Andreas (Bishop of Megara in Greece) 72.
Andreas Summaldason (Connected with one of the Gudrun documents) 155.
Andrew (Canon of Bergen or Nidaros and (?) Bishop of the Faroes) 69.
Anglesey 14.
Anljot (Father of Hafgrim, Bjarngrim and Hergrim) 31-2.
Arcimboldus *(Papal nuncio* in Germany) 73.
Argifossur (Shieling near Skopun on Sandoy) 3.
Argisa (Shieling near Kvívik, Streymoy) 3.
Ari Albriktsson (connected with one of the Gudrun documents) 155.
Aribertus (Cardinal-Priest of St. Anastasia) 163.
Arild Hvidtfeldt (Historian) 73-4.
Arnbjorn Gudleiksson (Referred to in certain of the Gudrun documents) 156-8.
Arne (Bishop of Skálholtur, Iceland) 66.
Arne Sigurdson (Bishop of Bergen) 66, 68.
Arne Svæla (Bishop of the Faroes) 69.
Arnold (Bishop of the Faroes) 69-70.
Arnora (Daughter of Arnbjorn and connected with one of the Gudrun documents) 157.
Asger (Archbishop of Lund) 61-2.
Astaldus (Cardinal Priest of St. Prisca) 163.

Aud the Extremely Rich or Deep-minded (Settler) 3, 5, 93.
Audfinn (Bishop of Bergen) 69, 165.
Augsburg (In Germany) 110.
Avignon (In France) 69.

"B"

Bárðr Petrsson (Scribe who wrote the *Sheep Letter)* 140, 145.
Baliol John (Claimant to the throne of Scotland) 68.
Baltic 13-4, 61.
Bardur Eiriksson (Accused person brought before the Norwegian King and the Bishop of Bergen) 72.
Barnes (Michael), Lecturer at London University 140, 145.
Basel (In Switzerland) 71.
Beiner (Father of Thorer) 6, 9-11, 13-5, 21, 42, 93, 100, 115.
Belfast (In Northern Ireland) ch. 16 n. 8.
Benedict IX (Pope) 44-5.
Bergen (In Norway) 5, 49-52, 54-6, 64-9, 72-3, 94-5, 156 nn. 2-3, 161, 168.
Bergenhus (Norwegian county) 66, 72.
Bergsven (Bishop of the Faroes) 65.
Bernhard (Missionary Bishop) 44-5, 62, 93.
Bernhard the Learned (Missionary Bishop) 44.
Bernhard the Saxon, or the Englishman (Missionary Bishop) 44-5, 93.
Bernhardus (Missionary Bishop) *see* Bernhard (Missionary Bishop).
Bernold (Bishop of Utrecht) 110.
Berwick (On the border between England and Scotland) 68.
Beym (In Dweold, Munster, Germany) 70.
Birna (Wife of Thorhal the Rich and later of Sigurd son of Thorlak) 30-1, 43, 46, 62.
Bjarngrim (Son of Arnljot) 30-1, 94.
Bjarni *see* Svínoy-Bjarni.
Bjørn (Neighbour of Sigurd son of Thorlak) 31.
Bjørn the Swede 14.
Boniface IX (Pope) 70.
Borðoy (Faroese island) 28, 84, Appendix 11 n. 10.
Borgund (In Norway) 68.
Brand (Son of Sigmund and Thuride) 21-2, 33.
Brattan (In Western Norway) 156-7.
Braunschweig (In Germany) 110.
Breakspear, Nicholas (Cardinal-Bishop of Albano, later Pope Adrian IV) 49, 63, 83, 161, 163, ch. 11 n. 44.

176

Breisach (In Germany) 110.
Brekkar (Suburb of Sandur on Sandoy) 166.
Bremen (In Germany) 44, 59-61.
Brester (Father of Sigmund) 6, 9-11, 13-5, 21, 42, 82-3, 93, 100, 115.
Brynjolvur Torbergsson (Priest on Sandoy) 158.
Britain 1, 75.
British Islands 102, 112.
British Isles 118.
British seas 1.
Bruce, Robert (Claimant to the throne of Scotland) 68.
Bruno III (Count of Braunschweig) 110.
Bue the Stout (A Jomsviking) 17.
Búi of Bergen 165.
Búi *alias* Búgvi Pattursson (Royal Official in the Faroes) 167.
Butzow (In Mecklenburg) 69.
Bygdøy (In the Oslo area) 66.
Bødvar the Clerk (Wrote the 1273 Decree of Magnus VI the Law Reformer) 139.

"C"

Canterbury (In England) 75.
Canute the Great (King of Denmark and England) 30, 44, 109, ch. 6 n. 33.
Carl of Møre (In Norway) 28-9, 32, 49, 84, 109.
Cecilia (Mistress and later wife of Brester Father of Sigmund) 6.
Celle (In Germany) 110.
Cencius (Bishop of Porto and St. Rufina) 163.
Census Camerarius (Historian) 63.
Chilianus (Bishop of the Faroes) 73.
China ch. 7 n. 7.
Christian I (King of Denmark) 73.
Christian II (King of Denmark) 55-6, 107.
Christian III (King of Denmark) 1, 56-7, 74, 107.
Christiania (Now Oslo) 53, 69.
Clement III (Pope) 163.
Clement IV (Pope) 163.
Cologne (In Germany) 66.
Conrad II (Holy Roman Emperor) 110.
Copenhagen 1, 56, 73.

"D"

Dacie *see* Denmark.
Dagfinnur Nikulasson (Connected with one of the Gudrun documents) 156.
Danorum *see* Denmark.
Davidsen, John (Archivist) of Torshávn ch. 12 n. 96.
Denmark 1, 6, 44-5, 53-6, 59, 61, 66, 70-4, 86, 93, 96, 100, 107, 109, ch. 6, n. 33.
Deventer (In Holland) 110.

Dicuil (Irish monk and author) 1-2.
Dímun 3.
Dolley, Michael (Numismatist) 109.
Donegal (County in Republic of Ireland) 2.
Dovrefjell (In Norway) 13.
Down (County in Northern Ireland) 111.
Drontheim *see* Nidaros.
Dugdale (Historian) 63.
Duisburg (In Germany) 110.
Dumfries (In Scotland) 68.
Dunaldur Haraldsson (Connected with one of the Gudrun documents) 158.
Dweold (In Münster, Germany) 70.

"E"

Eberhard (Bishop of Augsberg, Germany) 110.
Edward I (King of England) 68.
Edward the Confessor (King of England) 109, ch. 6 n. 6.
Egilbert *see* Eilbert.
Eilbert (Bishop of Farria and Fyn) 59-60.
Eilif (Archbishop of Nidaros) 69.
Einar (Son of Hafgrim and grandson of Leif son of Ossur) 39.
Einar the Sudreyan 6, 8, 22, 26, 79, 82, 93.
Eingjartoftum (In Vágar) *see* í Eingjartoftum.
Eldjarn Kamhat, *or* Hambhøtt 9, 21, 82.
Elbe (German river) 59.
Ellen (Man in the Middle Ages' report) 87.
Ellindur Filipsson (Mentioned in one of the Gudrun documents) 155.
England 44, 55-6, 68, 89, 99, 107, 109, 112, ch. 6 n. 33.
Ergibyrgi (Shieling near Akrar, Suðuroy) 3.
Ergidalur (Shieling near Hov, Suðuroy) 3.
Erik (Duke of Vadstene) 66.
Erik, Earl (Son of Earl Hakon) 14, 21, 36, 42.
Erik II (King of Norway, later known as "the Priest-hater") 52-3, 65.
Erik Glipping (King of Denmark) 66.
Erik Menved (King of Denmark) 66.
Erik III of Pomerania (King of Denmark, etc. and Duke of Pomerania) 169, Appendix 10 n. 14.
Erlend (Bishop of the Faroes, previously Canon of Bergen) 51-3, 65-8, 71, 103, 119, 140, 145.
Erlendr *see* Erlend.
Eske Bille (Chief official in Bergen) 56, 73.
Eskil (Archbishop of Lund) 59, 62, 64.
Ethelred II (King of England) 109.
Eugene II (Pope) 161.
Eugene IV (Pope) 72.
Eugenius (Pope) *see* Eugene II.
Euphemia (Queen of Rügen) 66.

Eystein II (King of Norway) 63.
Eystein (Archbishop of Nidaros) 64.
Eysturoy (Faroese Island) 3, 10, 15, 20, 29, 32, 84, 99-100, ch. 6 n. 30.

"F"

Fair Isle (Between the Orkneys and the Shetlands) 61.
Fámjin (On West coast of Suðuroy) 116-7.
Faria see Farria.
Farria (Believed to be alternative name for Helgoland) 59-61.
Farrie or Farrie (Believed to be the same place as Farria) 60-1.
Ffere see John Ffere or Seyre.
Finland 55.
Finn of Bergen 165, Appendix 8 n. 2.
Finngård (In Western Norway) 156-8.
Finnmark (In Northern Norway) 14.
Floki Vilgerdason (Viking explorer) 2, 93.
Florence (In Italy) 72.
France 55, 69, 107.
Franciscus (Papal Vicecamerarius and Cardinal-Priest of St. Clementis) 72.
Frederik I (King of Denmark) 55-6.
Frederik Barbarossa (Holy Roman Emperor) 60, 64, 94.
Frederyk de Friese (Bailiff in the Faroes of ex-King Christian II of Denmark) 55.
Frosta 16.
Fuglafjørður (on Eysturoy) 117, 170.
Fugloy (Faroese Island) 28.
Funningsbotnur (On Eysturoy) 84.
Funningur (On Streymoy) 170.
Furness (Abbey of) in England 68, 164.
Fyn (Danish island) 59, 72.
Fårö (Island in the Baltic) 61.

"G"

Galloway (In Scotland) 67.
Gawne, Miss M. (Of Peel, Isle of Man) 165.
Gaut the Red (Nephew of Thrand) 21-2, 27, 29-33, 82, 100, ch. 7 n. 16.
Gaute (Bishop of the Faroes) 65.
Gaute Eiriksson (of Norway) 81, 86, 168-9.
Gerlack Speckin (Canon of Butzow in Mecklenburg) 69.
Germany 61, 73, 96, 109.
Gevard (Bishop of the Faroes) 69.
Gilbert (Abbot of Rushen, Isle of Man) 67.
Gille, Earl (Administrator of the Sudreys) 19.
Gille, The Lawman (Of the Faroes) 26-30, 83, ch. 6 n. 10.
Gimsøy (In Norway) 170.
Godred II (King of the Sudreys) ch. 6 n. 10.

Gosler (In Germany) 110.
Goswin "the unjust son" (Believed to be Bishop of Skalholtur in Iceland) 72.
Gothian (Land of the Goths, see present-day Gotha in East Germany) 41.
Great Britain 112.
Greenland 26, 45, 59-61, 63, 66, 99, 161, ch. 6 n. 10.
Greece 72.
Gregory (Bishop of Sabina) 163.
Gregory IX (Pope) 163.
Greip Ivarsson (Of Hatteberg, Norway and sysselman in the Faroes) 81, 86, 111, 168-70.
Grim Kamban (First Norse settler of the Faroes) 2-3, 93.
Grimkil (Bishop of Trondheim) 44, ch. 6 n. 18.
Gronlondie see Greenland.
Grundlandonium see Greenland.
Gudbrandsson, (Canon of Nidaros) 71.
Gudbrandur Magnusson (Priest of Jala, Shetlands) 159.
Gudmund (Bishop of the Faroes) 46, 62-3.
Gudmundus (Bishop) see Gudmund.
Gudrun (Wife of Thorbjørn and sister of Svínoy-Bjarni) 5.
Gudrun (Daughter of Sigurd the Shetlander and sometimes referred to as "the Housewife of Húsavík") 54, 81, 87, 95, 103, 111-2, 155-9.
Gudrun (Daughter of Thrand) 36.
Guido (Cardinal-Priest of St. Chrysogonus) 163.
Guido (Cardinal-Deacon of St. Mary in Porticu) 163.
Gunnlaug Gudmundarson (Witness to Greip Ivarsson's mortgage) 169.
Gunnulv Audason (Member of the Law Thing at Skida, Norway) 169.
Guttorm (Lawman of Bergen) 86.
Guttorm (Son of Andras Guttormsen) 86.
Gaesa (Daughter of Sigurd and Birna) 43, 62.
Gøta (On Eysturoy in the Faroes) 3, 10-1, 20-1, 25, 30, 32-3, 170.
Gøtas see Gøta.

"H"

Hafgrim (Of Hov, Suðuroy) 6, 9-11, 14, 35-6, 42, 82, 93, 115.
Hafgrim (Son of Arnljot) 30-1, 94.
Hafgrim (Son of Sigmund and grandson of Leif son of Ossur) 39.
Hafgrim's Grave 10, 42, 115.
Hakon IV (King of Norway) 51, 64, 112, 139, ch. 10 n. 67.
Hakon V (King of Norway) 51-3, 66-7, 69, 75, 140, 145, 150 n. 1.
Hakon VI (King of Norway) 69.

178

Hakon (Duke) *see* Hakon V.
Hakon (Earl of North and West Norway) 13-7, 19-21, 36, 83, 93.
Hakon (Archbishop of Nidaros and previously Bishop of Oslo) 61.
Halgeir (At one time Bishop of Stavangar and later Bishop or pro-Bishop of the Faroes) 70-1.
Halsingaldie *see* Helsingland.
Halsinglandonium *see* Helsingland.
Halvan (Son of Eirik, priest on Suðuroy) 160.
Hamar (In Norway) 73, 161.
Hamburg (In Germany) 55-6, 73.
Hamburg-Bremen (See of) 43-5, 59-61, 64, 94, ch. 6 n. 18.
Hans (King of Denmark) 52.
Harald I Fairhair (King of Norway) 2.
Harald II Greycloak (King of Norway) 5, 13, 93.
Harald VI the Ruthless (King of Norway) 44, 109.
Harald Harefoot (King of England) 109, ch. 16 n. 6.
Harald Ironhead (Viking) 14-5.
Harald Hakonsson (Lawman of Skida, Norway) 169.
Haraldur Kálvsson (Lawman of the Faroes) 71-2, 86-7, 166.
Haraldur Siggasson (Priest of Sandur, Sandoy) 166.
Hardanger (County in Western Norway) 168.
Hardicanute (King of Denmark) 109.
Hartvig (Archbishop of Hamburg-Bremen) 61.
Hatteberg (In the parish of Skåle, Sunnhordland, Western Norway) 81, 168.
Hause (In the parish of Kinsarvik, Norway) 168.
Havard (Bishop of the Faroes) 69.
Hebrides 5, (Lewis, Skye, Islay and Mull groups of Scottish Islands) 2, 6-7, 63, 96.
Hedemark (County in Norway) 13.
Helgason, Jon (Author) 87.
Helgeland (In the southern part of the Norwegian county of Nordland) 14.
Helgoland (Island near the mouths of the German rivers Elbe and Weser) 59-61.
Helsingborg (In Denmark during the period of this history, but now in Sweden) 118.
Helsingland (In Norway) 60-1.
Helsingør (In Zealand, Denmark) 72.
Hemming (Bishop of the Faroes) 72, 93, 166-7, Appendix 9, Doc. 1 n. 5.
Henry VIII (King of England) 56, 107.
Henry (Cardinal-Priest of SS. Nereau and Achileus) 163.

Herbrand Ketilsson (Member of the Law Thing at Skida, Norway) 169.
Herbst, C.F. (Numismatist) 110.
Hergrim (Son of Arnljot) 30-1, 94.
Heri (Son of Sigmund and Thuride) 21-2, 33.
Herna (In Norway) 27.
Hestur (Faroese island) 54, 100.
Hilary (Bishop of the Faroes) 73, ch. 10 n. 82.
Hinze, *or* Henze, from Jutland (Member of the Law Thing at Skida, Norway) 169.
Holland 55, 95.
Holm Sigurdsson (Member of the Law Thing at Skida, Norway) 169.
Holmgaard *see* Novgorod.
Holstein (In Denmark during the period of this history, now in West Germany) 55.
Holtålen (In Juldalen in the Norwegian county of Sør-Trøndelag) 43, 118.
Hósvík (On Streymoy) 40.
Housewife of Húsavík *see* Gudrun (Daughter of Sigurd the Shetlander).
Hov (On Suðuroy) 10, 26, 42, 115.
Hoy (In Germany) 110.
Hoyvík (On Streymoy) ch. 6 n. 30.
Hubert (Archbishop of Canterbury) 75.
Hugh (Bishop of Ostia) 163.
Hundi, or Hvelp (Son of Earl Sigurd of the Orkneys) 19.
Hungary 109.
Húsar (On Kalsoy) 158.
Húsavík (On Sandoy) 53-4, 95, 103, 155-6, 158-9.
Hvolung (In Iceland) 73.
Høgni (Man in the Middle Ages' report) 87.
Hålogaland (In Norway) 50.

"I"

í Eingjartoftum 118.
Iceland 2-3, 26, 44-5, 55-6, 59-61, 63, 66, 69, 72-3, 79, 88, 93-4, 99, 107-8, 119, 161, ch. 6 n. 10, ch. 10 n. 31.
Icelandic Islands *see* Iceland.
Ignarium (Bishop of Tusculum) 163.
Inge I (King of Norway) 63-4.
Ingewald (Prior of Trondheim) 160.
Ingibjørg (Daughter of Arne, accused person brought before the Norwegian King and the Bishop of Bergen) 72-3.
Ingirid Oyvindardottir (Connected with one of the Gudrun documents) 156.
Innocent II (Pope) 60-1, 94.
Innocent III (Pope) 163.
Innocent IV (Pope) 163.
Innocent VI (Pope) 69.
Innvík (In the Norwegian county of Bergenhus) 72.

Ireland 2-3, 55, 72, 100, 107, 109.
Irish Sea 14.
Isle of Man 2-3, 45-6, 63, 67-8, 79-81, 84, 86, 95-6, 101-2, 107, 111, 116, 164, ch. 5 n. 3, ch. 11 n. 81, ch. 12 n. 37.
Islandie *see* Iceland.
Islay group of Islands (Group of Scottish islands) 6.
Islandonum *see* Iceland.
Italy 72.

"J"

Jakobsen, Jakob (Historian) 53, 73, 88.
Jakobsen, Peder (Farmer of Kirkjubøur) 52.
Jala (In the Shetlands) 159.
James III (King of Scotland) 55.
Janus Niklasson (Faroese "brother") 167.
Jóan Binarsson (Faroese priest) 157.
Jóan Nikalsson (Connected with the Gudrun documents) 157-8.
Jóan Ólavsson (Of Sandoy, member of the *Løgting*) 158.
Jóan Ólavsson II (Member of the *Løgting*) 167.
Jóannes Patursson *see* Patursson (Jóannes).
John (First Missionary Bishop in Trondheim) 44.
John (Archbishop of Tuam, Ireland) 72.
John I (First Archbishop of Nidaros) 64, 160, ch. 11 nn. 44-5.
John II (Archbishop of Nidaros) 51, 65, 67, ch. 10 n. 33.
John I the German (Bishop of the Faroes) 71-2, 87, 93, 166-7, Appendix 9 Doc. 1 n. 1.
John II the Dominican (Bishop of the Faroes) 70, 72.
John III the Chief (Bishop of the Faroes) 70, 72, 93.
John IV (Bishop of the Faroes) 73.
John (Cardinal-Priest of S.S. John and Paul) 163.
John (Cardinal-Deacon of S.S. Sergius and Bacchus) 163. John Ffere, or Seyre (Bishop of Man) 72.
Jones, Gwyn (Historian) 36, 42, ch. 10 n. 31.
Jutland 169.
Jämtland (County formerly in Norway, now in Sweden) 63.
Jørgen Hanssøn (Bailiff in Bergen of Ex-King Christian II of Denmark) 55.
Jorgensen, Dr. J. Balslev (Doctor) 116.
Jørundur (Archbishop of Nidaros) 65-6, 68.
Jørundur Skógdrívsson (Lawman of the Faroes) 86, 167.
Jåstad (In the parish of Ullensvang, Hardanger, Western Norway) 168.

"K"

Kálgarður (In Sumba, Suðuroy) 86.
Kalsoy (Faroese island) 28.
Kaltisen, Henrik (Archbishop of Nidaros) 44, 62, 64-6, ch. 10 n. 53.
Kermode, P. M. C. (Manx archæologist) 116.
Ketil Kristiansson (connected with one of the Gudrun documents) 155.
Kilkeel (In Co. Down, Northern Ireland) 111.
Kinsarvik (Parish in Hardanger, Western Norway) 168.
Kirk Braddan (In the Isle of Man) 67.
Kirkjubøur (on Streymoy) 43, 46, 52, 62, 64-5, 67-70, 94, 106, 116, 118-9, 165-6, ch. 6 n. 34.
Kjærland (In the parish of Skåla, Sunnhordland, Western Norway) 168.
Klaus Pedersøn *see* Pedersøn (Klaus).
Kleivgarður (On Sandoy) 166.
Koefoed—Jensen, L. (Architect) 119.
Kollafjørður (On Streymoy) 54, 84, 170.
Koltur (Faroese island) 170.
Koppen, Thomas (Held the Faroes in fief) 56, 96.
Krogh, Knud J. (Curator of the National Museum of Denmark in Copenhagen) 43, 45, 110, 118 ch. 11 n. 2.
Kunoy (Faroese island) 28.
Kvívík (On Streymoy) 100, 117-8, 170.

"L"

Lade (Near Trondheim in North-Western Norway) 14, 21.
Lagman (Godred I's deputy in the Sudreys) ch. 6 n. 10.
Langbek (Historian) 71.
Lateran (In Rome) 163.
Leif (Son of Ossur) 16-7, 21-2, 25-33, 39, 82-3, ch. 7 n. 16.
Leif (Son of Thorer Bresterson) 31, 94.
Leitet (Farm at Rossalandsstrand, Western Norway) 156.
Leo X (Pope) 73.
Lewis group of islands (Group of Scottish islands) 6.
Lítla Dímun (Faroese island) 10, 21, 100, 103.
Lodin (Bishop of the Faroes) 68-9.
Londonderry (County in Northern Ireland) 61.
Lothar (King of Saxony, Germany) 61.
Lothringen (In Germany) 110.
Lübeck (In Germany) 56.
Lund (In Denmark during the period of this history, now in Sweden) 49, 52, 59, 61-4, 71, 85, 145, 151 n. 22, 152-3.
Lunge, (Vincent, chief official in Bergen) 55-6.

Lupold (Clerk of Beym, Dweold, Münster) 70.
Lygra (In Norway) 27.
Lödöse (In Sweden) 72.
Løfall (Farm at Rossalandsstrand, Western Norway) 156.

"M"

Magdeburg (In Germany) 110.
Magnus, St. (Earl of the Orkneys) 119.
Magnus I the Good (King of Norway) 33, 39, 109.
Magnus II Haraldsson (King of Norway) 109.
Magnus VI the Law Reformer (King of Norway) 51-2, 65-6, 94-5, 139-40, 145, ch. 10 n.n. 26, 67, Appendix 3 n. 5.
Magnus VII Eriksson (King of Norway and also King of Sweden) 54, 69, ch. 11, n. 104.
Magnus Erlingsson (Connected with the Gudrun documents) 155, 159.
Man see Isle of Man.
Manfred (Cardinal-Priest of St. Sabina) 163.
Manna pass (On Suðuroy) 170.
Manx is the adjectival form of "Isle of Man."
Margaret I (Queen of Denmark) 54, 70.
Margaret (Princess of Denmark) 55.
Margaret (Woman in Middle Ages' report) 87.
Mark (Bishop of Sodor) 67-8, 81, 164, ch. 11 n. 81.
Martin see Matthew.
Matthew (Bishop of the Faroes) 64.
Maughold (In the Isle of Man) 46.
Mecklenburg (In Germany) 69.
Megora (Bishopric in Greece) 72.
Miðvagur (On Vágar) 84.
Múlin (On Borðoy) Appendix 11 n. 10.
Mull group of islands (Group of Scottish islands) 6.
Munch, P. A. (Historian) 45, ch. 11 nn. 2, 81.
Münster (In Germany) 70.
"Mururin" (Faroese name for the ruins of St. Magnus Cathedral at Kirkjubøur, Streymoy) 119-20.
Mykines (Faroese island) 170.
Myre (Farm at Rossalandsstrand, Western Norway) 156.
Møre (In Norway) 28-9, 32, 49, 84, 109.

"N"

Nicholas (Cardinal-Bishop of Albano) see Breakspear.
Nidaros (See in Norway) 49, 60, 62-4, 66, 69, 71, 160-3, ch. 9 n. 43, ch. 11 nn 14, 45, Appendix 6 n. 1, Appendix 8 n. 1.

Nikkajarðir (Farm in Sandur, Sandoy) 166.
Nikolaus (Archbishop of Uppsala) 68.
Nils (King of Denmark) 62.
Nólsoy (Faroese island) 170.
Nordfjord (In Norway) 50.
North Atlantic 1, 99.
Northbrigg (William, Bishop elect of the Faroes) 70, 93.
Northern Europe 73.
Northern Ireland 61, 102, 111.
Northern Islands (Of the Faroes) 28, 109, 170, Appendix 11 n. 10.
Norvie see Norway.
Norway 1, 5-6, 9-11, 13-7, 19-21, 26-7, 29-31, 33, 35-6, 39, 43-5, 49-56, 61, 63-4, 66-7, 69-70, 73-4, 80-1, 83, 86, 93-6, 100, 107, 109, 111, 117, 119, 139-40, 145, 150 n. 1, 161, ch. 6 n. 33, ch. 11 nn. 2, 14, Appendix 5 Doc. 2 nn. 2-5, Appendix 10 Doc. 1 nn. 6, 12, 14, Doc. 2 n. 9.
Norwegiorum see Norway.
Novgorod, or Holmgaard (In Russia) 10, 14, ch. 3 n. 9.
Nykøbing (On Zealand, Denmark) 72.

"O"

Odense (On Fyn, Denmark) 59.
Odo (Cardinal-Deacon of St. Nicholas at the Tullian Prison) 163.
Olaf I Tryggvason (King of Norway) 19-22, 36, 41, 44, 49.
Olaf II the Holy (King of Norway) 26-9, 44, 49, 81, 83, 94, ch. 6 n. 18.
Olaf III the Quiet (King of Norway) 109.
Olaf (Archbishop of Nidaros) 74.
Olaf (Bishop of the Faroes) 64.
Olaf Olafsson (Member of the Law Thing at Skida, Norway) 169.
Olafr hvítaskáld (Brother of Sturla Thordarson of Iceland) 108.
Olansgarfur (On Skúvoy) 116.
Olive (Daughter of Thorstein the Red) 3.
Olúva see Olive.
Oppland In Norway 51, 150 n. 1.
Orkdal (In Norway) 13, 16.
Orkneys 19, 45, 55, 63-4, 161.
Orm (Bishop of the Faroes) 59-60, 62-3.
Ormstein (Son of Thorgrim the Evil) 22, 25-6, 82.
Oslo 51, 66, 73, 140, 145, 150 n. 1, 161, ch. 10 n. 55.
Ossur (Son of Hafgrim of Hov) 11, 14-6, 35-6.
Ostia (In Italy) 163.
Outer Hebrides (Group of Scottish islands) 6.
Oyndarfjørður (In Eysturoy) 170.

181

"P"

Paasche ("Father", priest) 50.
Papil (In the Shetlands) 159.
Papilness (In the Shetlands) Appendix 5, Doc. 6 n. 3.
Pascall II (Pope) 61.
Patursson, Jóannes (Historian) 50, 62, ch. 11 n. 31.
Paul (Archbishop of Nidaros) 69.
Peel (In the Isle of Man) 67, 165.
Peter (Bishop of the Faroes) 65.
Peter (Prior of Trondheim) 160.
Peter Nikjalsson (Parish priest of Innvik, Norway) 72.
Pederson (Klaus, Chancellor to ex-King Christian II of Denmark) 56.
Petersen, Sámal (Antiquarian) 80.
Philip Gudbrandsson see Gudbrandsson.
Pløyen (Governor of the Faroes) 115, ch. 17 n. 4.
Portico (In Italy) 163.
Porto (In Italy) 163.
Principal Widow see Thuride.

"R"

Rafn the Sailor 10, 13, 93-4.
Ragnar (Missionary Bishop in Trondheim) see Ryngerus.
Ragnhild (Wife of Thorkel Barfrost alias Ulf) 13-4.
Ragnhild Hárvarðsdottir (Mentioned in the Gudrun documents) 159.
Ramsey (In the Isle of Man) 46.
Randver of Holmgaar (Viking) 14.
Rasmussen, Joannes (Antiquarian) ch. 17 n. 5.
Remagen (In West Germany) 110.
Riber, Jens (Evangelical Superintendent of the Faroes) 74.
Richard (Bishop of the Faroes) 70.
Richard (Bishop of Sodor) 164.
Roe (Bishop of the Faroes) 64.
Roe (River in Co. Londonderry, Northern Ireland) 61.
Rogaland (In Western Norway) 156, ch. 13 n. 7.
Rogalandsfylke see Rogaland.
Roland (Cardinal-Priest and Chancellor of the Holy Roman Church) 163.
Rolf (Bishop of Man) 45-6, ch. 9 n. 53.
Rome 63, 70, 73.
Roskilde (On Zealand, Denmark) 72.
Rossalandsstrand (In Norway) 156.
Rudolf. (Missionary Bishop, later Abbot of Abingdon) 44.
Rügen (In Germany) 60.
Rushen (In the Isle of Man) 67, 164.
Russia 16.
Russyn see Rushen.
Ryngerus (Missionary Bishop to the Faroes) 45, 62.

"S"

Sabina (In Italy) 163.
Saksun (On Streymoy) 53-4, 103, 170.
Sámal Petersen see Petersen.
Sandavágur (On Vágar) 116, 118.
Sandoy (Faroese island) 6, 31, 43, 53, 84, 103, 109, 118, 158, 166, 170.
Sandur (On Sandoy) 43, 84, 94, 109-10, 118, 158, 166.
Sandvík (In Suðuroy) 22, 25.
Saxony (In Germany) 61.
Scandinavia 59, 93-4, 100, 118.
Scheel, Dr. (Historian) 2, 49, 79-80.
Schrøter, Pastor (Antiquarian) 73.
Scotia see Ireland.
Scotland 55, 61, 67, 81, 99, 107.
Scredeundonum see Skridfinnerne.
Scriduindie see Skridfinnerne.
Selatrað (On Eysturoy) 84.
Serquirus (Bishop of the Faroes) 62, 64-5.
Setter see Setr.
Setr (In the Shetlands) 159.
Severin (Bishop of the Faroes) 71-2.
Seward (Missionary Bishop in Trondheim) 45.
Seyre see John Ffere or Seyre.
Seyrvágur (On Vágar) 118.
Seybágar (On Sandoy) 166.
Sheep Island (In the River Roe, Co. Londonderry, Northern Ireland) 61.
Shetlands 26, 51-5, 63, 69, 87, 93, 95, 140, 145, 150 n. 1, 156-7, 159, 168, Appendix 6 n. 2.
Siegfried (Missionary Bishop) see Bishop John (first Missionary Bishop in Trondheim).
Sigefrid the Younger (Missionary Bishop in Trondheim) ch. 6 n. 18.
Sigmund (Son of Brester) 6, 10-1, 13-7, 19-22, 25-6, 30-1, 35-6, 41-2, 82-3, 94, 100, 116.
Sigmund (Son of Leif) 30, 32, 39, ch. 7 n. 16.
Sigmund the Elder (Father of Brester and Beiner) 6.
Signar (Bishop of the Faroes) 69, 165.
Sigurd II the Talkative (King of Norway) 50, 63, 75.
Sigurd (Earl of the Orkneys) 19.
Sigurd (Son of Thorlak and nephew of Thrand of Gøta) 21-2, 27-33, 43, 62, 80-2, 100, ch. 6 n. 30, ch. 7 n. 16.
Sigurd the Shetlander 54, 81, 95, 155-9.
Sigurð see Sigurd (Lawman of the Shetlands).
Símun (Lawman of the Faroes) 86.
Símun Albriktsson (Connected with one of the Gudrun documents) 160.
Sjurður Birgisson (Connected with one of the Gudrun documents) 156.

182

Skálabotnur (On Eysturoy) 84.
Skálholtur (Diocese in Iceland) 66, 69, 72, 119.
Skania *see* Skåne.
Skarvanes (On Sandoy) 158.
Skegge (Son *or* grandson of Hafgrim grandson of Leif son of Ossur) 39.
Skien (In Norway) 81, 169.
Skofte of Streymoy (Neighbour of Sigurd and Birna) 31-2, 82.
Skoggard, Peder (Envoy of Vincent Lunge of Bergen) 55.
Skriddfinnene (In Norway) 60.
Skriddfinnerna (In Sweden) 60.
Skúvoy (Faroese island) 6, 10, 14-5, 17, 20-2, 25-6, 32-3, 42-3, 82, 103, 116, 170.
Skye group of islands (Group of Scottish islands) 6.
Skåle (Parish in Sunnhordland, Western Norway) 168.
Skåne (In Denmark during the period of this history, now in Sweden) 44.
Slauorum (The diocese of the Slavs) 60.
Slættaratindur (Mountain on Eysturoy) 99.
Snorri Sturluson (Historian) 108.
Snæúlf the Sudreyan 6, 9, 93.
Sodor (Diocese of the Sudreys) 6, 60, 164, ch. 11 nn. 80-1.
Sodor and Man (Diocese of) *see* Sodor.
Sogn (In Western Norway) ch. 13 n. 7.
Southern Jutland 55-6, 66.
Speckin *see* Gerlack Speckin.
Speier (In Germany) 110.
St. Brandonsvík (Near Kirkjubøur) 62.
St. John's (In the Isle of Man) 80-1, 84.
Stavanger (In Norway) 64, 70-1, 74, 161.
Steingrim (Father of Thorkel Barfrost *alias* Ulf) 13.
Steingrim the Halt (Son of Sigmund and Thuride) 21-2, 33.
Steingrim (Neighbour of Thrand of Gøta) 22.
Stevnuválur (Ancient meeting place of várting on Eysturoy) 84.
Stockholm 52, 86, 140, 151 nn. 25, 28-9, 152-3.
Stóra Dímun (Faroese Island) 10, 26-7, 80.
Storm, Gustave (Ecclesiastical historian) 70, 72.
Strendur (On Eysturoy) 170.
Streymoy (Faroese Island) 1, 6, 9, 15, 20, 30-1, 33, 53-4, 79, 84, 103, 115, 117.
Sturla Thordarson (Lawman of Iceland and historian) 51, 94, 108, ch. 10 n. 31.
Sudreyan, Person from the Sudreys.

Sudreys (The Isle of Man and the Hebrides —ie. the Lewis, Skye, Islay and Mull groups of Scottish islands) 3, 6, 19, 31, 63, 93-4, 161.
Suðuroy (Faroese Island) 3, 6, 10, 15, 22, 25-6, 39, 41-2, 74, 84, 88, 94, 115-6, 170, ch. 2. n. 13.
Suenorum *see* Sweden.
Sumba (On Suðuroy) 86.
Sunnhordaland (South-west part of the county of Hordaland, Western Norway) 168.
Sunnmøre (In Norway) 19.
Svein Magnusson of Sandoy (Member of the *Løgting*) 158.
Svein Markusson (Lawman of the Shetlands) 159.
Svein Vigleiksson (Member of the Law Thing at Skida, Norway) 169.
Sven, Earl (Son of Earl Hakon) 14, 21, 36, 42.
Sven (Bishop of the Faroes) 64.
Svend Estridsen (King of Denmark) 59.
Sverre (King of Norway) 50-1, 64, 75, 107.
Sverresborg (In Trondheim, Norway) ch. 9 n. 21.
Sverri Dahl (Archæologist) 33, 42, 115, ch. 6 n. 54, ch. 17 nn. 5, 10, 20-9.
Svinoy (Faroese island) 7, 15, 28, 100, 116.
Svinoy-Bjarni 5-7, 10, 15, 17, 22, 42-3, 100, 116.
Sweden 16, 44-5, 54-5, 60-1, 63, 66, 68-9, 117, ch. 11 n. 2.
Swedie *see* Sweden.
Syðragøta (On Eysturoy) 117.
Sørvágsvatn (Lake in Vágar) Appendix 11 nn. 5-6.

"T"

Teitr the Priest (Mentioned in the *Sheep Letter*) 140, 145.
Theoderik (Duke of Lothringen) 110.
Thiel (Now Tiel, in Holland) 110.
Tholf (Missionary Bishop in Trondheim) 45.
Thora (Mistress of Beiner) 6.
Thora (Daughter of Sigmund and Thuride) 16-7, 25-6, 31-2, 36, 39, ch. 7 n. 16.
Thoralf (Father of Ragnhild, wife of Thorkel Barfrost *alias* Ulf) 13.
Thoralf (Son of Sigmund and Thuride) 21-2, 26-7, 80, 83.
Thoralf Smør (Viking explorer) 2.
Thoralf of Stóra Dimun *see* Thoralf (son of Sigmund and Thuride.
Thorbera (Wife of Thorvald of Sandoy) 31.
Thorbjørn Gøtuskegg (Uncle of Brester and Beiner) 5-6.

183

Thord the Short (Nephew of Thrand of Gøta) 21-2, 27, 29-33, 82, 100, ch. 7 n. 16.
Thorer (Son of Beiner) 6, 10, 13-7, 20-2, 26, 82, 100.
Thorfinn (Earl of the Orkneys) 45.
Thorgrim the Evil (Farmer of Suðeroy) 22, 25-6, 82, 100.
Thorhal the Rich (Farmer of Streymoy and first husband of Birna) 30-1, 46.
Thorkel Barfrost *see* Ulf.
Thorlak (Brother of Thrand of Gøta) 6, 21.
Thorolf *see* Turolf.
Thorolf Butter *see* Thoralf Smør.
Thorstein the Red (Father of Olive *or* Olúva) 3.
Thorstein (Son of Thorgrim the Evil) 22, 25-6, 82.
Thorvald (Farmer of Sandoy) 31.
Thrand (Of Gøta) 5-7, 10-1, 14-7, 20-2, 25-30, 32-3, 35-6, 42-3, 49, 82-3, 93-4, 100.
Thuride (Wife of Sigmund) 13-4, 16-7, 21-2, 25-6, 31-3, 36, 39, 82.
Tinganes (On Streymoy) 1, 9, 15-7, 20, 26, 28-9, 32, 79-80, 82, 150 n. 6, ch. 2 n. 8.
Tjørnuvík (On Streymoy) 115, 117.
Tórar (Bishop of Skálholtur, Iceland) 69.
Tordur (Bishop of Greenland) 66.
Torkil Onundarson (Of Sandavágur on Vágar) 117-8.
Torlak Torhalleson (Bishop of Skálholtur in Iceland) 119.
Tromóður Andresson (Sysselman of Suðeroy) 160.
Tormóður Sjúðarson (Lawman of the Faroes) 86.
Tórshavn (On Streymoy) 1, 10, 26, 28, 41, 79, 88, 93, 115, 155, 160, 167, ch. 6 n. 30, ch. 12 n. 96.
Tranquilia (In Italy) 71.
Trondheim (In Norway) 6, 17, 21, 44-5, ch. 9 nn. 21, 43, ch. 11 n. 14, Appendix 6 n. 1, Appendix 8 n. 1.
Tróndur Dagfinnsson 155, 159.
Trongisvágsfjørður (In Suðuroy) 84.
Tschan, Professor Francis J. (Historian) 44.
Tuam (Archbishopric in Ireland) 72.
Turolf (Bishop of Orkney) 45-6, ch. 9 n. 53.
Tusculum (In Italy) 163.
Tynwald Hill (At St. John's, Isle of Man) 81, 84.
Tyssesøy (In the southern part of the Norwegian county of Bergenhus) 66.
Tønsberg (In Norway) 10, 13, 67, 80, 93.

"U"

Ulf, *alias* Thorkel Barfrost (Husband of Ragnhild daughter of Thoralf) 13-4, 16.
Ulfdal (Valley near Dovrefjelly central Norway) 13, 16.
Ullensvang (Parish in Hardanger, Western Norway) 168.
Ulph (Archdeacon of Trondheim) 160.
United Kingdom 111.
Unwan (Archbishop of Hamburg-Bremen) 44, ch. 6 n. 18.
Uppsala (In Sweden) 63, 68-9.
Urban VI (Pope) 70.
Utrecht (In Germany during the period in question, now in Holland) 110.

"V"

Vadstene (In Sweden) 66.
Vágar (Faroese island) 84, 116, 170.
Valdemar Atterdag (King of Denmark) 54, 70.
Valdemar (Duke of Southern Jutland) 66.
Vandil the Swede 14.
Vestmanna (On Streymoy) 170.
Við Hanusá 118.
Viðareiði (On Viðoy) 156, 158.
Viðoy (Faroese island) 28.
Vienna 68.
Vigbald (Bishop of the Faroes) 70, 93.
Vik (In Norway) 10, 13.
Vindasur (In the Shetlands) 158-9, Appendix 5 Doc. 5 n. 3.
Vitzlav (Prince of Rügen) 66.
Vordingborg (On Zealand, Denmark) 71.

"W"

Wales 86.
Weser (German river) 59.
West Africa 36.
West Germany 64.
West John F. (Historian) 87.
Whelp *see* Hundi.
Wigbold *see* Vigbald.
William (Bishop of the Faroes) 70.
Wilson David (Professor) 2.
Windos, *or* Windus, *see* Vindasur.
Wullenweber, Joachim 55-6, 96.
Wurzburg (In West Germany) 110.

"Y"

Yell *see* Jala.

"Z"

Zachariasen, Louis (Historian) 73.
Zealand (Danish island) 72, 74.

"Æ"

Ælfifu (English mistress of Canute the Great) 30.

"Ø"

Øravík (In Suðuroy) 84.